Globalization and Television

Globalization and Television

A Study of the Indian Experience, 1990–2010

Sunetra Sen Narayan

OXFORD
UNIVERSITY PRESS

OXFORD

UNIVERSITY PRESS

Oxford University Press is a department of the University of Oxford.
It furthers the University's objective of excellence in research, scholarship,
and education by publishing worldwide. Oxford is a registered trademark of
Oxford University Press in the UK and in certain other countries

Published in India by
Oxford University Press
YMCA Library Building, 1 Jai Singh Road, New Delhi 110 001, India

ISBN-13: 978-019-809236-0
ISBN-10: 019-809236-9

Typeset in Minion Pro 10.5/13
by Alphæta Solutions, Puducherry, India 605 009
Printed in India by G.H. Prints Pvt Ltd, New Delhi 110 020

In memory of my mother,
Esha Sen

CONTENTS

TABLES AND FIGURES

....

TABLES

FIGURES

FOREWORD

The last decade of the twentieth century and the first decade of the new millennium are especially significant in so far as mass communication in India is concerned. In the world's largest democracy, the entry of foreign television broadcasters and the gradual deregulation of the media more or less coincided with the advent of the phase of liberalization of the Indian economy. Even as different countries on the planet started getting closer to one another though an integration of their economic, financial, and trading systems, the 'mediascape' of India altered radically in an incredibly short span of time of two decades.

Contrast the fact that, till the early-1990s most Indian television viewers has access to only one broadcaster, the government-owned Doordarshan, with today's situation in which the government of India's Ministry of Information and Broadcasting has given permission to some 800 television channels to uplink and/or downlink to the country, and that around 300 channels which claim to be news and current affairs channels have invaded our homes and minds. The transformation that has taken place is truly dramatic. Earlier, in the mid-1980s, Doordarshan's expansion could not be rivalled by any television broadcaster anywhere in the world.

With the intensification of competition and privatization came a lowering of standards contrary to what capitalistic norms of free enterprise would have us believe since the media industry cannot be easily compared to industries that produce other products or provide services. After the boom in the media has come a period of deceleration, decline, and stagnation, accompanied by three phenomena. First, the dividing line between broadcasting and telecommunications is getting increasingly blurred (if not obliterated altogether). The flow of advertisement revenues ebb on account of recession or economic slowdown, leading to a shake-out in the name of consolidation. Finally, the exponential growth of the internet gradually encroaching into the space that was earlier the domain of 'traditional forms' of the media, notably print. These developments have raised a wide range of questions and concerns that are engaging scholars and professionals across the globe.

Sunetra Sen Narayan's study examines the political economy of television liberalization and globalization in the Indian context, looking into issues relating to the role of the state and regulatory mechanisms. After outlining the various theoretical approaches to globalization, localization, and the role of the state, she analyses their relevance in the context of broadcasting in India. Having contextualised a theoretical framework for examining the salient trends in the television and cable industry, the author then delineates the rise of the private sector in the country's television industry. Thereafter, she highlights the slew of issues pertaining to regulating this sector, issues that continue to be animatedly discussed and debated, and some of which still elude consensus.

The author is mindful that the amazing diversity of India requires a special recipe for media regulation. While at one level, legislation has sought to make the public broadcaster autonomous, in actual practice, Doordarshan is yet to become truly independent of the ruling establishment steeped as it is in the culture of sycophancy. At the same time, she points out that despite the upheavals in the communications environment, including wide-ranging technological changes and a growing role of the private sector, the state as a central actor has been able to consolidate its role. In this context, the author questions the extent to which the concept of a public sphere is valid and viable in the country at present, and the patterns of regulation that should evolve in the foreseeable future. She also raises the question as to whether the Indian state is extending or continuing its control over the broadcasting sector through establishing links with private broadcasters, and points towards future areas of investigation and research.

Paranjoy Guha Thakurta
New Delhi, June 2013

ACKNOWLEDGEMENTS

This book has grown out of my doctoral research at the Pennsylvania State University.

I owe a deep debt of gratitude to my doctoral advisor John S. Nichols. I would like to thank him for his expert guidance and encouragement. His questions and comments helped me to clarify my vision and hone my research. I thank Patrick R. Parsons for his insights into the philosophical and theoretical aspects of mass communications. I thank Robert La Porte for his interest in my research concerning the Indian subcontinent. I am grateful to all my teachers at Penn State. I would especially like to mention Stratford Smith, who was a great source of encouragement in the early years. I thank the Office of Fellowships, for providing financial assistance at the University.

Among friends who have provided unstinting help and support over the years, I thank Loubna Skalli, Sophia Said, and Vandana Aggarwal. I would also like to thank friends and colleagues at the Indian Institute of Mass Communications. Thanks are due to Shashwati Goswami, Vidhanshu Kumar, and Vinod Kapoor. I am grateful to Shalini Narayanan for her insightful comments on an earlier draft. I thank various officials and academics who spared the time to discuss issues with me. I would also like to thank my students whose questions keep me grounded. I would like to express my gratitude to everyone at Oxford University Press for their encouragement.

Finally, I thank my family who made this venture possible. I thank my mother Esha Sen, father G. K. Sen, and my mother–in–law Shantha Ramaswami for all their support. I thank my sister Selina and nephew Varun for their encouragement. Above all I thank my husband Badri and children Nayantara and Vikram, for everything.

INTRODUCTION TO
THE GLOBALIZATION OF
TELEVISION

The twentieth century has witnessed a major change in the nature of interactions between communities, regions, and nations across the world. This process of change has accelerated in the last two decades. The term 'globalization' is often used to describe this change. In an attempt to understand this term and its ramifications, social scientists have posited some of the most interesting theories of interactions across various political, economic, cultural, and social boundaries. While the concept of globalization has been a contested one, in the last two decades, contemporary theorists from a range of different political and theoretical viewpoints are converging on the idea that globalization is the distinguishing characteristic of the present moment (Durham and Kellner 2006: 579).

For many scholars, globalization has become the pivotal point for trying to make sense of the 1990s. In the view of some, these current theories on the subject of globalization have achieved the status of a '*Zeitdiagnose*'—a 'diagnosis of our times' (Scott 1997: 3). The concept of globalization lacks precision, even though it has already become a cliché, encompassing 'everything from global financial markets to the Internet, but which delivers little substantive insight into the contemporary human condition' (Held *et al.* 1999: 1). However, its hold over the popular imagination implies that this concept is at least worthy of investigation.

Featherstone and Lash inform us with regard to globalization, 'It has in fact in a very important sense been the successor to the debates on modernity and post modernity in the understanding of socio-cultural change and as the central thematic for social theory' (1995: 1). Even a perfunctory search of scholarly or popular literature on the subject of communications turns up the words global or globalization with increasing frequency. Local is used less often, but is the call-to-arms of the postmodernists.

GLOBALIZATION

What is globalization? While scholars may quibble about its exact meaning, there is, generally, a consensus that it is marked by characteristics such as financial sector integration, the accelerated growth of large transnational corporations, creation of global markets, and rapid changes in communications technology (Parikh and Shah 1999: 27). Most of these broadbrush-strokes are readily observable in the economic sector. However, globalization is also understood in more abstract and cultural terms such as the compression of time and space (Robertson 1995; Giddens 1990). One fairly comprehensive definition of globalization has been put forward by Held *et al.* (1999). These scholars suggest that globalization can be defined as, 'a process or set of processes which embodies a transformation in the spatial organization of social relations and transactions—assessed in terms of their extensity, intensity, velocity and impact—generating transcontinental or interregional flows and networks of activity, interaction, and the exercise of power' (1999: 16). Held *et al.* assert that globalization is a process that transforms social relations and transactions. The time and space dimensions are also included. It is significant that even the dimension of power finds place in this definition.

Is there indeed some reality behind the rhetoric? Are we becoming an increasingly global society with mass media and telecommunications contributing to this process? Alternatively, are we seeing processes of globalization and localization occurring simultaneously? Are we, as a world, heading towards cultural homogenization, or are distinct cultural forms still in existence or even rising anew? Are new forms of cultural hybrids emerging? Is globalization something new or is it a continuation of earlier processes such as imperialism and colonialism? These are some of the questions that are currently being debated in the social sciences. Theorists working in different disciplines are wrestling with these issues (Durham and Kellner 2006: 579–83).

POST-COLD WAR SCENARIO

The post-Cold War scenario does not exhibit the dualism and easy categorization associated with the Cold war period. International communications flows, which could largely be explained by the realist[1] paradigm in international relations during the Cold War, are now becoming harder to explain. An inquiry into new patterns (as in a post-Cold War era) of global politics, relations, or communications must begin from an examination of basic structures, concepts, and hypothesized relationships employed in understanding the old patterns. However, the ontological standpoint for interpreting the old pattern is open to question (Cox 1992). In the post-Cold War period, it is possible to question the realist foundations—Why states as the unit of analysis? Why balance of power? Why anarchy? And so on, in fact one may say, following Marx that 'all that is solid melts into air'. Indeed one may even question the concepts of order, and international in this more fluid era. It has been suggested that international emphasizes the interaction between states, while global is a looser and broader term (Cox 1992).

One fact that emerges is that the current period is one of reflection and soul-searching, while the search for a new heuristic device or formula to simplify the complex nature of reality, is proceeding unabated. Among the various formulations currently jostling for primacy in establishing a post-Cold War paradigm are models/concepts based on civilizations, economics, chaos, and states, to name just a few. Two models, conceptualized by Samuel Huntington and Francis Fukuyama respectively, are outstanding for the amount of attention they have received. These works are interesting because they are macroscopic, yet present different visions of a 'brave new world'. Huntington (1996) resurrects the civilization as the operational unit of analysis in a global system. Huntington,[2] following the tradition of Oswald Spengler and Arnold Toynbee, posits a model of the world order based on civilization units (Weeks 1993). In his opinion, with the passing of the Cold War, ideological conflict between nation-states will be supplanted by conflict between civilizations. His model seeks to provide an analysis of current international conflicts, as well as a method for predicting future conflicts. Huntington also claims to provide a theoretical basis for foreign policy analysis.

Fukuyama (1992) studies the issue of the spread of the ideal of liberal democracy worldwide. His provocative, if somewhat hastily constructed thesis, is that the ideal of liberal democracy has triumphed through the world with the collapse of the Soviet Union. This leads him to posit that the end of history is at hand, because humans have reached the terminal point of their ideological evolution.[3] The author cites the work of Hegel as a major inspiration, as Hegel viewed the 'liberal' order to be the highest stage in human history, arrived at through a process of evolution. Fukuyama's work seems to favour the emergence of a global dimension in politics.

Another model, which obliquely appears to support Fukuyama and the 'endist' view, is the global village model, which in its initial formulation dates back to Marshall McLuhan's writings in the 1960s. According to this model, advances in communications technologies and its convergence with data processing will lead to the world becoming a 'smaller' place, with the compression of distance and the potential cultural homogenization that some communications technologies can bring about (Hamelink 1996). The global village model is substantiated by some of the literature in international relations, which stresses complex interdependence in international politics (Nye and Keohane 1989). It is worth noting that cultural theorist Raymond Williams (1974), in a classic study of television, resisted the technological determinist approach espoused by McLuhan. In Williams' view, the 'medium is not merely the message', rather new technologies such as television offered the viewer opportunities for new forms of expression outside of the locus of control of transnational corporations and media moghuls.

James Rosenau (1990; 1992a; 1992b; 1997), the eminent international relations theorist, has some interesting observations to make about the system of world politics and notions of power and authority in the current period. Rosenau (1990) examines the turbulent nature of world politics. In this work, he suggests that the present era is a historical breaking point. He theorizes that macro-global structures have been bifurcated into 'the two worlds of world politics' (1990: 5). The two worlds refer to the state-centric system, which now coexists with a powerful, but more decentralized multi-centric system. In other words, non-state actors have ascended in importance.

For a sociologist such as Anthony Giddens (1990; 1991), globalization is a 'consequence of modernity'. However, Giddens (1990) characterizes the current period as one of 'late modernity' rather than post-modernity, because he believes that the world has entered an era where the consequences of modernity are becoming more radicalized and universalized than before. For Giddens, the hallmark of globalization is the compression of time and space.

The social theorist Arjun Appadurai (1990) has commented on the process of globalization. According to him, the complex dimensions of global cultural flows are important in understanding this phenomenon. He conceives of these dimensions as various 'scapes'.

While there is no consensus on the order of things in a post-Cold War, global era, there is general agreement on the fact that it is a period which has witnessed unprecedented change. In contrast to realism, with its emphasis on the nation-state, various non-state and non-systemic influences have been considered as determinants of a new paradigm. Realism has come under attack from many quarters, with critics offering their own visions of a brave new world based on civilizations, norms, chaos, economics, postmodern interpretations and others.[4]

Current theorizing appears to be eclipsing international with transnational, or global, as a unit of analysis. Processes such as globalization and rapid technological change, particularly with respect to information technologies, are increasingly being cited as the factors responsible for changing the relations between developed and developing countries. It is the contention of some scholars that telecommunications and broadcasting are increasingly becoming global in nature. Technological changes along the lines of digitization, convergence, fiber optics, and the use of satellites may be contributing towards this process. Matters are additionally complicated by the fact that global television and global telecommunications appear to be both a consequence, as well as a cause, of the process of globalization.

GLOBALIZATION, LIBERALIZATION, AND THE NATION-STATE

While the history of the Western state begins with the subject of the *polis* or city-state in ancient Greece, the role of the modern state has again become a focus of inquiry in the last two decades. The notion of national sovereignty has also been re-examined in the current period. The collapse of the Soviet Union and the rise of global capitalism are just some of the factors that have called into question the realist paradigm with its emphasis on the nation as a unit of analysis.

Is globalization a monolithic force that is slowly, but surely eroding the nation-state? In today's changing world, the meaning of sovereignty is being scrutinized. Attention has also been directed to the role of the state. While the dominant neo-liberal account maintains that market mechanisms are the most efficient and the state's activities should be curtailed, the statist response has been that the state is an actor with consolidation interests of its own. The state needs to function well, even if only to secure the proper functioning of markets.

These debates are particularly significant for many developing countries where historically, the state has controlled large sectors of the economy. In most instances, the broadcasting and telecommunications sector had also fallen under the states' purview. The pressures to bring about 'development' have added another dimension to the debate about the market versus the state. The whole paradigm of development has been called into question. The old import-substitution development model has in many cases been abandoned for a more integrative export-led model.

Worldwide, the frontiers of the state have been rolled back. In many instances, globalization has been tied to an increased reliance on the market, as compared to the state. Terms such as privatization, liberalization, and deregulation have come into common parlance. Public broadcasting and the state run Post, Telephone, and Telegraph

(PTT) model for the provision of telecommunications services have come under siege. However, it would be naïve to assume that an increased reliance on the market implies a straightforward reduction in the sphere of influence of the state. Deregulation has, in most instances, been accompanied by extensive re-regulation. Many developing countries have privatized or liberalized key sectors in their economies over the past decade. The PTT is no exception, and countries all over Latin America, East Asia, South Asia, and Africa have changed the way the telecommunications sector functions. Broadcasting has also been liberalized in many developing countries with new players coming in.

The new scenario is becoming harder to understand and it is also more difficult to make predictions in the area of electronic communications. Not only are there new players in the field, but there are novel regulatory problems arising out of new transnational information flows. Issues dealing with the Internet are a prime example. Factors such as digitization and convergence have also muddied the conceptual waters of the rationale for distinct broadcasting and telecommunications industries. Traditionally, the telecommunications industry (telephony) has been associated with interpersonal communication, while the broadcasting industry (radio and television) has been associated with mass communications. This distinction is beginning to blur, with the advent of new synergies between the two industries.

ECONOMIC ASPECTS OF GLOBALIZATION

If one examines the popular press, it would seem that globalization is occurring in every facet of our lives. The economy is becoming global with the growth of massive transnational corporations and wealth flowing ever faster across the world's financial markets. To illustrate the depth of the global economy, a few statistics are mentioned.

- One aspect of globalization is the flow of financial capital across countries. As Parikh and Shah inform us, 'private capital flows for direct investment and portfolio investment to developing countries have grown rapidly from $25 billion in 1990 to $150 billion in 1997. For low income countries, net private inflows have reached 4 per cent of GDP. Foreign exchange trading has seen a dramatic growth from about $15 billion a day in 1973 to an average of $1260 billion a day in 1995, seventy times larger than world trade per day' (1999: 27–8). According to the United Nations Conference for Trade and Development, Global foreign direct investment was about US $1, 122 billion in 2010.[5]

- Another aspect of globalization is the rising share of international trade in world output. During the period 1950–94, the volume of world merchandise trade is estimated to have increased at an average annual rate of more than 6 per cent, compared with an output growth of less than 4 per cent (WTO 1995). By 2007, international trade surpassed 50 per cent of global GDP for the first time (WTO 2008). This share has more than doubled over the period 1950–2007.

- Globalization is characterized by the changed manner of production wherein the producer is able to slice up the production process into many geographically separated steps. With regard to global production, Ramaswamy (1999) is informative, 'cross-border production by affiliates of Multi National Enterprises (MNEs) as a share of world manufacturing output rose from 12.7 per cent in 1982 to 17.6 per cent in 1992. The share of MNE affiliates in developing country GDP increased rapidly in the 1990s from 4.3 per cent in 1992 to 6.3 per cent in 1995' (1999: 192).

Thus, economic aspects of globalization include the acceleration of flows of financial capital across nations, the rising share of world trade in world output, and the changing nature of the production process.

CULTURAL ASPECTS OF GLOBALIZATION

Socio-cultural patterns are also not immune to the globalization influence. All the old bogeys about 'cultural imperialism' and the New World Information and Communication Order are now resurrected with boring monotony. American icons such as Coca-Cola,

McDonalds, or Disney have often been held up as the culprits responsible for cultural homogenization in other countries. Debates have also sprung up around the issue of whether globalization is primarily caused by Americanization, or by Westernization (Durham and Kellner 2006: 577–83). These views co-exist with the 'neo-liberalists' and the 'techno-evangelists' who sing the global hymn in a paean of praise. For them, the autarkic model of development is as dead as the dodo; the deeper integrated structures that characterize globalization as compared to the earlier phase of internationalization are viewed as being desirable. Yet another take on globalization is that it occurs through structural and cultural hybridization (Pieterse 2006).

The globalization issue has taken on a new garb in the last decade, but some of the concerns expressed by the developing countries date back to the 1970s. Dependency[6] theory sought to explain underdevelopment in Latin America in this period. A major round of debates with regard to international communications and information flows between countries centred on the technology of satellite broadcasting. Satellite communications had become a controversial topic in fora such as the UN and UNESCO during the 1970s and the 1980s (Smith 1990: 2–3). The developing countries had expressed their desire for a more 'balanced' flow of information via the New World Information Order (Masmoudi 1979).[7] According to Masmoudi, the imbalance in international information between the developed and the developing countries was multi-faceted, having both quantitative and qualitative dimensions. These inequalities would need to be redressed.

From its inception, the developing countries have viewed satellite communications as a medium for redressing the imbalance in information flows. Satellite television has furthered globalization of communications, as it need not confine itself to national borders. However, satellite technology can also be used as a catalyst for development; hence it is of crucial importance to the developing countries (Karunaratne 1982: 211; Hudson 1993). The growth of the Internet has also implied that the old debates about technology, development, and democracy have been resurrected in the new millennium. The globalization of communications has re-ignited the controversies surrounding the usage of communications technology for development.

GLOBAL MEDIA

Global media are another aspect of the globalization phenomenon. Transnational media conglomerates have consolidated their market share in recent years and have even spread into Eastern Europe and the countries of the former Soviet Union. Satellite broadcasting, by its very nature, is transnational. There is some evidence to suggest the recent inroads made by global television in the developing countries (Herman and McChesney 1997; Page and Crawley 2001; Straubhaar 2006).

Current issues have surfaced regarding the spread of the Internet also. The juxtaposition of the old and the new have created curious contradictions in the developing world, for example, the establishment of cyber cafes offering global connectivity inside a thirteenth century fort in the remote desert city of Jaisalmer in India. These cyber kiosks coexist peacefully with a lack of plumbing and elementary sanitation. One can only wonder at this aspect of 'development'. Mobile communications and new media are penetrating the developing countries. The rate of diffusion of these technologies is rapid, especially mobile telephony in Asia and Africa. This 'connectedness' is another aspect of globalization.

Whether considered to be desirable, or a force to be feared and reviled, it does appear that globalization is commonly being perceived as 'inevitable 'or 'irreversible'. Various social activists who have protested against the rising tide of globalization do not endorse this view. However, it is ironic that these activists may be organizing themselves and drawing support from like-minded groups, so much so that we may be witnessing the growth of a 'global civic community' or 'global citizens' where human rights are held to be more important than citizenship of a nation.

Certain non-governmental organizations (NGOs) have protested against the evils of globalization, but many NGOs are combining forces to build global activist networks. While the ideas of the global village and the global market may be passé, the concept of a global parliament was mooted in March 2001 at a meeting organized by the World Federation of UN Associations and the Brussels-based Earth Action, a Federation of 190 NGOs (Nagaraj 27 June 2001).

This kind of activism has contributed to the rise of the importance of the global sphere of activity and its intricate connections to the local level, often by-passing the national level.

LOCALIZATION

Along with the growing body of literature on globalization, there is renewed emphasis on the local as an area of study and often as a site of resistance. In contrast to globalization, Held *et al.* define localization as the 'consolidation of flows and networks *within* a specific locale' (emphasis added, 1999: 16). Thus, their definition clearly has territorial implications.

The ascendance in the importance of ethnicity and sub-national entities in the past two decades has contributed to the importance of the local. The environmental movement and notions of sustainable development have also emphasized the importance of communities with their essentially local connotations. What has emerged as a large area of interest in economics and political science is the decentralization of governance. The increased importance in local government and relations between the federal or central government and the local governments has acquired a new urgency in the last decade. In general there has been a demand for devolution of more powers to the local levels as compared to the federal government.

While there has been an explosion in communications worldwide in the last decade, there has also been a renewed interest in the overlap between communications, culture, and questions of identity. This has helped to bring the juxtaposition of global and local to the fore (Durham and Kellner 2006). The resurgence of the local has, in part, been funneled by the growth of the Internet and private broadcasting entities. The study of the diaspora emerging from the fields of sociology, anthropology, literature, and mass communications has also focused on the importance of local. As regards the Indian subcontinent, Indian writers in English, such as Salman Rushdie, and more recently Jhumpa Lahiri, have given new depth to the understanding of local and its relationship to global.

'Postmodernity', with all its ramifications, has often been the heuristic for understanding the category of local and of global/local media flows. Perhaps this is the rubric under which the contradictory character of modern media can best be subsumed. Postmodernity, which is characterized by traits such as pastiche and schizophrenia, could be a lens through which we could incorporate disparate, fragmented, and contradictory elements of the world we live in now (Jameson 1995).

However, Anthony Giddens, the eminent social theorist, differs. Giddens (1990) characterizes the current period as one of 'late modernity' rather than post-modernity, because he believes we have entered an era where the consequences of modernity are becoming more radicalized and universalized than before. While highlighting aspects of late modernity such as the compression of time and space, Giddens mentions sociological factors such as the dissolution of trust in the current era. Another sociologist, Robertson (1995), has explored the concept of globalization in depth and seeks to combine macro and micro levels in an interesting exploration of the global/local phenomena.

One accommodation between the opposing trends of globalization and localization has been achieved in the marketing literature through the concept of 'glocal'. Robertson (1995) suggests that glocal implies the strategies employed by transnational corporations where they adapt their global product or advertisement campaigns to local needs and markets.

RELATIONSHIP OF MEDIA TO THE STATE AND SOCIETY

Under scrutiny here is the relationship of the electronic media to the state. To take one step back, it is necessary to question basic premises about the role of media in society, made even more urgent in a period of unprecedented change.

Each media system is born of a particular socio-cultural milieu. To revert to a classic work by Siebert, Peterson, and Schramm (1963) we are informed that the press acquires the form of the social and political structures within which it functions. This is particularly so, regarding the system of social control whereby the relations of individuals and institutions are adjusted. Therefore, an understanding of these societal systems are necessary in order to understand the press, going further and examining basic assumptions of society such as the nature of man, society, and the state, the relation of man to the state, and the nature of knowledge and truth (Siebert, Peterson and Schramm, 1963: 1–2).

To apply their argument, we may assume that it has relevance for electronic media, as well as the traditional press. In other words, it is expected that the form of the media will differ across countries, because they arise in different social systems, with different philosophical underpinnings. For example, the media will be of a different form and will serve a different purpose in an authoritarian system of government as compared to a democracy.

The Toronto School

The nexus between the communications media and the state stretches back in time. The work of the Toronto school and that of Harold Innis in particular, offers an interesting perspective. Innis (1951, 1972) was an important theorist in the technological determinist tradition, who focused on the linkage between communication technologies and social processes. In his opinion, the history of civilization is best understood in terms of the history of various communications technologies. Innis attributes the salient features of successive ancient civilizations to the dominant modes of communication, each of which has its own bias in terms of societal form.

Innis' central thesis is that media such as stone or clay emphasize time, while media such as paper emphasize space. He believes that media that emphasize time support decentralization in organizational structures, while media that emphasize space support centralization in systems of government. Viewed from this perspective, the electronic revolution in communications technologies would only serve to be a centralizing agency, since such technologies emphasize space.

Thus, it would appear that an Innisian perspective might imply the reverse directionality, from communications to politics and social structures. This may be making a very strong case or reading too much into Innis. However, this conclusion may not be entirely without merit. The rapid proliferation of new communications technologies such as television, satellites, computers, ISDN, fax, and the convergence of computers and telecommunications in the post-World

War II period have impacted the societies in which they have sprung up. Historically, it has been observed that communications media have served a command and control function for the state (Innis 1951; Gillespie and Robbins 1994). Following this line of reasoning it would appear that ownership of the broadcast medium could confer great power to the owner. An examination of contemporary times has shown that the state still exercises control over national broadcasting in many countries. In times of crisis, control over the media is determined to be essential by the powers that be. 'There are good reasons why every competent military coup targets media for seizure'. (Baran and Davis 1995: 3).

The Realist Paradigm

As opposed to Innis, the realist paradigm in international relations, with its stress on the nation state, dominated the study of international communications during the Cold War. The importance of propaganda in the period following the Second World War was perhaps inevitable, as the nation-state was the primary unit of analysis in the realist formulation. Thus, propaganda outlets such as Radio Liberty and Radio Free Europe were the ideological apparatus to be employed in the service of the state, to serve its own interests (Kirschten 1995). Propaganda emerged as a major area of study within the field of communications during the Cold War.

On a more subtle level, the influence of the state was discernible in its shaping of the sociology of knowledge, or who could do the 'authoritative' talking in the field of mass communication research. For example, the U.S. government helped in legitimizing certain branches of knowledge, at the expense of others (Simpson 1994). In Simpson's words, 'some powerful factions of the government, notably the FBI and other domestic security agencies, aggressively repressed rival scientific concepts concerning communication, particularly those trends of critical thought they recognized as subversive' (1994: 9–10).

Whether one examines the interwoven fields of international communications and international relations from a functionalist perspective such as Laswell's or a critical perspective such as Schiller's, it would appear that the influence runs from international relations or politics, to international communications. In general, the paradigm of international politics is such that the nation state has been given pride of place, while the media and communications have played second fiddle. This is in contrast to the Toronto School, exemplified by the writings of Harold Innis and Marshal McLuhan.

The Piper

While ownership of the media confers power to the owner, the reverse side of the coin is that those who have power control the media. This view of the media is that, 'he who pays the piper calls the tune' (Parenti 1986; Altschull 1995). If the media is state-controlled, then, it is very likely that the agenda will be set by the state. In this context, it may be useful to draw upon Altschull's (1995) model of the press. The central theme in the symphonic model of the press that he proposes is that the press is a piper, but the tune being played is written by a higher power stratum. In other words, the press is a mere 'agent of power'. While one may debate the veracity of this statement, one fact that emerges is that the relationship between the media and the state is certainly a complex one, with mutual interaction and effects.

Soft Power and Authority

Other fundamental concepts such as power, the nation-state, and its authority are undergoing redefinition in this current era of globalization. Traditional notions of power as employed by statesmen and scholars ranging from Nicolo Machiavelli, Hans Morgenthau, and Kenneth Waltz have centered on notions of tangible resources (Mowlana 1996). The realist emphasis on military strength and 'hard power' seems to be somewhat anachronistic in the current period. Nye (1990) has suggested the concept of 'soft power', which sums up the present situation better. Soft power implies an inclusion of intangible sources of power, such as cultural, educational, ideological, and information technological factors. It has been suggested by Mowlana (1996) that soft power includes the concept of information as an intangible resource, implying that power is transferred from the capital-rich to the information-rich, with a consequent ascendance in importance of the information factor, as compared to physical resources.

In a broadening of the notions of power and authority, Rosenau (1990; 1992a) has some interesting observations to make. He informs us that the loci of authority have been relocated and restructured during the 1980s. Among the factors that come into play are the shift from an industrial order to a post-industrial order, the emergence of problems such as pollution, terrorism, currency crises, and AIDS, the authority crises that stem from the reduced capacity of states to deal with major political issues, the growing importance of subsystems or decentralization that have accompanied the weakening of states, and finally the feedback of the aforementioned factors on the skills and orientations of the individuals who comprise groups, and other collectives (Rosenau 1992a: 255).

In Rosenau's (1992a) opinion, authority has been relocated 'upward', toward transnational organizations, and 'downward', toward sub-national groups, with the implication that national governments are increasingly finding it difficult to resolve major issues and problems that afflict their societies.

CASE STUDY: INDIA

Issues dealing with globalization/localization, the state's role and liberalization in the electronic means of communicating have gained in importance with respect to the developing countries, in the last two decades. Some scholars have suggested that reforms in developing countries have clear political underpinnings. As Petrazzini informs us, with respect to reform in the developing countries, 'a long tradition of state intervention and politicized markets assured a pervasive role for politics' (1995: 5). It would appear that this argument can be extended to the broadcasting sector in developing countries as well.

Like in many other developing countries, the state in India exercised rigid control over the broadcasting sector till the 1990s. The surprise entry of Satellite Television Asian Region (STAR TV) in the Indian firmament as a spin-off of the Gulf War meant that the state could no longer play ostrich. It had to sit up and take note of new players and new issues. Unlike some other Asian countries, India never banned the reception of STAR TV signals. India's print media, unlike its broadcasting counterpart has a long history of autonomy. In this cultural milieu, an outright ban on transnational electronic signals may have been unacceptable. An indigenous cable industry sprang up higgledy-piggledy in the wake of STAR TV. To begin with it, was largely unauthorized and parasitic of foreign programming, having very little original programming. This opened up a Pandora's Box of new regulatory issues.

From a paltry couple of channels being aired by the state-controlled broadcaster Doordarshan prior to 1990, the Indian broadcasting scene had expanded to 75–100 channels by 2001 and it is growing rapidly. The television industry (defined as television distribution, television advertising, and television content) in India grew at the rate of 21 per cent over the period 2004–7, growing to an estimated Rs 226 billion in 2007 (FICCI and PricewaterhouseCoopers (PwC) Report 2008). The total number of television households increased from 102 million in 2004 to an estimated 115 in 2007 (FICCI and PwC Report 2008). In 2009, the valuation of the television industry stood at Rs 266 billion (PwC Report 2010). The television households increased from 118 million in 2008 to 124 million in 2009, representing a penetration of 60 per cent of the country (PwC Report 2010: 24).

Private broadcasters, both Indian and foreign are battling with the national broadcaster. Some private broadcasters have expanded and today, have not merely national, but global aspirations. A bouquet of regional language television channels is now being offered in addition to English and Hindi. The Cable industry has increased penetration and become a force to reckon with, serving an estimated 70 million homes in 2007 (FICCI and PwC Report 2008). This figure increased to 72 million homes in 2009 (PwC Report 2010). New delivery platforms such as Direct to Home (DTH) have come into existence and are gaining market share.

In the quest for a better understanding of these complex issues, this book primarily analyses the change in television in India over the period 1990 onwards, concentrating on the decade 1990–2000, as this period witnessed maximum change. In doing so, global, national, and local issues have been explored with respect to electronic forms of communications, using the Indian frame of reference. More spe-cifically, this book examines whether the authority of the state in the realm of broadcasting has been redistributed to global and local levels. The response of the state to any such redistribution is also the object of study.

This book opens with a general introduction and overview of the phenomena of globalization and localization, dwelling upon the relationship to the nation state. The first and second chapters review the literature at length and are culled from diverse fields including mass communications, sociology, anthropology, geography, economics, political science, and international relations. The third chapter outlines the parameters of television in India in the last two decades and seeks to contextualize it. The fourth chapter seeks to construct a framework for examining the broadcast and cable sector in India. The fifth and sixth chapters indulge in a detailed interpretation and analysis of the trends in the sector and discuss the emergence of private television broadcasting. The seventh chapter examines the regulatory policies of the state. In the last chapter, certain conclusions are reached, and implications of the study are considered. This book adopts a qualitative, interdisciplinary approach, and seeks to incorporate economic, political, social, and cultural dimensions with respect to communications, in the context mentioned.

After a long period of somnolence, events in electronic communications have occurred at breakneck speed in the post-1990 Indian subcontinent. A challenge that any researcher faces is that any work becomes obsolete even as it is written. Keeping this fact in mind, however, a theoretical analysis of the broadcasting scenario in post-1990 India may identify patterns that would help to establish policy guidelines for the future. It is hoped that this study would have specific lessons for South Asia, and some more general lessons for developing countries elsewhere.

NOTES

1. The realist paradigm considered the nation-state to be the primary unit of analysis. For a detailed exposition of realism see Kenneth Waltz (1979).
2. In *The Clash of Civilizations and the Remaking of World Order* (1996), Huntington emphasizes the civilization as the operational unit of analysis in a global system. According to Huntington (1996) a civilization is the 'highest cultural grouping of people and the broadest level of cultural identity people have short of which distinguishes humans from other species'. The author identifies seven or eight major civilizations that he considers to be of vital importance in the contemporary world.

These are, the West which includes Catholic and Protestant Europe, along with the United States, Australia, Canada, and New Zealand, Orthodoxy which includes Russia, modern Greece, and other countries subscribing to Eastern Orthodox Christianity, Sinic which includes China, Taiwan, Hong Kong, Singapore, and Japan, Hindu, which mainly consists of India and Sri Lanka, Muslim which is an amalgamation of various countries, Latin America, and 'possibly an African civilization' which would mostly consist of sub-Saharan Africa.

3. The terrorist attacks in New York and Washington on 11 September 2001 seem to have reignited interest in Huntington's thesis, contrary to Fukuyama and the 'endists' views.

4. For post-Cold War models emphasizing economics or the replacement of geo-politics by geo-economics see Harkavy (1995) and Thurow (1992). Ray (1989) and Mueller (1989) offer insights into models relying on norms. The importance of International Government Organizations in theorizing about a post-Corld War global order is studied by Jacobson, Reisinger, and Mathews (1986).

5. www.unctad.org

6. Dependency theory has at its foundation an inequality in interaction between entities, be it in the field of trade, commerce, or communications. This theory was based on a critique of imperialism with reference to the case of Latin America (Gunder–Frank 1969). Its broad frame-work analysed the economic relationships between developed and developing countries on a global scale. Dependency theorists have postulated the existence of two major entities, that is, the core or developed countries and the periphery or the developing countries, in the global capitalist system (Galtung 1971). Specifically, the dependency paradigm postulated that, as a legacy of colonialism, the developing countries were still dependent via economic structures on the ex-colonial powers. In the field of communications, the 'cultural imperialism' model, and its subset, the 'media imperialism' model, have argued that international flows of technology and cultural products have encouraged dependency, and actually impeded development in developing countries.

7. The New World Information and Communication Order (NWICO) is a major issue which was debated in the 1970s. The non-aligned movement, which consisted of many of the newly liberated nations of Asia and Africa, was a force behind the NWICO. This issue came into existence because of the developing countries perception that the

existing international information and communications structure was a hegemonic one. Facets of this hegemony included the quantitative imbalance in news flows between developed and developing countries, and the role of the information and communication order in creating and maintaining forms of neo-colonialism. Other issues in international communications which are linked to the NWICO are that of 'cultural imperialism' and development. The cultural imperialism view holds that international flows of technology and cultural products have encouraged dependency, and actually impeded development in developing countries. Issues such as the NWICO and cultural imperialism all revolve around the developing countries' concern for sovereignty, identity, and a shaping of their image in their own terms, in a manner conducive to their perception of development.

CHAPTER ONE

THEORETICAL APPROACHES TO GLOBALIZATION AND LOCALIZATION

....

GLOBAL

At a superficial level, it would appear that humanity is coming closer together, co-habiting a global village. Visions of the planet from outer space, transnational advertising campaigns, and even health or environmental issues such as global warming, genetic research, or AIDS seem to highlight a common denominator (Featherstone 1993). Robertson (1995) refers to this point of view broadly speaking as the 'homogenizers' in the globalization debates. The homogenizers include a number of Marxists and functionalists who implicitly believe in the notion of a world system. In large part they are concerned with the project of modernity. 'They look primarily at the presence of the universal in the particular, whether as commodification or as time-space distanciation' (Featherstone and Lash 1995).

The view of the homogenizers is contrasted with that of the 'heterogenizers' such as Edward Said (1978), Homi K. Bhabha (1990), and

Stuart Hall (1992), who are generally regarded to be 'postmodernists'. Heterogenizers generally would not subscribe to the notion of a world system. They 'will disclaim the distinction of universal and particular, and see the dominance of the West over 'the rest' as that of simply one particular over others' (Featherstone and Lash 1995). Robertson (1995) seeks to find a way of reconciling these divergent viewpoints by considering the dialectic between the global and the local. Pieterse (2006) also tries to strike a middle ground by looking at globalization as hybridization.

Global change is taking place along many dimensions: political, economic, social, technological and geographic (Bird *et al.* 1993). In the words of Eade, 'there is a widespread sense that the world is changing rapidly and drastically. While an awareness of change is nothing new, contemporary debates about *specific* changes raise novel issues' (1997: 1). Values and identities are now more than ever in a state of flux.

The process of globalization is 'proving difficult to pin down conceptually and to demonstrate empirically' (Harding and Le Gales 1997: 181). Even though there is no universally accepted definition of globalization, some recurrent themes, which have emerged out of different streams of inquiry, are that of the compression of both time and space (Eade 1997). For social theorists such as Giddens (1990, 1991), globalization is a 'consequence of modernity'. However, Giddens (1990) characterizes the current period as one of 'late modernity' rather than post-modernity, because he believes we have entered an era where the consequences of modernity are becoming more radicalized and universalized than before.

In exploring the relationship between globalization and modernity, Giddens (1994) and Beck (1994) use the concept of 'reflexive modernization'. Both Giddens and Beck believe that globalization and individualization are facets of the process of reflexive modernization. While Beck believes that simple modernization is the dis-embedding and re-embedding of traditional social forms by industrial social forms, he elaborates on the notion of reflexive modernization,

> It means first the disembedding and second the re-embedding of indus-
> trial social forms by another modernity...reflexive modernization, then
> is supposed to mean that a change of industrial society which occurs
> surreptitiously and unplanned in the wake of normal, autonomized

modernization and with an unchanged, intact political and economic order implies the following: a *radicalization* of modernity, which breaks up the premises and contours of·industrial society and opens paths to another modernity (Beck 1994: 2–3).

Thus it would appear that globalization via the concept of reflexive modernization corresponds to a period which has been labeled variously, 'post-industrial', 'information', or even 'post traditional' society.

Giddens (1990) approaches the issue from the field of sociology. According to him, the processes of 'distanciation' and 'disembedding' can explain space and time compression. Distanciation is a concept, which explains the terms by which 'time and space are organized so as to connect presence and absence' (1990: 14). The notion of disembedding refers to the way in which social relations are transformed from their local contexts, and restructured over indefinite spans of time–space. Gidden's notions allow for a dialectical relationship between the global and the local, and do not view globalization as necessarily leading to social homogenization.

What is globalization? Is globalization viewed positively, or negatively? Is it inevitable? What is the relationship of global with national and with local? These are some of the central questions that form the core of the inquiry about globalization. Giddens (1990) construes globalization to mean 'the intensification of worldwide social relations' (1990: 64). Holm and Sorensen define globalization as 'the intensification of economic, political, social and cultural relations across borders' (1995: 1). The advantage of this definition is that it views globalization as being multi-dimensional.

Some scholars who have studied the globalization process view it as being primarily uni-causal. Wallerstein's earlier work on world systems, emphasizing the economic factor falls into this category. However, Wallerstein's (1990) more recent work acknowledges the importance of culture. As opposed to Wallerstein's views, some scholars of international relations have acknowledged the importance of political factors, rather than economic factors in explaining the process of globalization.

One strand of thought on the process of globalization has emphasized the cultural imperialism thesis. According to this view, Western media, especially American media and cultural forms, were implacable in their effect on indigenous cultures, leading to cultural homogenization (Schiller 1991; Hamelink 1996). The problem with this view is that it does not take account of some of the subtleties of the globalization process, and its linkages with the local. Evidence of the emergence of cultural hybrids is also difficult to explain in the light of this thesis, which emphasizes an inexorable one-way flow from center to periphery (Pieterse 2006).

Other theorists have also conceived of globalization as being multi-causal, and do not subscribe to the view of either a cultural or an economic hegemon as being responsible for globalization. Appadurai's work, while giving a more central role to culture, belongs to the latter camp. In a seminal article, Appadurai (1990) explores the complex dimensions of global cultural flows. He conceives of these dimensions as various 'scapes'. *Ethnoscapes* refers to human flows such as immigrants, tourists, refugees, and others. *Technoscapes* implies the infrastructural flows, both mechanical and informational, produced by government organizations and national as well as multi-national corporations. *Financescapes* refers to the movements of global capital via structures such as currency markets, national stock exchanges, and commodity speculations. Appadurai goes on to talk about the existence of *mediascapes* and *ideoscapes*, which co-exist with the other terrains. *Mediascapes* refer to the electronic capabilities for the production and dissemination of information, as well as to the images created by the media. While *ideoscapes* also map images, Appadurai believes that these are often overtly political, and concern the ideologies of states and counter-ideologies of movements directed against the state. In Appadurai's words, 'the five terms I have coined set the basis for a tentative formulation about the condition under which global flows occur: *they occur in and through the growing disjunctures between ethnoscapes, technoscapes, financescapes, mediascapes and ideoscapes*' (emphasis in original, 301). To elaborate, Appadurai believes that the accelerated speed and scale of these flows have led to increasing importance of the disjunctures between flows in explaining the politics of global culture.

Global Media

In the field of communications, media players are operating in an increasingly globalized fashion. Herman and McChesney (1997) believe that there has been a restructuring of national media industries with the emergence of a global commercial media market since the 1980s. This system is dominated by three or four dozen large transnational corporations (TNCs), with fewer than 10 mostly U.S.-based media conglomerates dominating the global market. This global media order is characterized by the centralization of media power, commercialism, and an associated decline in the relative importance of public broadcasting (Herman and McChesney 1997: 1).

The emergence of large transnational corporations in the field of media is not a new phenomenon, but the rate of mergers and acquisitions across the spectrum of the media has stepped up in the last few years.[1] This trend runs parallel with a broader trend of mergers and conglomeration in the economy resulting in the growth of giant transnational corporations in the period 1990–2000. The application of neoclassical economic policies in the former Soviet bloc countries, as well as in many developing countries has further established the importance of laissez-faire ideology, associated with liberal democracies (Biersteker 1992). The implications are that the private corporations have expanded their sphere. This is evident even in the field of communications where many communications structures have changed hands from public to private ownership. As Herman and McChesney explain, 'Eastern Europe has been the site of a painful transition from a state dominated economy and media to one with increasing private ownership...TV programming is heavily westernized in both direct (imported) content and format...Despite strong nationalistic undercurrents, the elites in Russia (and elsewhere in Eastern Europe) are denationalized' (1997: 65).

Herman and McChesney's observations seem to point to the direction of cultural homogenization. The situation is similar to other East European countries such as Poland, Hungary, and the Czech Republic where western firms like Time Warner, Canal Plus, Disney, and Bertelsman have increasingly dominated television (Herman and McChesney 1997).

An important aspect of the globalization of communications is the increasing importance of advertising (Herman and McChesney 1997). This indicates a higher degree of commercialization present in the media, as compared to the earlier era where public broadcasting was the order of the day in many countries. In addition, the rash of privatization and liberalization afflicting most of the Post, Telephone, and Telegraph entities in the world, with their frequent acquisition by global telecommunications players imply an increased role for the market as compared to the state.

These facts would appear to fit in well with Fukuyama's (1992) thesis, which examines the spread of a liberal democratic order across the globe. The rhetoric of the information society also seems to match with Fukuyama's views. Fukuyama's model, however, is inadequate when it comes to explaining communications flows associated with phenomena such as ethnic movements and religious fundamentalism, the mainstay of Huntington's model. It is also not very useful in dealing with contradictions that may arise within liberal democracies.

As a counterpoint to the global/globalization views, there is a growing body of work that explores the conceptual category of local/localization.

LOCAL

The parameters of local are not very well defined in the sense that there are many interpretations of this term and it is also a somewhat contentious category. A large portion of the current literature on local/localization takes the issue of culture[2] as its central thematic. Hannerz, a social anthropologist, believes that there is currently a world culture, but there has not been a homogenization of systems of meaning. He believes that world culture is 'marked by an organization of diversity rather than by a replication of uniformity' (1990: 237). In his view, the world culture is formed through the growing bonds between various local cultures, as well as through the development of cultures, which are not connected to any particular territory. However, people can relate to this world culture in different ways. For example there are cosmopolitans and there are locals. Hannerz believes that the distinction between cosmopolitans and locals has existed in the sociologist's repertoire since Merton's (1957) classic study of a small town in the US during the Second World War. The importance of this distinction with respect to current studies on globalization is that the terms are contrasted and used to define each other. In other words, a cosmopolitan is that which a local is not.

Hannerz (1990) reminds us that historically, cultures have been conceived of as distinct structures of meaning, usually associated with territories. In this scenario, culture is assumed to be mainly a product of face-to-face relationships. An implication of this assumption is that the local is delineated as an ideal type. However, in the current climate, the ideal type of local may be more difficult to adhere to, as explained in the following passage from Hannerz:

> as collective phenomena cultures are by definition linked primarily to interactions and social relationships, and only indirectly and without logical necessity to particular areas in physical space. The less social relationships are confined within territorial boundaries, the less so is also culture; and in our time especially, we can contrast in gross terms those cultures which are territorially defined (in terms of nations, regions, or localities) with those which are carried as collective structures of meaning by networks more extended in space, transnational or even global. This contrast, too — but not it alone — suggests that cultures, rather than being easily separated from one another as the hard-edged pieces in a mosaic, tend to overlap and mingle. While we understand them to be differently located in the social structure of the world, we also realize that the boundaries we draw around them are frequently rather arbitrary (1990: 239).

It seems likely that as de-territorialized forms of social relationships arise; categories such as 'national' or 'local' may have to be re-conceptualized.

Dirlik elaborates on the notion of rethinking the unit of local. He refers to local 'as a site both of promise and predicament' (1996: 22). According to him, local could have promise as a site of resistance and liberation in a scenario of global capitalism. Conversely, Dirlik is wary that though local may hold the promise of liberation, it may also hold the seeds of oppression and parochialism. He emphasizes the fact that 'local' is not the conventional category, rather it is a contemporary concept that 'serves as a site for the working out of the most fundamental contradictions of the age' (1996: 23).

There has recently been a flowering of interest in the local. Some of the factors which may be responsible for the elevation in importance of the local in the last decade are social movements such as ecological, women's and ethnic movements, and intellectual developments associated with postmodernism (Dirlik 1996). Some scholars have repudiated modernist ideologies, as they associate the modernization project with repression of the local in the name of the universal. Those subscribing to postmodernist views would seek to reject the 'meta-narratives' of modernization and development. Modernist theories primarily viewed local derogatorily, as areas of rural backwardness, to be transformed by progress. This view also held sway in the early writing on communication and development by individuals such as Lerner, Schram, and Rogers. It is interesting to note that the modernist devaluation of the local prevailed in both bourgeois and Marxist social sciences in the decades after World War II (Dirlik 1996).

Local Media

Since the parameters of 'local' are not well defined as indicated ear-lier, the category of 'local media' also poses conceptual challenges. In some ways, the category of local media would emphasize culture, in others it could be a site of resistance. It may be useful to define it in a contextual manner. For example, it has been argued that the use of communications media such as audio and video cassettes were vital to the Iranian Revolution (Mowlana 1996; Sreberny–Mohammadi 1997). These are examples of local media in the manner in which they were circulated. However, the same tapes if aired on a national channel may not necessarily be local. Traditional forms of commu-nication such as folk art, storytelling, and puppetry have associations with the local.

In the context of India, All India Radio (AIR) the government controlled broadcaster has a category of 'local radio stations'. In April 2010, the number of local radio stations in India numbered about 86. They appear to have been defined as local according to the power of the transmitter, that is, between 1 and 10 kilowatts of power. They started being commissioned from the 1980s onwards. While the first such local radio station to be commissioned was at Nagercoil in Tamil Nadu in 1984, the bulk of the local radio stations were com-missioned in the 1990s.[3] In terms of content, programming is very similar to other higher powered stations of All India Radio.

Media have also been defined as 'big' or 'small' (Schramm 1972). While 'big' media are associated with the mass media, 'small' media generally are associated with participatory and public means of communication as opposed to that controlled by the states or large corporations (Sreberny–Mohammadi and Mohammadi 1997). After touching upon the concepts of global and local, we arrive at the intersection between them.

GLOBAL VS LOCAL

The relationship between the global and the local has often been couched as opposite poles, or a dualism. One example of this line of scholarship is Barber's (1992) view on the subject. According to Barber, globalization, or 'globalism' is defined as the opposite of localization, or 'tribalism'. In his pithy phrases, the New World (dis) Order can be summed up by the principle of homogenizing global-ization or 'McWorld',[4] which necessarily exists in tension with the opposite principle of fragmentation, or 'Jihad'.[5]

By contrast, Robertson (1995), who has written widely on the topic of globalization mentions the terms 'glocal' and 'glocalization', which seeks to combine the universal with the particular. These con-cepts seek to combine global and local into some form of a blend. He believes that these ideas were popularized during the 1980s, growing out of the Japanese business practice of adapting a global outlook to local conditions.[6] In Robertson's view, globalization need not inevitably be opposed to localization. Instead he maintains that globalization has involved the creation and incorporation of locality, thus the concept of glocalization could replace the concept of glo-balization. In his opinion, the form of globalization is related to the ideologically laden notion of world order. According to Robertson, the two seemingly opposing simultaneous trends of homogenization and heterogenization are actually complementary and interpen-etrative. He expresses the opinion that 'glocalization can be, in fact, is, used strategically, as in the strategies of glocalization employed by contemporary TV enterprises seeking global markets (MTV, then CNN, and now others)' (1995: 40).

In this respect, Robertson's views resonate with Giddens (1990) notions of the dialectical relationship between the global and the local.

The view that we are currently in a 'new world-space of cultural production and national representation which is simultaneously becoming more *globalized* (unified around dynamics of capitalogic moving across borders) and more *localized* (fragmented into contestatory enclaves of difference, coalition, and resistance) in everyday texture and composition' is expressed by Wilson and Dissanayake (1996: 1). Their views can be considered to be postmodernist, and find echoes in the writings of many others that take culture to be their focal point in the study of the global/local.

The dimension of power in the interactions of different levels and players, as in local, national, and global is a crucial one. Featherstone and Lash argue that it is important to become familiar with the nuances of the process of globalization and seek to develop theories, which incorporate the different power potentials of the various players. Different entities, such as nation-states, multinational corporations, and international organizations, have different resources (economic and cultural) and seek to set different agendas. 'Not every nation-state can be fitted easily into a developmental sequence derived from Western experience of tradition-modernity-post modernity, indeed the application of these concepts to other non-Western contexts may well be flawed and misses the politics of knowledge where a dominant particular is able to represent itself as the universal' (1995: 3).

Other fundamental concepts such as power, the nation-state, and its authority are undergoing redefinition in this current era. Traditional notions of power as employed by statesmen and scholars ranging from Nicolo Machiavelli, Hans Morgenthau, to Kenneth Waltz have centred on notions of tangible resources[7] (Mowlana 1996). Deutsch (1966) proposed the idea of power as a currency in interactions between political systems built on the notion of tangible resources, as well as intangible resources. As with the realists, tangible resources could be measured as countable voters, size of the army, military hardware, and other measures. Intangible sources of power could include skills, morale, intensity of support, and other factors.

The realist emphasis on military strength and 'hard power' seems to be somewhat anachronistic in the current period. Nye (1990) has suggested the concept of 'soft power', which sums up the present situation better. Soft power implies an inclusion of intangible sources of power, such as cultural, educational, ideological, and information technology factors. Mowlana (1996) seeks to present the notion of power as an integrated whole, a combination of hard power, as well as soft power. He clarifies that a more holistic notion of power includes economics, technology, politics, cultural products, educational products, military hardware, as well as intangibles such as belief and value systems, ideology, knowledge, and religion. It has been suggested by Mowlana (1996) that soft power includes the concept of information as an intangible resource, implying that power is transferred from the capital-rich to the information-rich, with a consequent ascendance in importance of the information factor, as compared to physical resources. He expresses the opinion that the process of globalization can be best understood within the context of intangible sources of power. Thus, Mowlana highlights the linkages between communications, power, and globalization.

In a broadening of the notions of power and authority, James Rosenau (1990; 1992a; 1992b; 1997), the eminent international relations theorist, has some interesting observations to make. In an early work, Rosenau (1990) examines the turbulent nature of world politics. In this work, he suggests that the present era is a historical breaking point. He theorizes that macro global structures have been bifurcated into 'the two worlds of world politics' (1990: 5). The two worlds refer to the state-centric system, which now coexists with a powerful, but more decentralized multi-centric system. In other words, non-state actors have ascended in importance.

Rosenau identifies three main dimensions of world politics that are conceptualized as its main parameters. The micro-parameter operates at the level of individuals and consists of the orientations and skills by which citizens and members of non-state organizations link themselves to global politics. The macro-parameter refers to the 'constraints embedded in the distribution of power among and within the collectivities of the global system' (1990: 10). The mixed parameter refers to the 'nature of the authority relations that prevail between individuals at the micro level and their macro collectivities' (1990: 10). In this formulation, Rosenau suggests that all the parameters identified above are undergoing transformation.

In order to develop his theory of world politics, Rosenau utilizes concepts such as authority, control, and legitimacy. These would appear to derive from an essentially Weberian notion of the state.

For the sake of clarity, the formal definitions of these concepts as formulated by Rosenau are laid out in the following section.

- The key concept used by Rosenau is that of control. According to him,

  'the exercise of control in other words implies attempts on the part of one actor to modify, preserve or otherwise affect the orientations or actions of another. Thus, it is a concept rooted in interactions, and its existence can be determined empirically only by observing the degree of correspondence between what the controller does and how the object of the control responds' (1990: 183).

  It is also suggested that there is a continuum of control techniques ranging from brute force and other forms of physical coercion at one end to scientific proof and reason at the other. Other techniques, which lie between these two extremes, include appeals to shared values, trade-offs, bargaining, economic sanctions, and others. In a parallel fashion, the responses of the actors towards whom the techniques are directed can also be placed along a continuum ranging from agreement and compliance to disagreement and defiance. The other responses lying between these extremes include avoidance, conditional agreement, delay, apathy, and others.

- A closely allied concept, which is central to Rosenau's model, is authority. Authority, considered to be an outcome of control relations is defined as,

  that set of premises and habits on which macro leaders are entitled to rely on to obtain automatic compliance from their followers. Authority relationships in other words, are those patterns of a collectivity wherein some of its members are accorded the right to make decisions, set rules, allocate resources, and formulate policies for the rest of the members, who in turn comply with the decisions, rules and policies made by the authorities (1990: 186).

  Authority relations exist in formal structures such as constitutions, bylaws, statutes, and judicial decisions. They also exist in informal settings. Rosenau's interpretation of the term authority resonates with Weber's (1978) definition of authority as the probability that an order with a specific content will be followed by a group of persons.

- Rosenau (1990: 183–4) prefers to use the concept of control rather than power in his model, as he feels that relationships between actors revolve around this dimension. He implicitly takes cognizance of the power factor as the term capabilities refers to the possessional side of power, while control refers to the relational side.

- The concepts of control, authority, power, legitimacy, and coercion are all interrelated. Legitimacy is also a dimension that has to be taken into account in this model. In Rosenau's words,

> 'ordinarily, acts of authority are clothed in some degree of claimed legitimacy: the contention that the policies or actions are undertaken by appropriate officials and conform to recognized principles and accepted rules. If the claim is not accepted, that is, if legitimacy does not attach to the acts of leaders, authority is unlikely to sustain habits of compliance for long. Without legitimacy, authority can evoke compliance only by the use of brute force' (237).

Rosenau's usage of the term legitimacy owes a debt to Weber (1978). Legitimate authority according to Weber (1978) describes an authority, which is obeyed partly because it is regarded by the subordinate actor as obligatory or exemplary in some way.

Rosenau (1990; 1992a; 1997) informs us that the loci of authority have been relocated and restructured during the 1980s. Rosenau (1992a) believes that the sweeping changes that occurred in the arena of world politics during the 1980s, or 'the lurch toward change and accommodation that unfolded on a global scale', were multi-causal (1992a: 253). Among the factors that come into play are:

- global dynamics, such as the shift from an industrial order to a post-industrial order, with its associated emphasis on information technologies,
- the emergence of problems such as pollution, terrorism, currency crises, and AIDS,

- the authority crises that stem from the reduced capacity of states to deal with major political issues,
- the growing importance of subsystems or decentralization that have accompanied the weakening of states,
- and finally the feedback of the aforementioned factors on the skills and orientations of the individuals who comprise groups, and other collectives (Rosenau 1992a: 255).

In Rosenau's (1992a) opinion, authority has been relocated 'upward' toward transnational organizations and 'downward' toward sub-national groups, with the implications that national governments are increasingly finding it difficult to resolve major issues and problems that afflict their societies. Rosenau explains,

> If the new order is a response to the need for structures that accommodate both the powerful centralizing and decentralizing forces unleashed by the dynamics of technology, and it is founded on transformed processes whereby legitimacy and authority are generated and sustained, its form consists of an ungainly, asymmetrical set of global structures that accord a lesser (though not trivial) role to the state-centric system and a greater (though not overpowering) role to a newly emerged multicentric system (Rosenau, 1992: 256).

Rosenau (1990; 1992a) stresses the importance of the role played by new communications technologies in informing individuals, and adding to their analytical and emotional skills, which empowers them vis-a-vis the state. In particular, Rosenau believes that global television and computers have had a great impact on individuals. He introduces the concept of micro actions at a local level causing macro outcomes, due to greater interdependence and faster communications. Thus, Rosenau (1992a; 1992b; 1997) emphasizes the importance of communications as an explanatory variable of change in the last decade. These inter-linkages between the micro and macro levels are yet another way of conceptualizing the global/local problematic.

Teheranian (1997) suggests the dual nature of communications technologies. He informs us, 'information technologies, however, seem to have a Janus-like dual face. Historically, they have contributed to both democratic and counter-democratic trends in society.

Hence there is the promise of a Democratic Revolution alongside the perils of a Control Revolution' (1997: 77). In other words, communications can serve as an agent of domination, centralization, and neo-imperialism; it can also be the harbinger and enabler of emancipation. It would appear that the paradoxical nature of communications, especially mediated communications, is evident in its global, as well as its local manifestations.

In the last few years, new forms of accommodations between the global and the local are occurring in communications media; joint ventures between transnational players and local players, the appearance of culturally hybrid media products and the proliferation of 'local interest' websites in cyberspace, as well as the explosion in social networking to name just a few.

GLOBALIZATION, LIBERALIZATION IN BROADCASTING

As we look back and ponder, television has undergone a massive transformation from an essentially scarce national medium in the 1950s to a prolific international medium post 1990 (Smith 1998). Smith (1998) is of the opinion that while television once provided the core of a nationally authorized culture; in the 1990s it moved beyond the jurisdiction of the government. Globalization of television is evident in the shift towards an advertising based, commercial paradigm as well as a shift in the content as in programme genres, which tend towards globalized models or patterns (Straubhaar 2006: 681).

One of the major ideological debates in the field of broadcasting in the last few decades has been over the issue of ownership of the medium. Three distinct models have emerged: competitive commercial service, license-fee funded public service, and a mixed policy (Smith 1998). New technologies suggest that traditional broadcasters the world over will face commercial rivals. However, Smith (1998) does not believe that public service and state-run systems will perish, merely that they will have to define special roles for themselves.

The importance of television is evident in the fact that no other medium can match it for audience size in the developed nations. According to one estimate 98 per cent of homes in the developed world possessed a television set by 1990 (Smith 1998). It had also made massive inroads in the developing countries in the last decade.

Television households appeared to be growing fastest in Asia, and Africa, followed by Central America, over the period 1984–94. It is important to note that there have also been changes in the organizational structure and content of television, over the past decade.

Privatization, liberalization, and deregulation have implied a growing commercialization of television. Thus, Barker (1997: 4) argues that the favouring of commercial television by de-regulatory policies have implied that state television services, especially public service broadcasting entities have suffered a crisis. Similar issues are confronting the governments of many developing countries such as India, in the current period. One major area of difference, however is that in South Asia, the state-run broadcaster has to grapple with commercial television, from foreign entities, as well as domestic commercial broadcasters.

The growth of global television has in part been the result of technological change. Communications satellites, a particular type of information technology, are used extensively in the transmission of telephony, broadcasting, and data flows. They have greatly helped in the globalization of communications (Stewart 1991: 33). Before the development of satellites, fibre optic cabling and digital compression, television was a local/national outlet (Verna 1993). Technological advancements such as the development of digital compression to transmit analogue signals have changed the modes of transmission and helped to revolutionize the TV industry.

Satellites have added to the global/local cocktail. Satellite feeds allow local TV news shows to blend world events with local electronic news gathering (ENG) reports, restructuring TV network news. Economic imperatives also dictated a more aggressive pace of syndication and multi-national programming, increasing the worldwide nature of non-network programming (Verna 1993).

Scholars such as Dahlgren (1995) and Barker (1997) point out the need to study television in a manner, which would delve into the connections between economic, political, social, and cultural dimensions of society, as a multi-dimensional process. At the institutional level, it has been suggested that global television involves both national systems and transnational television. The argument has also been made that changes in technology have led to new methods of distribution for television which, coupled with increased political and industrial support for market solutions have emasculated national regulatory environments.

Verna (1993) cites some early examples of 'global casting', which set a trend. These were Live Aid, an international music programme in 1985, followed by Sport Aid, Prayer for World Peace, the 1990 Goodwill Games and others. The enabling technology was international satellite links. Verna (1993) defines global casting as TV transmission from multiple points to multiple locations on earth, usually live, with tape inserts, allowing a maximum number of viewers/listeners around the world to share the television experience (1993: 3). The technological factors spurring the growth of global television are important, however, other aspects of TV, namely content, also have to be taken cognizance of.

At the level of content, television has been called global in the sense that similar narrative forms or genres, notably news and soap operas, circulate worldwide (Barker 1997: 6–7). The global audience is large for the categories of music, sports, and news (Verna 1993). News oriented channels such as CNN and BBC World have come into their own in the last two decades. CNN's coverage of the 1991 Gulf War helped to establish it as a global brand name. The soap format and game shows have proved to be very popular in South Asia, as in other parts of the world. Talk shows have also proven to be popular across the globe.

Other trends in programming are expansion into multiple language fields and increased co-productions. For example, the Oprah Winfrey show was often shown in more than 60 countries, often dubbed in different languages. MTV is in a class of its own. The Warner Amex Satellite Entertainment Company in USA started it in 1981. By the early 1990s, MTV had 54 million viewers in the US and 50 million additional viewers in 39 countries. MTV represents the 'glocal' dynamic in the sense that it is co-produced to match its target audience in each country.

Countries like the United States fall at one end of the spectrum, since its commercial imperatives have led to the establishment of many familiar genres. The BBC, on the other hand, is still of interest as it exemplifies the public service model that many broadcasting systems aspire to. India now appears to be teetering between the two poles. Developing countries are currently experimenting with different reform measures in both radio and television. India is a regional leader in South Asia. Understanding India's experience will undoubtedly help throw light on other countries in the region.

Press freedom as defined by Freedom House, was not significantly correlated with the economic standing of the country in Asia during the 1990s. The US-based Freedom House measures press freedom by an indicator that is dependent on laws that influence media content, political pressures and controls on media content, economic influences over media content, and repressive actions against the media. For example press freedom is higher in the low-income countries of South Asia (with the exception of Maldives, Bhutan, and Pakistan) than in the middle-income countries of South-East Asia (barring Thailand, Philippines, and Indonesia). By this standard, India, Sri Lanka, Bangladesh, Nepal, and pre-Musharraf Pakistan fall into the 'partly free' category. In general, political pressures and controls on media content are high across South Asia, except for the print media in India (Gunaratne 2000: 2). In 2010, Freedom House categorized India as 'partly-free' in its annual survey of media independence in 197 countries. This index assesses the degree of print, broadcast, and internet freedom in every country examined.[8]

The history of television in South Asia has shown a predominance of state control. Historically, the audio–visual medium has been state run in the South Asian countries of India, Pakistan, Bangladesh, and Nepal. Sri Lanka is an exception since it initially started as a private venture. From the mid-1980s and accelerating in the early 1990s, there has been an increasing accommodation of private interests in the audio–visual medium (Thomas 1998). Many South Asian countries had some foreign assistance in setting up their television systems.

*   *   *

Television in South Asia expanded and by the mid-1990s had become a nation-wide service in most countries. Notwithstanding the differences between the various South Asian television systems, there were some commonalties in terms of ideologies and structures of broadcasting. In the words of Thomas (1998: 203), 'The iron-hold that state broadcasting structures maintained over audio–visual space in South Asia was routinely legitimized in the language of public service, national security and state prerogative. While the need to extend an affordable broadcasting service to national audiences was, to some extent a noble sentiment, this was soon exploited for political reasons'. Thomas (1998) points out that throughout South Asia, television functioned as an instrument of propaganda for the ruling political party, even though there were different types of governments in power across the region. The *de facto* liberalization brought about by satellite television in the late 1990s has forced the state broadcaster to re-evaluate its role across South Asia in the new millennium.

NOTES

1. For a detailed analysis of increasing monopoly in the media, see Ben Bagdikian (1996).
2. The concept of culture is a controversial one. What is culture? Definitions abound, for an analysis of this contentious subject see James Dewey (1934); Clifford Geertz (1973); Raymond Williams (1958); Stuart Hall (1992); Frederic Jameson (1995). In Dewey's opinion, works of art are formed through an interaction with experience. He argues for a view of culture, which derives out of this particular view of art. Dewey thus broadens the horizon of culture, incorporating its symbiotic relationship with the environment. The eminent anthropologist Clifford Geertz (1973) has indicated that he is opposed to a very inclusive definition of culture, on the grounds that such a definition may obscure more than it reveals. The concept of culture espoused by Geertz is in essence a semiotic one. In his words,

> 'Believing with Max Weber, that man is an animal suspended in webs of significance he himself has spun, I take culture to be those webs, and the analysis of it to be therefore not an experimental science in search of law, but an interpretive one in search of meaning' (1973: 5).

To reiterate, Geertz endorses the view of culture as a symbolic system, but one in relation to the behaviour of individuals and groups, within the logic of everyday life. In Raymond Williams' pioneering work *Culture and Society* (1958), he attempts to achieve a better understanding of social organizations and relationships through the mediation of culture. Williams examines how the notion of culture has historically undergone many changes. The term culture, for example, changed in meaning through the spectrum of natural growth, a state of perception, attaining an ideal, intellectual development, terminating in Williams' own description of culture as a 'whole way of life'. This view of culture is as a continuous, evolving process, resulting in the establishment of shared meanings through the community.

Stuart Hall (1990), an important figure in British cultural studies has indicated that notwithstanding cultural studies preoccupation with culture, no single unproblematic definition of culture has emerged. He argues that the concept of culture remains a complex one—a site of convergent interests, rather than a logically or conceptually clarified area. Frederic Jameson (1995), in his study of postmodernism, has expressed one of its distinctive features to be the erasure of the dividing line between high culture and popular culture. Jameson's views of culture seem to be narrow in scope, harking back to earlier times, when culture and art were equated with artefacts such as books, painting, architecture, and so on. Although Jameson refers to the concept of culture explicitly, it appears to be a somewhat restricted view.

3. Available at www.allindiaradio.gov.in.

4. The concept of McWorld obviously has connotations of globalization and the convergence of a world-view as represented by the global McDonalds Corporation.

5. The principle of Jihad as conceptualized by Barber refers to the centripetal tendencies brought into motion by an ethnic movement or a religious war. The term derives from the Islamic concept of a holy war.

6. Robertson's notion of glocalization first grew out of a body of work in marketing literature.

7. Realism considered the nation-state to be the primary unit of analysis. It utilized the assumption that the back-drop against which nation-states acted, was one of international anarchy, implying that there was no central authority (Waltz 1979). Nation-states vied with each other to establish supremacy within this anarchical system. The architect of this approach was Hans Morgenthau, who maintained as early as 1948, that balance of power between nations was the crucial variable that determined war and peace. Moreover, power was based on various factors, but military power was of major significance in the power equation (Waltz 1979).

8. Available at www.freedomhouse.org.

CHAPTER TWO

THEORETICAL APPROACHES TO THE ROLE OF THE STATE

Although current scholarship is widely divergent on the role the state[1] should play in the current period of changed global/local conditions, there is, at least, general agreement on the need to re-examine the role of the state. Beck (1994) suggests the modern state is something of a paradox. He believes that on the one hand the modern state is withering away, but on the other it is more urgent than ever, implying a metamorphosis of the state. In his words, 'that is how one can sketch and fill out the image of a state that, like a snake, is shedding the skin of its classical tasks and developing a new global "skin of tasks"' (Beck 1994: 38). In Beck's opinion, the classic state is giving way to a 'negotiation state, which arranges, stages conversations, and directs the show'. Other scholars have also considered the changing face of the state.[2]

GLOBALIZATION AND THE NATION-STATE

It has also been suggested that the notion of national sovereignty requires close scrutiny in a post-Cold War world. An interesting view on the current state of international politics is provided by Buzan and Segal (1996) in their concept of 'postmodern' states. Buzan and Segal hold the view that in postmodern states, the government no longer controls a major function, namely that of controlling the economy. These management functions have been taken over by the private corporations. In their opinion, postmodern states still retain the trappings of modernity such as national borders and sovereignty, but they are more receptive to cultural, political, and economic interactions than modern states. The characteristic features of postmodern states are pluralism and individualism; national identities are no longer as cohesive as in modern states. Multiculturalism and fragmented/multiple identities come into existence, partly fueled by the drive to legitimize the 'other', be it in the realm of race, class, gender, or religion (Buzan and Segal 1996). Thus it would appear that some scholars are attempting to re-conceptualize the role of the state in a post-Cold War world.

Karl Polanyi's work in the 1930s and the 1940s may shed some light on the contemporary globalization *problematique* and the role of states. His model, which considers the interplay of economic and political forces, may be relevant even today because of the following factors identified by Scott (1997). Firstly, the globalizing tendencies of market societies are analysed along with an explicit analysis of their political and regulative institutions. Secondly, globalization is conceived as one possible outcome for a capitalist society, 'the realization of which requires conditions that are both contingent and political' (Scott 1997: 8). Lastly, although the collapse of communist regimes has cast doubt on its viability as an alternative to liberalism, Polanyi's views suggest a way out of the trap of cultural fragmentation and the celebration of consumerism.

The central features of Polanyi's model are as follows. The primary hypothesis is that markets destroy the way in which economic life is structured, typically as local relationships of reciprocal obligation. The second hypothesis is that markets come into existence as the explicit outcome of political action and through the actions of states. Polanyi believes that all markets are regulated, as the state institutions set the rules of the game. Lastly, his model indicates that the social disruption caused by markets will lead to social collapse, or authoritarianism, or 'in the re-introduction of political mechanisms for regulating the market and protective restrictions on its scope of operation' (Scott 1997: 9). Scott (1997) considers Polanyi's work to be relevant even in explaining the current phase of globalization. He points out, 'although these arguments were developed to explain the rise and nature of the first "free market utopia" (Britain as it was conceived by Manchester economics)...the general points he makes remain relevant to what might be called the "second free market utopia" (i.e. a single global market as it is conceived by contemporary neo-liberalism)'. In other words, while analysing globalization, ideas are perhaps as important as societal processes and economic trends and globalization remains a contested and unrealizable project (Scott 1997: 9).

Therefore, Scott (1997) derives inspiration from Polanyi to suggest that in addition to social and economic forces, globalization also flows from an idea, specifically that of the free market. A reading of Polanyi in current circumstances also implies that states have a more versatile repertoire of action than that conceived by realism. Nation-states have to play a contradictory role as; they are instrumental in establishing markets, and also have to provide protection against the effects of markets. To clarify, as the market expands via deregulation and other measures, society may mobilize itself in various ways. One reaction could be the emergence of new regulatory bodies at the local and/or the interstate level (Scott 1997).

The relationship between globalization and the nation-state has been the subject of recent inquiry by political scientists. The nation-state of old is being subjected to new pressures from areas as diverse as transnational corporations, transnational political institutions such as the UN, supranational military and trade organizations (witness Kosovo and NATO intervention), and global social movements. The spread of neo-liberalism in economics has implied that the ideology of the market has gained vis-à-vis the state. Is the death knell of the nation-state being sounded? It would seem that an obituary at this point in time is somewhat premature. I am in agreement with Holton (1998) when he says that the issue of the nation-state has become controversial. Transnational organizations and processes relying on highly mobile capital and labour owned by multinational companies have reduced the resources available to nation states. However, the nation-state, whether in the Western world or elsewhere, has proved to be more resilient in economic matters than some predicted. Transnational entities must still work with national governments in establishing their goals. Also, nation-states have looked as much to regionalism, as in the European Union (EU) and the more recent North American Free Trade Association (NAFTA), as to global arrangements. In Holton's words, 'globalization, it seems, has not yet overrun the nation-state. Indeed...individual governments, interest groups, and individuals have in many ways helped to create or harness global processes and networks to their own advantage (Holton 1998: 6).

The Withering away of the State

According to international relations scholars Palan, Abbott, and Deans (1996), the literature on the relationship between the state and globalization falls into three broad categories. The first group 'interprets globalization to mean a qualitative transformation of the environment of accumulation from essentially nationally dominated "economies" to an "economy" and "society" which span the entire world and are largely impervious to political borders. For this rather diverse group, the state appears exposed and outflanked' (1996: 1). This view, which emphasizes the impotence of the state, has been described by Palan *et al.* (1996) as the 'withering' or the 'hollowing out of the state' thesis. They believe that this thesis is supported by a number of arguments, some of which may be incompatible. In part, this view stems from the neo-liberal rejection of the Keynesian state. There are some ambiguities present in this view, as expressed by Palan *et al.* (1996), 'there is a suggestion therefore that the thesis is as prescriptive as much as it is descriptive, that the more one accepts the decline of the state, the more one reinforces such decline' (1996: 2).

The withering away of the state view is also supported by political economists such as Ohmae (1993) who contend that technology is the driving force which has changed the dynamics of economic activity, to larger units, possibly some forms of 'regional states'. Sassen (1991), however, talks about the emergence of global cities, in a kind of neo-medievalism, funnelled by economic and technological factors. These cities, generally, have large financial markets, which cater to investors from different nations.

Globalization as a Fad

In contrast to this view, another group of scholars believes that talk about globalization reflects a fad, and is not based upon any significant structural changes in the international economy. The work of Chase-Dunn (1994) and Jackson and James (1994) are examples of this line of thinking. The critique of this view offered is that it is historically insensitive and does not provide us with the theoretical tools needed to deal with phenomena such as global corporations and global financial markets (Palan *et al.* 1996).

The Resilient State

A third strand of literature on the theme of globalization and the state seeks to reconcile some of the other views. Some of the recent literature in international political economy supports the notion of a resilient nation-state, which though chastised by global processes, has adopted policies to ensure its consolidation and survival. Cerny's (1990, 1995) work on the 'competition state' is a case in point. According to this view, instead of viewing the state and globalization as polar opposites, the flexibility of the state in adapting to new conditions is underlined. In other words, it may actually be in the state's interest to encourage the forces of trans-nationalization—for example by wooing foreign investment.

Palan *et al.* (1996) sum up the third view as follows, 'the idea that the entire institutional, cultural, political and psychological notions about society can simply be brushed aside by the "forces of the market" is not credible. The third school argues that both society and the state are changing, but that such change should not be confused with decline. The state can be besieged but it can fight back and reorganize itself. In fact, social structures and historical experiences have proved to be far more resilient than was normally assumed' (1996: 3–4).

The renewed emphasis on states as organizational structures and as potentially autonomous actors surfaced in the 1980s. In a milestone work prophetically entitled *Bringing the State Back In* editors Evans, Skocpol, and Rueschemeyer (1985) point out that 'current work, however, increasingly views the state as an actor that, although obviously influenced by the society surrounding it, also shapes social and political processes' (1985: 7).

Skocpol (1985) describes the emphasis on states as being a relatively new phenomenon. In her opinion, politics and governmental activities were largely understood in society-centered terms, characteristic of the pluralist and structure–functionalist perspective dominant in the United States in the 1950s and 1960s. The 1960s saw the neo-Marxists engage in debates about the 'capitalist state'. These alternative conceptualizations widened our understanding about the various socioeconomic functions performed by the capitalist state, for example as an instrument of class rule, an objective guarantor of economic accumulation, or an arena for political class struggles. Notwithstanding this more nuanced view of the functioning of the state, Skocpol (1985) believes that most neo-Marxist writers on the state have society-centered assumptions, where states are shaped by classes and class struggles so 'many possible forms of autonomous state action are thus ruled out by definitional fiat' (1985: p. 5).

While the nature of the state has been the subject of debate in the twentieth century,[3] emphasis on the state as independent actor has resurfaced in the last two decades. To sum up, over the period of the nineteenth century, up to the post-World War II period, Western social science did not accord salience to the importance of states as autonomous organizational actors. Even phenomena such as authoritarianism and totalitarianism were explained in terms of theories emphasizing economic backwardness, or 'traditional' values.

Relation between Society and State

Rudolph and Rudolph have commented on the interaction between the state and society in a classic work (1987: 61). They believe that the state–society relationship can be located on a continuum ranging from complete State domination of society to complete societal domination of the State. Further, they identify four potential positions on the continuum; totalitarian, in which the state completely dominates society, creating and controlling social formations, maintaining a closed milieu, and using force without restraint; autonomous, in which the state can be self-determining because it is relatively free from societal forces, the limits on its freedom to act being legitimacy and consent; constrained, in which the state's freedom to act is limited not only by legitimacy and consent but also by the representation of organized social forces; and reflexive or heteronomous, in which the state lacks self -determination because it is dominated by society, whose organized interests or classes appropriate state authority and resources. A state's location on the continuum depends on historical circumstances, including ideology, leadership, conjunctural effects, and the balance of public and private power.

Furthermore, Rudolph and Rudolph (1987) emphasize the fact that state formation is a continuous process located in history, leading to the occurrence of states in a variety of forms, characters, and styles. They endorse Peter Nettl's (1968) view of the polymorphic state, and his use of the term 'stateness' to imply that high and low 'stateness' depends on historical experience, institutional legacies and political culture.

Various factors have contributed to the decline in the importance of society-centered views of social change and politics. Some of the factors identified by Skocpol (1985) are, firstly, the 'Keynesian revolution' from the 1930s to the 1950s which led to national macroeconomic policies and expanded public social expenditures in the industrialist capitalist democracies. Secondly, many new nations emerged as the yoke of colonialism was thrust away over the 1950s to the 1970s. These post-colonial nations subscribed to patterns of political organization and policy choices that were not merely limited to the Western liberal democratic model. Lastly, by the mid-1970s, Britain and the United States were facing intense international economic competition. The renewed interest in states as actors and society-shaping institutional structures surfaced at this juncture.

What then is the state[4]? In Max Weber's classic formulation, 'states are compulsory associations claiming control over territories and the people within them' (Skocpol 1985: 7).[5] Organizations performing administration, legal, extraction, and coercion functions lie at the heart of the state. The structure of these organizations varies across countries. Skocpol envisages the state as being more than the government, as it affects many aspects of civil society. However, the state is not all encompassing as other agents and organizations also affect social relationships and politics. Skocpol seeks to illuminate two important trends in current scholarship examining the role of the state. The first pertains to state autonomy, while the second examines the capacities of states as actors in achieving policy goals.

'State autonomy' as defined by Skocpol, implies the formulation and pursuit of 'goals that are not simply reflective of the demands or interests of social groups, classes, or society'(1985: 9). Various explanations have been put forward as to the parameters of the state's actions with respect to formulation and pursuit of goals. Some of the reasons mentioned by Skocpol (1985) are, the drawing of states into transnational structures and international flows of communication may lead state officials into pursuing new strategies, even against stiff resistance from various interest groups; States may also pursue reform, arising out the need of states to maintain control and order. Regarding the possibility of such activities, Skocpol contends, 'it seems that organizationally coherent collectivities of state officials, especially collectivities of career officials relatively insulated from ties to currently dominant socioeconomic interests, are likely to launch distinctive new state strategies in times of crisis' (1985: 9). In addition, she points out that state autonomy is not a fixed factor in any governmental system, rather it is a variable. When the capacities of states to implement policies are studied, again various factors come to mind. Amongst these are sovereign integrity and the stable administrative–military control of its territory, loyal and skilled officials, and adequate financial resources (Skocpol 1985).

Evans and Rueshemeyer (1985) have also undertaken a study of the important variables of state autonomy and state capacities, in the context of newly industrializing nations. They point out the reasons why state intervention is required for economic transformation in a capitalist context. One is Durkheim's argument that the market requires normative underpinnings in order to function at all. The rise of institutional economics, and in particular the work of Douglas North, stands testimony to the importance of institutions, including norms. Yet another argument for the necessity of state intervention is the problem of public or collective goods. Even in the ideal model of perfect competition, the problem of public goods exists, and increases as the market model deviates from perfect competition (Evans and Rueschemeyer 1985). They believe that the problem is compounded in the Third World, where the dominant class is often oligopolistic, having transnational rather than local interests and an agrarian elite, whose interests are as patrimonial as they are profit seeking.

In a more nuanced look at the functioning of the state, Evans and Rueschemeyer (1985) reveal the contradictory tendencies that may operate to undercut state capacities. Like Skocpol (1985), they basically subscribe to a Weberian definition of the state. 'We consider the state to be a set of organizations invested with the authority to make binding decisions for people and organizations juridically located in a particular territory and to implement these decisions using, if necessary force' (1985: 47). In their opinion, the capacity of the state is determined by:

> Although our definition of the state is cast in formal terms of authority and enforcement, we recognize that across a range of historical circum-stances—in ways that vary substantially—the state *tends* to be an expres-sion of pacts of domination, to act coherently as a corporate unit, to become an arena of social conflict, and to present itself as the guardian of universal interests. Clearly, these tendencies stand in contradiction to each other and cannot all at once come into their own...The crucial underlying point is that the efficacy of the state will always depend on the pattern in which these contradictory tendencies are combined, both in its internal structure and in its relation to the social structure as a whole. (Evans and Rueschemeyer 1985: 48)

The salient point that emerges from their discussion is that the state must acquire a certain degree of relative autonomy from the dominant class in order to achieve economic transformation. In this sense, the work of Evans and Rueschemeyer (1985) resonates with that of Skocpol (1985). Some of the social structural conditions favouring greater autonomy as identified by Evans and Rueschemeyer are firstly, a division within the dominant class, secondly, increased pressure from the subordinate class vis-à-vis the dominant class.

THE STATE AND PRIVATIZATION, LIBERALIZATION, AND DEREGULATION

The key role of the state with respect to privatization, liberaliza-tion, and deregulation has been recognized and more recently been formalized. Some scholars have stressed the role of the state in the context of telecommunications reform in developing countries

(Petrazzini 1995; Mody, Bauer, and Staubhaar 1995). Others have examined the role of the state with respect to broadcasting reform (Chatterji 1991; Thomas 1993; Golding 1995).

Petrazzini (1995) has concentrated on the important variables of the relative autonomy of the state and the degree of power concentration within the state in order to explain the state's effectiveness in implementing telecom privatization policies. He has studied these processes in various developing countries ranging from Argentina, Mexico, South Africa, and Malaysia to Thailand. Petrazzini's main conclusion is that while political factors such as state autonomy and power concentration were important explanatory variables in understanding the privatization of state owned telecommunications enterprises, economic variables offered a more accurate explanation of liberalization success.

In their study of the changing role of the state, Mody and Tsui (1995) conceptualize the state–market interactions as 'pendulum swings that are an integral part of the historical capital accumulation process' (1995: 179). They characterize the current phase of privatization in telecommunications as private sector participation at the invitation of the state. Contrary to the withering away of the state thesis, Mody and Tsui (1985) believe that a change in ownership in particular sectors of the state economy is an attempt to strengthen the state fiscally. In their words, 'if export-led growth does not occur, or profits do not materialize when good times return, the pendulum could swing back' (1985: 180). Mody and Tsui maintain that decisions regarding ownership of telecommunications derive from national and international accommodations between members of the powerful state, national capital, and foreign capital. They are in accord with Skocpol (1985), Evans (1985), and Rudolph and Rudolph (1987), in that they consider the state to be a 'central actor with survival and consolidation interests of its own' (1985: 184). Mody and Tsui are of the belief that in contemporary capitalist society, the political power of a state is increasingly dependent on its economic wealth. In other words, it is in the state's own interest to support and advance the accumulation of national capital. They also envisage the modern state's activities to largely consist of structuring and subsidizing national capital toward profitable and transnational patterns of production and distribution.

Recent scholarship on the newly industrializing countries (NICs) has highlighted the role played by the state in encouraging economic growth (Applebaum and Henderson 1992; Palan *et al.* 1996). State strategies in support of economic development in various countries range from encouragement of domestic competitiveness via provision of infrastructure and subsidies of Research and Development (R&D) to financing of basic research (Mody and Tsui 1995). Palan *et al.* (1996) also suggest that there is neither a worldwide shift from one state-form to another, nor is there a universal model of a competition state emerging. Instead, they outline a number of competitive strategies that are pursued by states:

- states may wish to join together in large regional blocks;
- they may adopt the 'development state' model;
- they may embrace the 'social democratic' mode of selective integration into the world economy;
- a select number of states may seek to dominate their regional economy or even the world economy to achieve hegemony;
- they may try to exploit their cheap and abundant labour to attract foreign capital;
- they may seek to exploit a parasitical niche in the world market such as tax havens
- they may be structurally impeded from joining the competitive game at all (Palan *et al.* 1996: 5)

While the first four strategies are primarily open to OECD countries, poorer or weaker countries may adopt the latter three strategies. To explain a little further, countries such as Japan, Taiwan, and South Korea have been considered to have 'developmental states'. States joining together to form regional blocks have been exemplified by the cases of the EEC and NAFTA. The 'social democratic' mode of selective integration has been pursued by a number of European welfare states in the 1980s such as Sweden, Finland, Norway, Switzerland, Austria, and others. Countries as diverse as Singapore, Hong Kong, Malaysia, Philippines, Mexico, Sri Lanka, Thailand, Tunisia, and India have used the strategy of employing cheap and abundant labour. Many countries in the Caribbean and others such as Bahrain and Liberia have pursued the 'parasitical' or tax-haven strategies.

To reiterate the main trends in current scholarship, alongside the analysis of the processes of globalization/localization there is a growing body of work, which focuses on the changing role of the state. The interesting question here is if as Rosenau (1992, 1997) suggests, there is a relocation of power away from the nation-state towards the global and local levels, how does the state react to this loss in control?

One area in which the examination of the role of the state has become crucial in the last two decades is that of electronic communications. With the large-scale technological convergence that is taking place between computing and electronic communications, the globalization and liberalization of telecommunications is also of interest to students of broadcasting liberalization.

THE STATE IN INDIA

Partha Chatterjee's (1993, 1997, 2010) work sheds some light on the nature of the Indian state. He argues how colonialism has influenced the process of imagining the nation. In fact, he explores the particularities of post-colonial societies, differentiating these from Western-centric theories. Chatterjee (1999) differs from Benedict Anderson's notions of nationalism and imagined communities.

In Chatterjee's words, 'the most powerful as well as the most creative results of the nationalist imagination in Asia and Africa are posited not on an identity but rather on a *difference* with the "modular" forms of the national society propagated by the modern West' (1999: 5). To elucidate, he believes that in the context of India, anti-colonial nationalism creates its own domain of sovereignty within colonial society before it battles on a political plane with the colonial master. This is achieved by bifurcating the social institutions and practices into two dimensions, the material and the spiritual. The material or 'outside' domain encompasses the economy, statecraft, science, and technology; an area where the West had emerged as superior to the East. The implication of the West's superiority in this domain is that the successes are to be studied and replicated in the East.

The spiritual or 'inner' domain on the other hand is the seat of cultural identity, which requires preservation to maintain its distinctiveness from the West. Chatterjee (1999) is of the view that this division is a basic feature of anti-colonial nationalisms in Asia and Africa. He believes that the colonial state does not extend its influence over the 'inner' domain of national culture, but rather this spiritual domain is the site of the emergence of 'modern' national culture and nationalism. In other words, his belief is that in this essential domain, the nation is already sovereign, even when it is colonized. This aspect is missed by conventional histories which emphasize nationalism as beginning with the struggle for political power. The dimensions of the inner domain of national culture included language, secondary and tertiary education and the family. To sum up, Chatterjee is opposed to the imposition of 'Western universalism' in the imagined state in post-colonial Asia and Africa.

NOTES

1. The history of the western state begins in ancient Greece with the writings of Plato and Aristotle on the subject of the *polis* or city-state. The ancient Roman Empire added the notion of a legal system through the concept of *res publica* or commonwealth. The modern concept of state emerged in the 16th century with the writings of Niccolo Machiavelli and Jean Bodin. Their views characterized the state as the centralizing force whereby stability could be ensured. The opinions of a range of reformers and philosophers such as John Locke, Jean-Jacques Rousseau, Thomas Hobbes, G.W.F. Hegel, Immanuel Kant, and Karl Marx have had an impact on the modern conceptualization of the state.
2. For a discussion of the resilience of the modern state see Cerny's (1990, 1995) work on the 'competition state'.
3. Joel Krieger (1993) identifies the salient view-points to emerge in a discussion on the nature of the state. These are Anglo-Saxon liberalism, Marxism, and Germanic Realism. Most versions of liberalism view the state with suspicion and extol the virtues of society. This view generally offers society-centered explanations because the polity is not considered to possess an independent reality. Marxism also offers society-centered accounts of politics, where the character of the social classes depends on the mode of production which they utilize. The 'withering away of the state' thesis owes its existence to Marx. The third perspective loosely labelled German realism envisages the state to be an actor in its own right. The state is also viewed to be a guarantor of survival (1993: 879).

4. For a classic study of the state see Harold Laski (1960).

5. More modern definitions of the state by social scientists also include the elements suggested by Max Weber. For example Joel Krieger (1993) identifies three elements in the composite definition of the state, 'First, a state is a set of institutions which possess the means of violence and coercion...Second, these institutions in principle control a geographically bounded territory, usually referred to as a society...Third, the state monopolizes rule-making within its territory' (1993: 877).

CHAPTER THREE

CONTEXT OF
BROADCASTING IN INDIA

The theoretical framework for this book derives from the confluence of different streams of literature dealing with globalization/localization, liberalization in electronic communications, and the role of the nation-state. This study seeks to understand the links between these issues in the context of a particular country—India. The time frame chosen for the study is from 1990 to the present day. This period is particularly interesting because it marks a period of liberalization in the Indian economy, as well as in the communications sphere.

THE INDIAN SCENARIO — A BRIEF BACKGROUND

Situated in South Asia, India is the seventh largest country in the world, constituting an area of 3.3 million square kilometres. It is the second most populous nation in the world, with a population that is currently over one billion [1.21 billion in 2010, according to the

Human Development Report (2010)]. India's population has a rural bias, with the urban population standing at only 30 per cent of the total population in 2010 (Human Development Report 2010). As India has only 2.4 per cent of the world's landmass, but over 16 per cent of the world's population, it stands to reason that it has a very high population density (Viswanath and Karan 2000).

The fact that India is an incredibly diverse nation is a cliché worth recording here. There is diversity present in every facet of life; spanning religion, language, geography, ethnic composition, culinary traditions, and other areas. Historically, India has been open to many influences ranging from invasions by Turks, Central Asians, Persians, and others, to colonial influences from France, Britain, and Portugal. While India has a long history, with the Indus valley civilization predating Christianity, its strategic location and natural resources have ensured interaction with traders and invaders throughout its history.

There are 18 major languages, and many dialects (844) spoken in India. These include languages from the Indo–Aryan group of languages, such as derivatives of Sanskrit, and languages with Dravidian roots. Though Hindi was specified as the official language of the Union in 1950, English is also allowed for official purposes, and is the primary language of commerce. Notwithstanding the multitude of languages spoken on the subcontinent, the country's overall literacy rate was only 61 per cent in 2005 (Human Development Report 2007–08). However, there are variations across regions, and between genders. Males show higher rates of literacy than females, and southern states such as Kerala show higher rates of literacy than northern states such as Bihar. The fact that India has a vibrant oral culture also has implications for the broadcast media.

India is also a land of many religions. There is a large Hindu majority constituting 82 per cent of the population, followed by minority groups of Muslims, Christians, Sikhs, Buddhists, Jains, Zoroastrians, and others (Chatterji 1991). Issues pertaining to language and religion in India have important political and cultural ramifications. Hence, these linguistic, religious, and other aspects of diversity have special implications for broadcast regulation.

India is a secular, democratic republic, comprising 26 states and six union territories. India's form of government is primarily based on the British system of parliamentary democracy. India has a mixed economy, with the presence of both private and public sectors. Notwithstanding Nehru's legacy of socialism, India has pursued strategies of deregulation and liberalization since the early 1990s. This is particularly true of the decade following the budget plan released in 1991.

THE INDIAN ECONOMY

In the year 2000, India was the 10th most industrialized country in the world. It also had a high level of technological development, evidenced by its vibrant software exports. India has its own space programme, and it was the sixth country in the world to have ventured into outer space. However, the Indian economy and social conditions are marked by contradictions, where highly industrialized enclaves coexist with traditional and less developed communities (Viswanath and Karan 2000). By 2005, India ranked fourth in the world according to its Gross Domestic Product (GDP) in terms of purchasing power parity (Human Development Report, 2007–2008). It remained at this position till 2010.

The guiding beacon of India's industrial policy has been a belief in a mixed economy. This implies that there are three categories of products produced within the industrial sector—those which are produced only by government enterprises, those which are produced both by the public and private sector, and those which are produced only by the private sector. The Indian government's policy since the 1950s has emphasized centralized planning, with large scale growth in the size of the public sector (Chatterji 1991). Nehruvian socialism implied that the state occupied the 'commanding heights of the economy'. In the post-Independence period, the government established a licensing system for the private sector, as a protection against monopoly abuse. Thus, the state exerted control over sectoral resource allocation through industrial licensing and import permits. Public investment was of vital importance in the industrial sector. High tariffs and quotas were put in place to protect domestic industries. These were largely dismantled in the reforms after 1991, with the exception of a few strategic industries (Panda *et al.* 1999).

India is still a largely agricultural nation, with agriculture accounting for about two-thirds of the labour force, but only about one-third of the GDP in the late 1990s. The Indian agricultural sector has seen fluctuations in its fortune over the last two decades. The annual growth rate in this sector was 4.7 per cent during the period 1992–7 which slipped to 2.1 per cent during 1997–2002.[1] The annual growth rate for agriculture during the 11th Five Year Plan, that is, 2007–8 to 2010–11, averaged about 3.2 per cent (Sharma 2011).

By 2009–10, the share of services in GDP had increased to 57 per cent, while that of industries and agriculture stood at 28 per cent and 15 per cent, respectively. The share of labour force by occupation stood at approximately 52 per cent in agriculture, 14 per cent in industry, and 34 per cent in the services sector.[2] It is important to recognize that agriculture still employs about half the population. These statistics are a crude measure, which show that productivity in the agricultural sector is not high. They also serve to illustrate the fact that there are two Indias—a rural one characterized by agriculture, low productivity, and lower levels of literacy, and an urban one with the reverse characteristics.

Notwithstanding the many poverty alleviation schemes implemented, a large portion of the population still lives below the poverty line. A recent estimate of poverty by a committee headed by S.D. Tendulkar, put the figure as high as 38 per cent in 2009, based on indicators such as health, education, sanitation, nutrition, and income (Chauhan 2009). There has been much land-reform legislation introduced in India after 1947, but less than half the peasantry owns its own land, and problems of tenancy, sharecropping, and landlessness remain. The much-touted 'Green Revolution' has not been an unqualified success in India, in comparison with other Asian countries. Again, the prevalence of low productivity, illiteracy, and poverty has special implications for broadcast and telecommunications regulation in India.

In a marked departure from earlier policies, the state embarked on a liberalization initiative in the early 1990s. The impetus for reform came from the fact that India was facing a severe balance of payments crisis at the time. The industrial sector underwent restructuring and consolidation post-1991. In the first five years post the reforms, industrial growth increased sharply, but it slowed to 4.5 per cent in the next five years. In 2001–2, industrial growth rate was only 2.7 per cent, but then it rose to 7.1 per cent in 2002–3 and 9.8 per cent in 2004–5.[3]

In the decade starting 2000, India sustained fairly high rates of economic growth, till the global economic downturn of 2008. The Indian economy then recovered, exhibiting close to 9 per cent growth in 2010. The Information Technology sector in India has expanded, contributing significantly to India's GDP growth in the last decade. According to a finding of the NASSCOM Annual Survey on performance of Indian Information Technology, Back Processing Office industry, this sector reached US $58.8 billion in 2008–9.[4]

While liberalization in the economic sector in India post-1990 is the background, this has been accompanied by liberalization in the communications sector as well. McDowell (1997) has provided a broader definition of liberalization, rather than one described as merely an increase in competition. In his study of communications policy change in India he says, 'the term "liberalization" refers here to a process of changing state, social and economic institutions so that there is an increased use of individual choices and market mechanisms to guide social, economic and political life' (1997: 2). There has been a revitalization in private-sector initiatives across the board in the last two decades. In order to better understand changes in the communications sector, it is first instructive to examine the political background to India's economic reforms.

THE INDIAN POLITY

The modern states of India and Pakistan were two sovereign countries created from the British Empire in August 1947. At that time many princely states were merged into these two nations. The territorial boundaries of independent India were created out of the 'mode of transfer of power from British colonial rule and of political negotiations between the leaders of independent India and the rulers of the princely states' (Chatterji 1997: 5). In 1956, the former provinces of British India were reorganized as states and union territories on the basis of linguistic principles.

The Constitution of India was formulated in 1950 by the Constituent Assembly, which was composed mainly of Congress members. The constitution provided for a sovereign legislature elected by direct universal suffrage, and the guarantee of a set of fundamental rights for all citizens. The form of the government was a parliamentary democracy, with an executive responsible to the Parliament, and an indirectly elected President as the head of state. The real power, however, lay with the Prime Minister and the council of ministers who were members of Parliament. There was also a provision for an independent judiciary with powers of judicial review of laws made by the Parliament. Although the Constitution was a federal one, the distribution of powers was heavily tilted towards the union, rather than the states. In general, it has been suggested that the Indian Constitution was far more centralized than most federations elsewhere (Chatterji 1997).

The national legislature of India is bicameral, consisting of the *Rajya Sabha* (Council of States) and the *Lok Sabha* (House of People). The Rajya Sabha has a total of 245 members. While the legislative bodies of the states elect 233 members, the president nominates 12. The Lok Sabha has 545 seats. With the exception of two nominated members, these members are directly elected on the basis of adult suffrage. Elections are to be held at five-year intervals, unless the Parliament is dissolved prior to its full term (Viswanath and Karan 2000).

Government administration was carried out in a manner which provided continuity from the colonial period. The new service called the Indian Administrative Service was modelled on the colonial Indian Civil Service, the 'steel frame' of India. Basically, the elite cadre of the national services and the bureaucracy of the provincial services provided administration. The primary unit of the administration apparatus was the district, which was responsible for the maintenance of law and order, and developmental work.

At the time of Independence, the Congress was a mass party with good organizational structure at various levels such as the village, district, provinces, and all-India committees. At this juncture, the Congress had responsibility for running the central government, as well as most of the state governments. After Independence, the Congress party emerged as the hegemon of a dominant party system (Rudolph and Rudolph 1987: 129).

Jawaharlal Nehru was the Congress party's president when he became the first Prime Minister of India. During Nehru's period of governance, the provincial party units of the Congress were able to assert a large degree of autonomy, as compared to the central party leadership. The salient feature of Nehru's leadership was the 'developmental state', with large-scale intervention of the centre in the economy. Nehru's brand of socialism envisaged a planned economy, albeit a mixed one, where the state would control the 'commanding heights' of the economy. Thus, the state was directly responsible for industries such as minerals, metals, heavy machinery, chemicals, fuel, power, and transport. This developmental strategy rested on the foundation of rapid industrial growth. A Planning Commission was established, relatively independent of the central government, with the task of defining goals, strategies, and investment planning with regard to development (Chatterji 1997).

The Congress party was dominant at both the centre and states till 1967, and won the first three general elections. The strategy of rapid industrialization however had its drawbacks. These included food shortages, and a foreign exchange crisis by the mid-1960s. Perhaps it is not surprising that in the 1967 elections, Congress managed to win only 54 per cent of the seats in the Parliament and it failed to win a majority in nine states. The new situation meant that centre–state relations assumed greater importance in Indian politics (Chatterji 1997). The period following the 1967 elections saw the Congress party struggle with internal power skirmishes and defections. In 1969, these power struggles culminated in the Congress party split-ting into two factions, the Congress (Organization) or Congress (O), and the larger bloc Congress (Requisitionists) or Congress (R). Indira Gandhi, then Prime Minister of India, was associated with the Congress (R). The 1971 elections saw Indira Gandhi sweep into power on the populist mandate of removal of poverty.

It would appear that the Congress party grew more centralized in its functioning under Indira's leadership. In fact, it has been sug-gested that Indira Gandhi was responsible for the de-institutionaliza-tion of the Congress party, as her political decisions seemed to stem from controlling power struggles within the party, rather than any ideological commitment to strengthening the party (Rudolph and Rudolph 1987: 134).

Unlike in the pre-Independence era, when institutions of health, education, and social welfare were set up by voluntary action, or by nationalist political organizations, in the Indira Gandhi period, it was almost universally expected that the state would perform this role. Second, the Nehruvian strategy had emphasized public undertakings in capital goods and infrastructure. Consequently, agricultural growth was not emphasized until there were food shortages in the mid-1960s. Indira's government sought to tackle these problems by ushering in the 'Green Revolution'. This revolution encompassed state subsidies of seeds, irrigation, and fertilizers, geared toward the strategy of rapid increase in food grains production. Mainly, the larger farmers in parts of Northern India adopted these strategies. It has been suggested that the Green Revolution created a new player in national politics—the rich farmer (Chatterjee 1997).

However, the government ran into heavy weather in the early 1970s. The Indira Gandhi government responded in mid-1975 by imposing the 'emergency' or an authoritarian regime, which lasted till early 1977. This strategy resulted in an erosion of legitimacy of the government as the 'emergency regime accelerated state as well as party deinstitutionalization by substituting fiat for a government of laws and fear for consent' (Rudolph and Rudolph 1987: 137). The 1977 elections brought the united opposition, the Janata Party to power. However, the Janata Party failed to remain united, and to provide strong competition to the Congress.

The Congress returned to power in 1980. Indira Gandhi was assassinated in October 1984. Indira's son Rajiv Gandhi led the Congress-I to a decisive electoral victory two months later. Rajiv's subsequent actions appear to be harder to interpret than Indira Gandhi's. He appeared to encourage some objectivity in procedures and to discourage further de-institutionalization of the Congress party. He was also responsible for emphasizing information technology in the Indian development context. Sadly, history repeated itself and Rajiv Gandhi was also assassinated in 1991.

The decade that followed was one of divisive and coalition politics. The early 1990s saw caste and communalism come to the fore with the Mandal Commission Report and the destruction of the Babri Masjid in 1992. There was also growing disaffection in Jammu and Kashmir. The Bharatiya Janata Party (BJP) won the national elections in 1996, but was unsuccessful in forming a stable government because it lacked a majority; a coalition government led by the Janata Dal came into being.

The BJP was victorious in the election of 1999. The period that followed was one of coalition governments and dissolution of the Parliament before it completed its full term. They held power till 2004. Throughout the 1990s and the early 2000s, India liberalized the economy. The result was an accelerated growth rate, and increase in per capita income. Foreign Direct Investment and the share of services in the GDP also rose. The Congress party won the elections in 2004 and 2009. However, they had smaller electoral margins, which implied they were constrained as compared to the period when they had a huge share of the vote. There was continuity in their policies in terms of emphasis on universal education and rural poverty alleviation during this decade. The pressures of coalition politics have impacted the Congress government's ability in policy formulation adversely in the last decade.

COMMUNICATIONS IN INDIA

The print media has historically enjoyed a high degree of freedom from government interference in India. Up to about 1990, the government in India had controlled broadcasting and telecommunications, after which they were liberalized. The quantum of change in the area of broadcasting and telecommunications has been phenomenal in the last two decades.

The Indian Press

The press in India is an influential force in the developing world, since it is among the oldest and freest presses in South Asia (Chen and Choudhury 1992). Up to the time when India achieved its independence from the British (in 1947), the spirit of nationalism gave impetus to the growth of the press. During this period, the main objectives of the Indian press were the promotion of social and political reform and nationalism. The link between the use of the press, and influence on public opinion is evident in the fact that during India's freedom struggle, Mahatma Gandhi used his position as editor of various weekly newspapers to propagate his views of freedom and nonviolence, thus sparking political activism.

The freedom of press enjoyed by Indian journalists continued after 1947, since the first Prime Minister of India, Jawaharlal Nehru, advocated it. Initially, the post-Independence press supported the government's efforts at nation building. After Independence, the government also institutionalized regulation of the press through bodies such as the Press Commissions, appointed in 1952 and 1977, the Press Council set up in 1965, and the office of the registrar of newspapers (Viswanath and Karan 2000).

Press freedom, however, suffered a setback in mid-1975 when the then Prime Minister, Indira Gandhi declared a political emergency. Freedom of speech and of the press was curtailed. Over the period of the next 18 months, the government imposed restrictions on the press by detaining journalists, expelling some foreign correspondents, and even dissolving the Press Council. The end of the Emergency signaled a period of vibrant growth and freedom for the press (Viswanathan and Karan 2000).

Today, there is vast diversity prevalent in the print media; facets of which include linguistic diversity, as well as ideological stances. According to one estimate, over 2000 daily newspapers were published in India in the mid-1990s (Encyclopedia Britannica 1995). English language newspapers and journals continue to enjoy prestige and influence, undoubtedly a legacy of Colonialism. According to Chen and Choudhury (1992), in 1987 the Hindi press had a total readership of 14 million, while the English press had a readership of 10 million. The distribution of the print media reflects an urban bias with about 80 per cent of the circulation being accounted for by cities, even though they have only 20 per cent of the country's population. The four major metropolitan areas of Delhi, Bombay, Calcutta, and Madras, accounted for about 30 per cent of newspapers published in India (Chen and Choudhury 1992). Although the English language press does not lead in terms of circulation, it is influential in the formation of public opinion, as indicated by scholars such as Chen and Choudhury.

According to one estimate, India had about 39,000 publications including dailies, weeklies and monthlies by the end of 1996 (Viswanath and Karan 2000). This represents an increase in over 50 per cent from 1987. Even though there is great diversity in the publication of different kinds of newspapers, regional press in languages other than English or Hindi has made great strides in the last two decades. This has affected broadcasting as well. Viswanath and Karan inform us that regional newspapers such as *Malayala Manorama, Amrita Bazar Patrika, Eenadu, Navbharat Times*, and *Punjab Kesari*, have adopted marketing strategies such as the introduction of innovative editorial features, regional or zonal editions, and language use. They have also diversified into television, and are competing with national and international channels (2000: 95). While there has been a boom in regional media, globalization and liberalization have also forced print media to adopt new technologies and marketing strategies.

In 1998, *The Times of India* was the top circulating newspaper in the country, with a circulation figure of 1,296,000. It was followed by regional dailies such as *Malayala Manorama, Gujarat Samachar*, and *Punjab Kesari*. By 2007, the circulation figure of *The Times of India* stood at 13.5 million. In the year 2007, the print media industry stood at Rs 149 billion, with a growth rate of 16 per cent, as compared to the previous year (FICCI and PwC Report 2008). In 2009, the print industry was estimated to be about Rs 161.5 billion in size. The highest readership and circulation figures were garnered by Hindi dailies in this period. It is predicted that regional markets will play a key role in the growth of the print media in the next few years. (PwC Report 2010).

One of India's plus points is undoubtedly the freedom of press that is prevalent in the country. According to the New York based organization Freedom House, India ranked high among the 'most free' countries regarding freedom of the press in 1988 (Stephens 1992). In the opinion of Chen and Choudhury (1992), control exercised by the government over the press in India is weak. The pluralistic tradition in India's print media, unfortunately, did not carry over to the broadcasting and telecommunications sector, which till the 1990s continued to be dominated by the state. In 2010, Freedom House categorized India as 'partly free' in their annual survey of press freedom across the globe.[5]

India abounds with paradoxes. It has a relatively free press (Lee and Wang 1995). However, the state in India has had a monopoly on radio and television right from their inception. For a long time, the government owned the broadcasting authority,[6] with Doordarshan as its television wing reigning supreme. Doordarshan's programming for the most part consisted of limited channels, airing soporific fare. Socialist mores were emphasized with a stress on education, health, family planning, and agriculture. Entertainment got short shrift, and there were only two channels available. Another paradox is that although entertainment figured so low on the television programming priorities, Bombay had one of the most prolific film industries in the world.

The year 1997 marked the fiftieth anniversary of India's Independence. It may be argued that India witnessed more change in its telecommunications and broadcasting sector in the decade 1990–2000, than in the previous four decades. The rhetoric of liberalization gained credence in elite Indian circles in this decade. In the Indian economy, the broad scope of deregulation and liberalization across the board has been accentuated in the area of telecommunications. These developments should be reviewed in a global context, where the synergies between telecommunications, data processing, broadcasting, and new information technologies underline the importance of holistic regulation of all these areas.

The History of Television Broadcasting in India

Broadcasting in India began with the practice of amateur broadcasting in 1923. By 1927, broadcast stations were established by the Indian Broadcasting Company in the metropolises of Bombay and Calcutta. The lion's share of the company's revenue was derived from radio licenses. Since the total number of radio licenses actually declined in the late 1920s, the Indian Broadcasting Company's finances were adversely affected, and it went into liquidation in 1930. The government acquired its assets, and the Indian State Broadcasting Service came into existence. Broadcasting in India continued to be at low ebb between 1930 and 1935 (Chatterji 1991). Broadcasting in India was given new impetus under the leadership of Lionel Fielden of the BBC, who took charge as Controller of Broadcasting in 1935. Under Fielden's guidance, the All India Radio (AIR) network consisting of medium-wave radio stations at principal centres was set into motion.

The birth of television in India came about in 1959. To begin with, 21 television sets were provided in rural locations near Delhi.

Following this, UNESCO provided 50 sets, which were also installed in rural areas. During 1960–1961, an educational experiment was carried out under UNESCO's auspices, which was designed to air content aimed at changing the audience's attitudes toward particular issues (Chatterji 1991: 51). The first phase of television in India was marked by the social objectives of education for farmers and children.

Television's rate of diffusion was slow in the 1960s. This is illustrated by the fact that AIR's second TV transmitter was set up in Bombay only in 1972. The rate of expansion of television picked up impetus after 1975, with TV centres being set up in the cities of Madras, Lucknow, and Calcutta. In 1976, AIR's television service called Doordarshan was set up as a separate entity, headed by its own Director-General (Chatterji 1991).

The Satellite Instructional Television Experiment (SITE) was an important milestone in the growth of Indian television. In the SITE experiment, the United States' National Aeronautics and Space Administration's (NASA) Applications Technology Satellite (ATS-6) was used to broadcast TV programmes to receivers in 2,400 villages (Singhal and Rogers 1989). Doordarshan produced the programmes aired over the ATS service, and they consisted of a mix of educational, news, general interest, and cultural programmes.

The SITE experiment illustrated the importance of the usage of satellites in expanding television coverage in India. This experiment assisted in paving the way for India's own communications satellites. NASA launched the Indian National Satellite, the INSAT-1A in 1982. This satellite was functional for a short period. It was used for the broadcast of radio and television programmes. Another multi-purpose satellite, the INSAT-1B was launched for the purpose of providing television broadcasting in India in 1983. Over the period 1984–1985, 120 television transmitters were installed in India to increase television coverage via the INSAT-1B satellite (Singhal and Rogers 1989: 62).

Along with the expansion of television coverage through the use of INSAT-1B, some other momentous events were taking place. Indian television changed from a black and white format to a colour format in 1982. The impetus for this change came from the fact that India was hosting the Asian Games in 1982, and colour television suddenly entered the public consciousness. Commercial sponsorship of programmes was also encouraged after 1980. In the mid-1980s, indigenous soap operas (some of which combined education with entertainment) became popular. The one programme that really became a milestone was the programme *Hum Log*. Mythological serials also followed. According to Singhal and Rogers (1989), in 1988, approximately 90 million, or 12 per cent of the population watched television regularly, while about 500 million or about 62 per cent of the population lived in areas covered by television broadcasts. This represents a high rate of diffusion of television if we compare these figures to the paltry percentage of population that had access to television in 1960. The 1990s ushered in a totally new era in Indian television, and the foreign owned and operated STAR TV was largely responsible for initiating this change. The last two decades have seen a total transformation of the television environment with the entry of new players, channels, technologies, and audiences.

*   *   *

India is a very complex and diverse country. It has an ancient civilization juxtaposed with contemporary cultural influences from the rest of the world. It is secular, and although it has a Hindu majority, the number of Muslims in India is substantial. Western liberal ideas and forms of governance were superimposed on India's traditional society at the time of Independence and also during the period it was colonized by the British. The Nehruvian ideals of socialism and non-alignment added yet another layer of complexity to the Indian experience. India's autarkic economy suddenly threw its doors open at the beginning of the 1990s. In this decade, the political structure also saw the ascendance of factors such as religion, language, and caste. The decade starting from 2000, saw India's emergence as a force to be reckoned with, as it managed to sustain high rates of economic growth.

In tandem with the liberalization that was occurring in other sectors of the Indian economy, the communications sector, especially electronic communications, underwent a sea change in the last two decades. Both telecommunications and television broadcasting were state-owned monopolies till the 1990s. Post-1990, liberalization has been seen in both these areas. The advent of satellite television has made a huge difference to the broadcasting scenario in India.

Competition from international satellite television providers and private domestic broadcasters has broken the Indian government's monopoly over broadcasting. The invasion of the Indian skies by Satellite Television Asian Region (STAR TV), and other international and domestic players has now filled the homes of millions with diverse programmes. A large cable TV industry in India has also sprung up in the wake of satellite broadcasting. The most visible response of the state in the decade following 1990 has been the granting of 'autonomy' to the national broadcasting organization (Prasar Bharati).

Rosenau's (1990, 1992, 1997) theoretical framework has been adopted to understand developments in the Indian broadcasting scenario because it seems best suited to illumine the chain of events in the last two decades. The bi-modal distribution of authority towards the global and the local levels as theorized by Rosenau, appears to have validity in the Indian context. An alternative theoretical model deriving from dependency theory and cultural imperialism was not utilized, because it failed to take into account the rise of local enterprise and domestic broadcasting. It is also difficult to accommodate the appearance of culturally hybrid media products within a classic centre-periphery analysis.

In addition, the Indian case with its low volumes of trade and foreign investment does not fit into the typical dependency scenario. An economic analysis, relying primarily on labour and capital as the chief players, does not do justice to the reality in India, because of the importance of the state as the third actor (Skocpol 1985; Evans and Rueschemeyer 1985; Rudolph and Rudolph 1987). The political economy of the Indian state also has certain unique factors such as the importance of caste-based politics.

NOTES

1. Available at www.India.gov.in.
2. Available at www.India.gov.in.
3. Available at www.India.gov.in.
4. Available at www.nasscom.in (accessed July 2009).

5. Available at www.freedomhouse.org/report/2010.
6. The government owned broadcasting authority had two main divisions—Doordarshan (DD), the television division, and All India Radio (AIR), the radio division. In 1997, the broadcasting authority was formally granted autonomy, and these divisions continue to exist as divisions of the Prasar Bharati Corporation.

CHAPTER FOUR

DEVELOPMENTS IN BROADCASTING AND CABLE, 1990–2010

THE RESEARCH FRAMEWORK

Global change is occurring along many frontiers; economic, social, political, and cultural. An interesting aspect of global broadcasting and telecommunications networks is that they both contribute to the process of globalization, as well as are, in part, the result of globalization. Communications researchers are currently evincing interest in various aspects of global media (Sreberny-Mohammadi 1996; Sreberney-Mohammadi *et al.* 1997; Mohammadi 1998; Herman and McChesney 1998; Smith and Patterson 1998; Thussu 1999; Durham and Kellner 2006).

The rapid growth of broadcasting, cable, and the Internet in the last two decades has indicated the importance of the electronic medium of communications. This growth has been linked to broader processes of globalization, liberalization, and privatization. In this new, liberalized environment, the role of the state has come under close scrutiny. From the literature reviewed in various disciplines including communications, sociology, anthropology, economics, and political science, on the themes of global/local processes and the role of the state, certain trends have emerged. These are:

(1) the phenomenon of globalization (variously defined) is accelerating in tempo over the period of the last two decades;
(2) the current era of 'globalization' has many facets impinging on the economy, polity, culture, society, and media of a particular country;
(3) globalization, somewhat paradoxically, has been accompanied by a resurgence of the 'local';
(4) the complex interactions between global, national, and local processes have affected the state;
(5) the response of the state has been varied, but in many instances the state has been resilient, and the 'withering away of the state' thesis has in fact not been uniformly supported by the empirical evidence.

The process of broadcasting and telecommunications liberalization has been studied widely in the context of the developed countries. More recently, the reform process in developing countries has drawn academic interest. However, the political processes underlying reform[1] in both areas have been inadequately explored in the developing country context. This study examines the television and cable industry in India as a site for the study of intricate interactions between the global, local, and national forces, as well as the response of the state. The present study, seeks to address the existing lacunae in the literature, by:

(1) presenting a comprehensive overview of the broadcasting sector in India over the period 1990–2010;
(2) examining the global/local processes at work with respect to broadcasting and cable in India;
(3) developing an understanding of the global/local ramifications of the liberalized communications environment on the Indian state, and
(4) studying the Indian state's response.

(5) making conjectures about the wider implications of the global/ local processes and the role of the state with respect to broadcasting in India.

Firstly, a better understanding of the Indian scenario may enable us to comprehend developments in other countries undergoing change in the broadcasting sector. Secondly, a better understanding of the above mentioned processes in the broadcasting sector may shed some light on the nature of globalization, local resurgence, and the role of the state in the current era.

As an aspect of the global/local *problematique*, the underlying objective of this study is to understand whether a redistribution of control has occurred with respect to the electronic communications sector regarding the state at the national level, vis-à-vis the global and local levels. Rosenau's (1990, 1992, 1997) framework regarding the relocation of authority away from the national and towards both the global and local levels has been applied to the case of a specific sector and a specific country, namely a case study of broadcasting and cable in India, from 1990 onwards.

This study relies on multiple research methods in order to investigate the status of the broadcasting and cable industry and the actions of the state[2] in India. Although some elementary quantitative techniques have been utilized for data analysis, the issues are primarily explored through qualitative means. Since this area is best pursued through an interdisciplinary perspective, accordingly, an attempt is made to pull together threads from the disciplines of communications, politics, sociology, economics, and culture, amongst others. The project also concentrates on production and distribution aspects of broadcasting and cable, and only makes conjectures about consumption.

In order to investigate the central questions, this study relies on documentation/archival research, textual analysis, elite interviews, and content analysis. A plurality of qualitative methods has been employed in an attempt at triangulation (Jankowski and Wester 1991). For example, textual analysis of government documents, parliamentary proceedings, and industry reports have been read against data generated from elite interviews. This has, in turn, been compared to results of content analysis of programme schedules of the national broadcaster. It must be emphasized that the present study is exploratory in the sense that there are few academic[3] studies in the field whose path it can follow.

As indicated earlier, Rosenau (1990, 1992, 1997) suggests that in a shrinking world, authority has been relocated away from the nation-state, toward a range of other actors, both transnational and sub national. The terms global and local are employed here to indicate these categories. Rosenau (1992) indicates that the authority of the state is linked to factors such as control and legitimacy. Following Rosenau, this study utilizes the concept of control as an indicator of authority.[4] The following questions come to mind:

(1) In India, post-1990, is control devolving to global/local levels in the broadcasting sector? This leads to the next issue. If indeed there is a relocation of authority away from the nation-state, the pertinent question is;

(2) How has the state responded to these changes? The state in this context has been studied as the Central Government.

In the light of the earlier discussion of communications, information technologies and soft power, it is assumed here that control over the means of communication bestows power to the owner (Deutsch 1966; Nye 1990; Mowlana 1996). A relocation of power and authority would therefore be interpreted as relocation, or change in ownership in the means of communicating, advertising revenues, and audience share, whether in the sphere of cable or broadcasting. Thus, authority or control is partly considered in its economic dimension as ownership/control. Although it is recognized that power is also prevalent in its ideological dimension, as in Gramscian notions of hegemony and Althusser's conceptualization of ideological state apparatuses, that is not the main focus of this study. Authority or control is also considered in the realm of regulation or policy formulation, a classic function of the state.

To revert to the primary question, in the last decade in India has the control over broadcasting increasingly gone to:

(1) transnational or international players and/or;

(2) local players, with a reduction in control for the central government?

These phenomena has been investigated and analyzed by examining the following dimensions:

(1) ownership;

Rosenau's (1990) model refers to ownership as capabilities or the possessing side of power. This is related to authority and control via the capabilities, which help one actor to modify or affect the orientations or actions of another actor. With respect to the present study, ownership over the broadcast and cable medium would imply having the means of control vis-à-vis other actors, that is, other broadcasters and the audience. A change in ownership would generally imply a change in the ability to exert control for the particular actor who was the owner. This study begins by mapping out the broad contours of the broadcast and cable industry in India in the last decade. The major players are identified at different points of time in this dynamic scenario.

(2) audience share/revenues;

The concepts of authority and control refer to the right of certain actors to make rules, allocate resources, and formulate policies, while others comply with their decisions. In other words, indicators such as audience share and advertising revenues reflect control and authority relationships via the attempts or abilities of an actor to 'modify, preserve or otherwise affect the orientations or actions of another' (Rosenau 1990: 183).

In terms of the broadcast and cable media, audience shares and advertising revenues are indicators of the popularity of the media. If viewership figures and advertising revenues are low for a particular broadcaster, it implies a low capacity to effect change or ensure compliance via its messages as far as the audience is concerned. The implication would be that declining advertising revenues and audience share figures would reflect a decline in control and authority relationships and vice-a-versa.

(3) content—considered broadly as in television listings and genres, as well as broad categories such as education or entertainment;

In an examination of the relocation of the loci of authority/control away from the state and towards transnational and sub-national actors in the realm of television, some examination of content is necessary. To elucidate further, the state's sphere of control with respect to broadcasting would also depend on the 'programming' being aired and whether such 'programming' met the state's objectives. For example the emphasis on 'developmental programming' by the state in the period following Independence implied that the programmes that got priority on All India Radio dealt with rural development and education. The Indian state officially subscribes to the view that education and information are preferred categories of 'programming' as compared to entertainment because they work towards the state objective of development.

While a detailed analysis of 'programming' aired over major television channels including a study of particular programmes would no doubt be desirable, content has been considered broadly in terms of major genres in this research project for practical reasons. This study examines the categories of education, information, and entertainment with respect to the erstwhile national broadcaster Doordarshan in order to examine whether the state's objectives have been pursued 1990 onwards.

(4) regulation/policy formulation and implementation.

Regulation, policy formulation, and implementation come under the rubric of formal authority relations in Rosenau's (1990) model. In fact these areas are considered to be classic functions of the state. The former two factors are primarily economic, while the latter two are a mixture of economic and non-economic factors.

Regarding the investigation of the state's response, the domain under consideration is the state's behaviour. In order to understand and analyse the state's response, this study considers variables such as state autonomy and the capacity of the state to formulate and implement policies (Skocpol 1985; Evans and Rueschemeyer 1985; Evans 1985; Rudolph and Rudolph 1987; Petrazzini 1995; Mody, Bauer, and Straubhaar 1995). The Central or Union Government of India has been operationalized as the state in this research project. To be more specific, the actions and opinions of the various ministers for information and broadcasting and the bureaucracy of this ministry have been analysed as a vital part of this case study.

METHODOLOGY

A research project such as this one is important for our understanding of the different processes at work in the evolution of a media industry over time. Research projects that explore topics in the realm of communications policies, 'require not only sensitive historical and contemporary analyses rather than a mere narrative recitation of events, but also a contextualization of the emergence of ideas, technologies and policies' (Hansen *et al.* 1998: 66). The present study attempts to take cognizance of these guidelines.

The methodology adopted in this study is qualitative in essence. The hallmark of qualitative research is that it normally looks for patterns of interrelationship between many categories. It is better suited to answering, or investigating, ambiguous questions. In broad terms, qualitative research is concerned with language, meaning, and process (Kirk and Miller 1986). For the meaningful study of communications in its wider social, political, and cultural context, methods of qualitative and 'thick' description are of benefit (Geertz 1973).

Since the focus of the study is on understanding the operation of processes—global, national, and local in a specific context—a case study method is adopted. As Yin (1984) informs us, the case study used as a research tool contributes to our knowledge of individual, organizational, social, and political phenomenon.

Drawing upon multiple sources including literature research, newspaper and magazine articles, governmental documents, and fieldwork, this study explores several facets of the broadcasting scenario in India in the last decade. Archival research was undertaken in some libraries and governmental institutions in India. It also included interviews with a range of government officials, private broadcasters, cable operators, and media analysts based in India.

DEVOLUTION OF CONTROL

To reiterate, in India, post-1990, is control devolving to global/local levels in the broadcasting sector? In order to tackle this central question, an overview of various broadcasters, cable systems, and the channels available currently in India has been undertaken. This has been compared to the status of the industry two decades ago. As indicated earlier, the issue of devolution of control to global and local levels is indicated by the entrance of foreign broadcasters as well as the domestic private broadcasters and the domestic cable industry. 'Global' in the context of this research study is understood to be transnational broadcasters whose programming is receivable in India. In addition, the majority ownership is not Indian. Global also has the connotation of content, which is not indigenous.

For the purpose of this study, 'local' is associated with programming in regional languages by private broadcasters as well as the local cable channel. In addition, the majority ownership is Indian. Local is also associated with content which is indigenous. The concept of 'glocal' is also useful as many aspects of broadcasting in India fall under this category. In the context of the present study, the concept of 'glocal' as applied to television covers a range of combinations of global and local categories spanning marketing techniques, genres, language, and even distribution aspects.

For the greater part of the decade spanning 1990–2000, the category of 'national' was associated with the state controlled broadcaster, Doordarshan. In this period there was a direct correlation between the influence of the state and the actions of the broadcaster. After the broadcasting authority, Prasar Bharati, gained formal autonomy in 1997, this path of influence became indirect. The categories of 'global', 'national', and 'local' are inherently problematic in the current era of satellite television and technological convergence. They will be explicated at length in the following chapter.

The role of the state is investigated by examining pertinent legislation, parliamentary processes, ministerial statements, and also the actions of the state-owned broadcaster. The national broadcaster, Doordarshan, was directly controlled by the state for the greater part of the decade spanning 1990–2000.

An elementary quantitative analysis has been done to lay the groundwork. Parameters such as revenues and audience share have been analysed to suggest recent changes as compared to 1990. Some simple quantitative techniques have been used when the data for the number of players and the audience shares/advertisement revenues available in the different segments of the industry have been analysed. The data is then interpreted as to the redistribution of authority as represented by the dimensions of ownership, advertisement revenues, and content of programming.

The devolution of control is also examined within the realm of broadcast and cable policies and specifically an examination of regulation.

THE STATE'S RESPONSE

How has the state responded to these challenges? The state, in this context, has been defined as the central government. The analysis here is a little more complex. In order to understand the response of the state to changed circumstances, it has been necessary to delve into processes of policy formulation and legislation in the communications sector, as well as the reactions of the national broadcaster, which was finally granted 'autonomy' only recently. This study has examined details of various government legislations and reports, including the Prasar Bharati Act of 1990, the Cable Act of 1995, and other proposed legislation on communications. A textual analysis of various legal documents, records of parliamentary proceedings, and industry reports has been undertaken. This is combined with data generated by interviewing media elites.

The governments' agenda of development programming (emphasizing education and rural development) for the national broadcaster has also been examined in terms of broad categories such as educational and entertainment programming.

POLICY RESEARCH

The response of the state can be investigated by sifting through various policies, which are pertinent to the broadcasting and cable sector. As Hansen *et al.* (1998: 67) inform us, 'broadly defined, communication policy analysis seeks to examine the ways in which policies in the field of communication are generated and implemented, as well as their repercussions or implications for the field of communication as a whole'. However, they caution us that rarely is policy analysis an exploration of a coherent package of ideas and strategies.

In fact Hansen *et al.* (1998: 66–7) suggest that sometimes policies are unwritten and may have unintended consequences, or may even be contradictory.

All these factors come into play when examining the role and the behaviour of the state in the Indian context. One must also state explicitly that the decade of the 1990s has been one of political upheaval in India, which has witnessed a rapid turnover of governments. This has added a great deal of complexity to the analysis as entire governments, cabinets, and bureaucracies have changed, making the analysis of a particular set of policies particularly difficult.

The study of media in a multi-ethnic, secular country, which is also host to a bewildering array of languages, is a daunting task. The role of the media in a developing nation, which is attempting to pursue democracy and development simultaneously, is even more problematic. Keeping the degree of complexity in mind, this research project has attempted to study the research questions in as holistic a manner as possible. As outlined here, policy research is a combination of various research methods, some of which are described at greater length in the following sections.

ARCHIVAL RESEARCH/DOCUMENTATION

In order to conduct the study, archival research, content analysis, textual analysis, and elite interviews have been used. The secondary data consists of existing published material from a number of scholarly journals, newspapers, books, magazines, company annual reports, and the Internet. Internal research documents from the concerned ministries in India have also been utilized. However, it is more difficult to get data on the advertisement revenues and audience ratings for different satellite television companies,[5] which are not publicly listed. The cable industry is particularly disorganized and it is very hard to get any details as to advertisement revenues and programming on the local cable channel.

The Indian popular press in English has been referred to widely. These include the following publications: *The Times of India, The Indian Express, The Hindu, The Hindustan Times, India Today,* and *Outlook.* These can all be classified as elitist in the Indian context. Other key documents referred to have been various industry reports, governmental bills and acts concerning the broadcasting sector. 'The Lok Sabha Debates', a publication which provides the proceedings of Parliament sessions, have also been widely referred to.

TEXTUAL ANALYSIS

The research methods adhered to have been primarily qualitative. As part of the case study, textual analysis of documents and newspaper articles has been used as a method of analysis. The documents analysed in detail have included the Prasar Bharati Act of 1990, the Broadcasting Bill of 1997, the Communications Draft Bill of 2000, the Supreme Court judgment delivered in the Hero Cup case of 1995, and The Lok Sabha Debates. There have been some influential committee reports, which have addressed issues in the broadcasting and cable industry at the suggestion of the government. These include the Verghese Committee Report, the Joshi Committee Report and the Shunu Sen Committee Report. These have been examined and analysed.

Another important source to be analysed textually is the publication series entitled 'The Lok Sabha Debates' which provides the reports of the proceedings of the Lower House (comparable to the House of Commons) of Parliament. These have been analysed for the relevant periods.

CONTENT ANALYSIS

Content analysis is yet another arrow in the quiver of the communications researcher. As Stempel III (1989: 124) suggests, 'content analysis is a formal system for doing something that we all do informally rather frequently, drawing conclusions from observations of content'. This research method is concerned with a systematic analysis of communications content. An often quoted definition of content analysis is provided by Berelson (1952: 18), 'content analysis is a research technique for the objective, systematic and quantitative description of the manifest content of communication' (quoted in Stempel 1989: 125).

A content analysis of television programming has also been undertaken for the national broadcaster[6] for the period 1994–2001.

This period was chosen depending on the availability of data. Data available prior to 1994 is not easily comparable with the post-1994 period in terms of categories of programming. Doordarshan's audience research wing really started gathering data on its programming on a regular basis only from 1993 onwards. Therefore, the annual reports of Doordarshan were analysed for the period 1994–2000. The annual reports of Doordarshan were utilized to tabulate data regarding categories of programs telecast on the flagship channel 'DD1'. They gave an indication of macro changes in programming, such as number of hours of broadcast and broad categories of programming such as information, education, or entertainment.

Detailed television listings for sample weeks in 1994, 1996, and 2001 were also analysed with a view to uncovering finer changes within the categories of programming. Williams (1974) classic study of television examined the distribution of types of television programmes in channels such as BBC 1 and BBC 2 in the UK and the KQED in the USA. The channel chosen for scrutiny in this study was DD1, or Doordarshan's flagship channel, since this channel has the highest reach and it is also the best-established channel. Prior to achieving autonomy, DD1 was also closest to being the voice of the central government. The programming available on DD1 has been divided into broad categories such as information, education, and entertainment.

The sample of programme schedules chosen for detailed analysis has largely been a function of availability. Repeated visits to the Doordarshan's offices in Delhi elicited programme schedules for sample weeks in 1994 and 1995. These have been compared to the programme schedules for 2000/2001 with a view to examining the change in the quantum and type of entertainment programming as compared to educational and information-based programmes over time.

In addition, an analysis delving into genres such as soaps, quiz or game shows, and news currently available on the international and regional/local broadcasting channels has also been undertaken.

ELITE INTERVIEWS

An important research method which can be employed in projects which examine policy is to conduct interviews with certain 'key individuals whose understanding of the subject matter might prove helpful in interpreting events, documents and the like' (Hansen *et al.* 1998: 75). Hansen *et al.* clarify that these key individuals could be chosen from the ranks of regulators, civil servants in the relevant ministries, academics, or journalists.

Accordingly, this book seeks to analyse events in the broadcast industry in India by conducting several in-depth interviews with media elites. Persons interviewed included government officials in the Ministry of Information and Broadcasting and Prasar Bharati Corporation, executives in the private broadcast companies, cable operators, academics, and journalists. Many interviews were conducted with media elites. In addition there were also numerous meetings with other officials and executives who wished to remain anonymous and declined to be identified. Their insights were valuable in arriving at a better understanding of many broadcast-related processes.

In conclusion, the research is based on an integration of the data concerning the number of players, audience shares, advertisement revenues, and hours/genres of programming with textual analysis and interview data as to the reaction of the international (for example Sony), national (for example Doordarshan, and the Central Government), and local players in post-1990 India.

Given the paucity of previous academic studies and the constraints to conducting research in this area, this study had few precursors on which it could be closely modeled. Therefore, the research methods used were eclectic; efforts have been made to ensure reliability and validity by exercising self-reflexivity and examining alternatives.

NOTES

1. For a detailed examination of the political processes underlying tele-communications reform in selected developing countries see Petrazzini (1995).

2. Brian McVeigh in *The Nature of the Japanese State; Rationality and Rituality* (1998) explores Japan's Ministry of Education in a case study which then draws conclusions about the nature of the Japanese State. The author explores ideological and institutional linkages in this ministry to arrive at an 'anthropological understanding of the state'. In a parallel

fashion, the research project identified here focuses on the Ministry of Broadcasting and Information in India in order to arrive at conclusions regarding the response of the state in India.

3. An important work by David Page and Willam Crawley (2001) studies the impact of satellite television in South Asia. The research methodology adopted by these scholars includes elite interviews, focus groups, and surveys.

4. For a detailed examination of Rosenau's interpretations of the concepts of authority, control, power, and legitimacy see the second chapter.

5. For example repeated attempts to contact STAR TV officials in India did not bear fruit and ultimately this researcher had to rely on estimates of STAR TV parameters from other published sources.

6. While an analysis of content genres for the large private broadcasters, over the last 7–10 years would have been informative, programme schedules for these periods were not available. In addition, private broadcasters primarily air entertainment with some information programming, so a consideration of the broad categories of information, education, and entertainment would not have been meaningful for them.

CHAPTER FIVE

SALIENT TRENDS IN TELEVISION AND CABLE, 1990–2010

BACKGROUND

The print media played an important role in the creation of a nationalist discourse in India. From the late eighteenth century, newspapers such as the *Bengal Gazette* helped usher in modernity and forge a national identity. The press came to play a pivotal role in the nationalist movement, which gained momentum in the 1940s. Publications had sprung up in a number of Indian regional languages, vociferously arguing the cause of freedom from the colonial yoke. Mahatma Gandhi himself used the Gujarati as well as the English press to champion the cause of freedom (Thussu 1998).

At the time of Independence, Jawaharlal Nehru's ascendance in the political firmament implied that he was able to put his own stamp on the nation-building programme. His ideas were of supreme importance in the national discourse. These dissipated by the 1980s, in the face of challenges from Hindu fundamentalism, domestically, and globalization, internationally. Ian Talbott, a political scientist who has studied the subcontinent, identifies the main ideas at work in the Indian nation-building exercise:

> Secularism and democracy occupied the leading positions in the nationalist pantheon, followed by statism, socialism and non-alignment. They were regarded as the hallmarks of a modernising and progressive Indian nation-state eager to cast aside both its 'traditional' and colonial past. By adopting them, India would, in Nehru's telling phrase, be able to clothe herself in the 'garb of modernity' (Talbot 2000: 167).

Nehru subscribed to a statist outlook, which stressed the role of the government in order to attempt modernization and nation-building. The Nehru period was characterized by a developmental state, with intervention in the economy, planning, and attempts at directly promoting the welfare of the population (Chatterjee 1997: 12). Public services such as education, health, and transport were to be provided by the state. The planned economy elements were inspired by the socialist regimes such as the Soviet Union.

The emphasis was on a secular state,[1] which would provide equality of opportunity for everyone, regardless of his or her gender, caste, or religion. The goals of the secular state would be reached through legislative enactment,[2] the state-controlled media—All India Radio (AIR) and Doordarshan (DD)—and by positive discrimination for the 'Untouchables'[3] (Chatterjee 1997: 171).

After Independence in 1947, the press continued its watch-dog role in the infant democracy. The broadcast media (at that time only AIR), however, was actively enrolled in the task of 'nation-building' and was entrusted with the somewhat problematic job of creating a 'national consciousness' by the government (Thussu 1998). It must be borne in mind that the dual system of a private press and state-controlled broadcasting were thought to be suitable for a number of historical, political, and cultural factors. The traumatic birth of the nation where the violence of Partition (creation of modern India and Pakistan) caused displacement of over 15 million persons implied that AIR was entrusted with the unenviable task of developing a 'national consciousness' at a time when wounds were fresh.

The importance assigned to the state-controlled broadcast media in creating a national consciousness was evident across South Asia. Page and Crawley (2001: 26), in their study of television in South Asia, have argued that the electronic media have played a central role in the shaping of national identity. Central governments have used them as an integrative force, reinforcing nationalism and reinterpreting the histories of the colonial and pre-colonial periods. Content and language were important factors in this exercise.

Notwithstanding these lofty ideals, what followed, unfortunately, was often state propaganda, which flagrantly served the needs of the political leadership. In India, development was high on the state's agenda and the early emphasis on education and information flowed from this. Television was born in this scenario, as a part of AIR in 1959. The state television channel, Doordarshan, also followed AIR in its official goals of creating a national consciousness and national unity.

The raison d'être of the television industry when it first started out in India was to create a 'national consciousness' and disseminate developmental programming. It was envisaged to be a partner in progress, actively supporting 'government plans and programmes for bringing about social and economic change and to protect national security, as well as advance the cause of national integration' (Sinha 1996: 303). The ideology of DD[4] and of not developing domestic competition to the national broadcaster was not really questioned right up to the nineties.

By the mid-1980s, India had witnessed a leaching away of some of its modern founding ideas. Factors such as caste and communalism came to the fore in the 1990s (Chatterjee 1997: 35). The rise of *Hindutva*[5] (Hindu pride or chauvinism) in the 1980s was symbolized in the struggle over the building of the Ram temple at the site of the disputed Babri Masjid (mosque) in Ayodhya.[6] This dealt a mortal blow to secularism as conceived in the Nehruvian ideal. The caste factor also re-surfaced with new urgency in the early 1990s.[7] The V. P. Singh government ground to a halt over the disruption caused by the affirmative action type of policies for the 'backward castes' recommended by the Mandal Commission in the early 1990s.[8] The economic crisis facing the Congress government in 1991 added to the social unrest.[9] Talbot draws a link between the rise of Hindutva and pressures from within and without, 'Inchoate upper-caste anxieties arising from the "Mandalization" of politics and the breakdown of order and society under population pressures and globalization were displaced onto a demonised Muslim "other"' (2000: 175). By 1990, the Indian middle class had expanded and a pent-up demand for consumer goods came into existence. Thus, the twin planks of Nehruvian idealism, namely secularism and a socialist economy were called into question in the period following 1990.

The broadcast media reflected some of these changes in the 1980s and 1990s. Programming by DD tended to favour national values, at the cost of regional and local flavours, right up to the mid-1990s. Hindi language programming was favoured, while regional languages were ghettoized in small time slots. Regarding news, DD and AIR favoured the broadcasting of news reports in Sanskritized Hindi, at variance with the Persianized Urdu of Pakistan Television. DD aired short clips revolving around the theme of India's greatness (*Mera Bharat Mahaan*) from the late 1980s onwards. These, again, reinforced the idea of the nation as they showed national icons such as Mahatma Gandhi, and later day heroes such as cricket stars (Talbot 2000).

In terms of content, DD aired serials based on the ancient Hindu religious epics Ramayana and the Mahabharata from 1987 onwards, which made a phenomenal impact on the audience (Rajagopal 2003). It has generally been acknowledged that the version of the Ramayana aired by DD promoted a homogenized version of the epic, which gave a fillip to the Bharatiya Janata Party's (BJP) aims. The BJP is the Hindu nationalist party, which gained prominence and came to power in the 1980s. The nexus between television and politics is indicated by the fact that the BJP leader, L. K. Advani, appropriated the imagery of the DD's Ramayana for political purposes.[10] In an interesting real life episode, Deepika Chikalia who played the reel life 'Sita' or female protagonist in the serial was awarded a BJP ticket in the parliamentary elections in 1991 (Talbot 2000: 185–187). Thus, the broadcast media and politics became closely entwined with the Ramayana spin-offs.

The decade of the 1990s has been one of unprecedented change as far as television in India is concerned. The change is stark, both qualitative as well as quantitative. In 1990, Indians watched primarily one channel, namely Doordarshan, aired nation-wide. It was owned and rigidly controlled by the Government of India. In 2001, urban Indians could tune into over 70 channels on an average cable system. By early 2009, this number had swelled to 360 channels, with applications for another 160 awaiting government approval.[11] According to another estimate, the number of channels grew from 389 in 2008 to 461 in 2009 (PwC Report 2010: 29). There has been an explosion in television, both broadcast and cable. It is no longer the monopoly of the government with private broadcasters increasing in popularity at the cost of DD. The change from monopoly to competition has implied that broadcasting has become increasingly market-driven. New indicators for measuring success such as advertising revenues have become important compared to vague notions of public service used in the earlier era. In this new competitive environment, content in general and the old-fashioned portrayal of 'national' culture in particular has undergone redefinition.

At the vanguard of this army of new broadcasters are foreign players like STAR and Sony and domestic players like Zee. The fare provided now includes programming in English, Hindi, all the major Indian languages, and some foreign languages. In an interesting development, some private broadcasters have encouraged the use of 'Hinglish', an illegitimate hybrid linguistic entity deriving from Hindi and English. The menu of channels runs the gamut from movies, news, fashion, infotainment, religion, children, and education to sports. The state-owned television broadcaster was finally granted autonomy in 1997 and the autonomous Prasar Bharati Corporation came into existence. These wide-ranging changes have had their impact on the content of DD. Competition and global genres have affected the erstwhile national broadcaster.

The same decade has seen the rise of the information technology (IT) industry in India. The growth of this sector is being actively encouraged by the state. From the paltry 1.4 million Internet users in India in 1998, there has been an exponential increase with an estimated 80 million users in 2009.[12] The telecommunications sector, from being a complete monopoly a few years ago, has undergone corporatization and liberalization. Wireless telephony has shown high rates of growth. Convergence is also occurring in a compressed time-frame. Barely a few years after the cable industry established itself, cable systems in the larger cities were offering over 70 channels.

The Central Government and state governments are actively pursuing an IT agenda as the path to progress. This is particularly true of the more forward looking states in South India such as Andhra Pradesh, Karnataka, and Tamil Nadu which are actively wooing foreign direct investment and joint ventures in this sector. Even the state government of the Union Territory of Delhi is pursuing a pro-active IT policy. Cyber shops are being established to expand the populace's access to the internet; e-governance is being encouraged by the novel *Bhagidari* scheme. Delhi is emerging as an important cyber hub (Sharma 2000).

Globalization is occurring along many axes as far as the mass media and telecommunications are concerned. Local enterprise is also paving the way for unique partnerships between the global, regional, national, and the local levels. Liberalization in the Indian economy has resulted in the growth of unprecedented consumerism in the last decade. The electronic media have helped to usher in this change. Simultaneously, the television has itself reflected new influences, both transnational and sub-national. The marketing strategies adopted by multinational corporations (MNCs) for selling consumer products have also become integral to the marketing of media products on the Indian sub-continent. According to Page and Crawley (2001: 24) who have conducted a comprehensive study of satellite television in South Asia, television advertising has helped to create new markets for products as well as re-branded consumer goods in South Asia.

Analysing the broadcast industry in India is a complex process that must straddle many areas—politics, economics, marketing, culture, and also the domestic film industry. We begin with an examination of the latter three factors in the succeeding sections. After investigating factors, which have impacted the broadcasting sector such as marketing and the domestic film industry, the major broadcasters/channels are studied along the dimensions of ownership, advertisement revenues and programming content. The major broadcasters are DD, STAR, Zee, Sony, NDTV, and regional broadcasters such as Sun TV. STAR and Sony represent transnational or global categories of broadcasters, while Zee, Sun, and other regional broadcasters represent local categories. An analysis of the cable industry is included, as this is the main conduit for the distribution of satellite channels.

This section is followed by a detailed analysis of DD undertaken to examine its organizational structure, finances and programming over the period 1990–2001. The beleaguered broadcaster was directly controlled by the state till 1997. Even after Prasar Bharati was granted formal autonomy, the broadcaster continues to be dominated by mandarins in the Ministry of Information and Broadcasting. It is also the only broadcaster with a terrestrial infrastructure. Thus, it is associated with the category of national.

The discussion is concluded with an analysis of the major trends in the broadcast industry in the last decade and an interpretation of the issues and events through Rosenau's framework.

MARKETING AND CULTURE

The MNCs in India realized that a local twist is required for marketing global products in the 1990s. This is true for products ranging from foods and beverages to media products. For example both Coca-Cola India and PepsiCo India have introduced locally developed products in order to meet customer demand in the last few years (Sharan 2009). India is not unique in this respect; marketers in Asia have followed this formula. Foods across Asia are preferred in their local variants—kimchi pizza in Korea, teriyaki burger in Japan, and spiced up Chinese food in India (Bhardwaj 2000). The 'glocal' strategies are an eclectic blend that have no respect for the 'purity' of language, sartorial styles, palates, and ideologies. What is interesting is that a parallel has been drawn between categories such as food, consumer durables, and media and cultural products.

The 'go forth and multiply, locally' strategy is in part precipitated by the need to achieve volume leadership in a highly competitive market (Rath 2000). In the period following liberalization in 1990, when the MNCs knocked on India's door, the marketing strategy was simply an extension of their global one—emphasis on international style and quality. This strategy was not very effective. The successful MNCs are those who were quick to adapt to the market.

The strategy pursued by MNCs now helps them to become relevant to the Indian conditions and address the price issue. The Indian middle class at around 250 million in 2000 was large in absolute terms, but its purchasing power was not comparable to

Western societies. The plan was to launch new product forms or to enter new categories, as the Indian market was too big to be ignored. Most consumer goods MNCs are increasing the volumes of products that are created specifically for the local market (Rath 2000). Concomitant with the new 'glocal' product line is the localised advertising strategy.

Some examples of innovative marketing of hybrid products in India in the decade 1990–2000:

- McDonald's introduced the vegetarian *McAloo Tikki* burger in India, using the traditional Indian potato cutlet. In fact the McDonald's Indian menu is 75 per cent different from its Western counterparts (Dasgupta 2000).
- Pizza Hut marketed a 'Jain' pizza in Western India, which excluded the use of garlic, mushrooms, and onions as toppings.
- Domino's introduced pizzas with distinctly different regional variations within India—pizza with mustard sauce and sardines in the East, butter chicken and *paneer makhani* pizzas in the North and *chettinad* pizzas in the South (Dutta-Sachdeva 2000).
- Coca Cola sponsors popular events by the regional brand leaders such as the beverage *Fanta* in Tamil Nadu.
- Kellogg India faced with indifferent sales of breakfast cereals in India entered a new category of biscuits, an extension of its *Chocos* cereals.
- Lacoste, a global brand-name for T-shirts and sportswear has launched ethnic *kurtas* in India, an exception to its normal marketing strategy. This is based on perceptions of strong socio–cultural patterns (Rath 2000).
- Proctor and Gamble has launched India-specific versions of its detergent Ariel, with ingredients to tackle dirt 'unique to the Indian milieu' (Rath 2000).
- In a departure from the usual practice, mega advertiser Hindustan Lever Limited (HLL) has purchased the re-telecast rights for the mythological serial *Om Namah Shivay*. This is the first time that the telecast rights for a serial are being purchased outright by an advertiser, rather than acting as a sponsor. HLL had been acting as a sponsor for *Om Namah Shivay*, which

had run on DD for the period 1997–2000 under the title *Wheel Bhakti Vandana–Om Namah Shivay* (Thakur 2000).

- Indian pop and regional pop music has come of age. MNC music companies such as Sony music, Virgin Records and Magna sound (a licencee of Warner Music) had backed regional artists singing in languages such as Bengali, Punjabi, Tamil, and Marathi. Maneet Jolly, the Marketing Manager of Magna sound, reasoned, 'most music companies have now realized that to sell a singer as a national figure is a difficult proposition, so they have started focusing on regional singers' (quoted in Dutta-Sachdeva 2000).

The glocal combinations in the marketing of consumer products have also spilt over into media and cultural products[13] as will be examined later.

During the post-liberalization period, Gross Domestic Product (GDP) grew at an average annual rate of 6.4 per cent between 1992–2000. Consumption, especially of Fast Moving Consumer Goods (FMCGs) also increased over this period (Brahmankar and Gupta 2000). Consumerism is on the rise in India, as indicated by retail expenditure figures. According to an A. C. Nielson survey, there has been an almost 45 per cent increase in time spent by Indian men and women in purchasing non-grocery products over this period. Other surveys illumine different facets of the same phenomenon (surveys quoted in Walia 2000). This aspect is particularly important when the survival of so many television channels is dependent on advertising revenues.

The increased emphasis on regions within India by MNCs is partly in acknowledgement of the increase in buying power in the smaller towns and rural areas. According to a study by Brahmankar and Gupta (2000), rural India has a share of about 55 per cent in total consumption of FMCGs. Over the period 1992–93 to 1997–98, rural India showed a growth rate of over 12 per cent per annum with respect to consumption of FMCGs. This is a healthy growth rate by all accounts. This is growing in tandem with the penetration of media in smaller towns and the rural areas. Another facet of this regional emphasis is the rise to prominence of regional political parties, as compared to the earlier scenario of a nationalist party ruling with a large majority.

According to the CII–BOOZ Report (quoted in *Mint*, 17 December 2010: 14) about FMCG, the Indian FMCG industry in 2010 accounted for 1300 billion rupees or 2.2 per cent of the country's GDP. This sector has grown by 12 per cent annually in the last decade. This growth is attributed to several factors including healthy GDP growth, increased rural incomes, opening of rural markets, urbanization and changing consumer lifestyles. The current rate of growth is expected to continue, over the next decade with the FMCG industry forecast to touch Rs 4,000 billion by 2020.

The increasing amounts of advertising expenditures in the last decade are inextricably linked to the rising levels of consumption. While there were at least a dozen companies that had spent over US $23 million (Rs 100 crore) in 2000, a single company, namely Hindustan Lever had spent close to US $186 million (Rs 800 crore) in advertising in this year (Khanna 15 June 2000). Even the harbinger of globalization, McDonalds, is estimated to have spent Rs 200 million on advertising in the year 2000. A large portion of this total ad spend was reserved for brand-building commercials on satellite TV channels such as Zee, Sony, MTV, AXN, and STAR. In line with the localization of the fare, the advertisements for McDonalds are local in character, targeting the family (Arathoon 2000). Media analysts also argue that corporate ad spend on TV, especially by FMCG companies is on the rise. It would appear that cable and satellite TV channels have attracted loyal audiences with a high level of purchasing power.

The advertising industry in India in 2007 was estimated to be Rs 196 billion (FICCI and PwC Report 2008). This figure suggests a growth of 22 per cent over the previous year. By 2010, the advertising industry stood at Rs 247.5 billion (PwC Report 2011). The overall entertainment and media sector in India stood at Rs 646 billion in 2010. Television, radio, and the Internet have shown steady rates of growth over the last five years, but film has actually exhibited slowing down in growth rates in 2009 and 2010 (PwC Report 2011: 7). Television advertising constitutes one of the largest segments in advertising in India. This segment stood at about 41 per cent of the total advertising pie in 2010. The top three categories of products advertised in 2010 were toilet soaps, mobile phone service, and social advertisements.

Other sectors which were prominent advertisers on television in 2010 were food and beverages, personal care, and hygiene products and services. Coco Cola India Ltd. was the foremost advertiser in the food and beverages segment, while Hindustan Unilever Limited topped the advertisers in the personal care category (PwC Report 2011: 31).

Television has changed advertising strategies. While about 70 per cent of the advertising budget would have gone to print, the rest being divided amongst other media 30 years ago, in 1999–2000 the share of TV of the total advertising spend was closer to 38 per cent (Khanna 15 June 2000). The share of TV advertising as a percentage of the Indian advertising industry in 2006 had gone up to 41 per cent, while that of print stood at 49 per cent (FICCI and PwC Report 2008). In 2010, there were an estimated 134 million homes in India with television sets. This was divided up between markets with 64 million TV owning homes in urban India compared to 70 million in rural India.[14] The latest trends in entertainment programming are responding to the heterogeneity in the ownership of television sets. High viewership is being reported from middle and small town across India, so programming is reflecting stories set in these locales.[15] The proliferation of TV channels has only served to make the media planner's life a nightmare. With the paucity of empirical data plaguing the broadcast industry, advertisers found it hard to make decisions in the 1990s. For example there were two competing rating systems on viewership data, one based on respondent's diaries while another based upon electronic monitoring by respondents.

To summarize, consumerism has been on the increase in India in the last two decades. Television and cable have both contributed to this process, as well as been impacted by it. Culturally, appropriate marketing of consumer products has led to the rise of 'glocal' marketing strategies. These have even spilt over into the electronic media with an increased commodification of cultural products.

BOLLYWOOD—THE INDIAN FILM INDUSTRY

In attempting to map out the contours of India's broadcasting industry in the last two decades, the Indian film industry has to be taken into account, as it is a major source of content. The importance of the film industry in India's popular culture cannot be over-stated. This has had a huge impact on television programming in the past and its importance is evident even today.

India's film industry, unlike television, has been market driven right from its inception. This industry has been regulated on the basis of the Cinematograph Act of 1952, which covered the area of censorship. However, the film industry managed to avoid the iron hand of the state by indulging in a large degree of self-censorship. Thus themes perceived to be controversial, were avoided by most filmmakers right up to the early 1970s. The film industry also consciously (if a trifle self-consciously) tried to promote the statist objectives of Hindu–Muslim unity and Nehruvian goals of nation-building during these decades (Talbot 2000). It is a point worth recording that even before television became very popular, the film industry affected radio broadcasting. Film songs were very popular on AIR even in the sixties.

The last three decades have seen a change in emphasis in Indian cinema. Indian cinema has reflected some of the disillusionment with the state-led model of modernization. There has also been an increasing recourse to sex (with the obligatory soaked *sari* scene) and violence marked by such films as *Bobby* and *Satyam Shivam Sundaram* (Talbot 2000: 189). Amitabh Bachchan, the superstar of Indian cinema starred as the 'angry young man' in a number of films in the 1970s and the 1980s, where he stood up for the rights of the downtrodden.

The 1990s saw a reduction in rural themes, and less emphasis on poverty. Films such as *Dilwale Dulhaniya Le Jayenge*, which was essentially a romance, brought in the importance of the diaspora audience. The sensitive issue of Hindu–Muslim relations was actually explored in the film *Bombay* released in 1995. The political problem of secession and terrorism formed the backdrop of films such as *Roja, Fiza,* and *Mission Kashmir,* all produced in the 1990s. A film such as *Satya,* which shows the Bombay underworld, is an example of the gangster genre which was released in 1998.

The themes in the next millennium have grown more experimental, in some ways more realistic, showing maturity and a range of different themes and styles. A film such as *Dil Chahta Hai* which was released in 2001 shows the urban youth and their preoccupations in a film about male bonding. It marks a departure from earlier films in terms of story and style. It is a quintessentially urban film with no family conflicts, rural locales, and so on, a mainstay of films in earlier decades. The hit film *Lagaan*, which also released in 2001, was a historical film which showed both colonialism and cricket. It gained international renown when it was nominated for an Oscar for best foreign film. The two comedies *Munnabhai MBBS* and *Lage Raho Munnabhai* broke new ground in this decade as they were both critical and commercial successes. The latter film explored the complex issue of civic reform by Gandhian principles, delivered in a comedy format.

The fate of many television channels today is linked to India's Hindi film industry located at Mumbai, which has acquired the somewhat inane sobriquet of 'Bollywood' (derivative of Bombay and Hollywood). The title of the industry may not be as ridiculous as it appears because a lot of the films churned out by this prolific industry are in fact a promiscuous combination of Hollywood themes with suitable Indian cultural adaptations. The big three private satellite broadcasters—Zee, Sony, and STAR have a close affinity to Bollywood. It is a symbiotic relationship that even DD has pursued actively. In fact, a programme officer in DD remarked, 'forget about educational programming, all we are using now are *filmi* programs from Bombay' (DD programme officer 2000). The new entrant in 2000, called B4U (which stands for Bollywood for you) unashamedly relied on the film industry as its raison d'être. Even STAR TV launched a 24-hour classic Hindi movie channel in 2000. The golden oldies of Bollywood are being given a new lease of life on STAR Gold which targets the above-thirty demographic (Bamzai 2000c).

One observer, commenting on Indian TV programming which was heavily dependent on Bollywood remarked that, 'the humdrum countdowns, the hackneyed and fluffy interviews and even the soaps, that appear to break new ground but are tired regurgitations of the old formulas had turned Indian television into an extension of Bollywood' (Bhatia 2000). Given this scenario, it is a worthwhile exercise to examine the broad contours of Indian entertainment emanating from Bollywood.

The Indian film industry is prolific, producing over 800 films a year with total revenue of Rs 27 billion in 2000 (Kohli-Khandekar

2010: 118). A market for Indian films already exists in USA, UK, South Africa, and UAE. Potential markets in other countries such as Australia, New Zealand, Fiji, Singapore, Mauritius, Hong Kong, Malaysia, Kenya, and Indonesia have also been explored. Tamil films have proven to be popular in Japan (*The Economic Times* 2000a). The Indian film industry has shown vigorous growth over the last decade as is evident from the fact that in 2009, Hindi films released numbered 235, while 1053 films were released in Tamil, Telugu, Kannada, Punjabi, Gujarati, Bengali, and other Indian languages (PwC Report 2010: 56).

The Indian film industry grew to Rs 96 billion in 2007, with domestic box office collections representing the lion's share of total revenue, standing at 72 billion in 2007 (FICCI and PwC Report 2008: 98). India is currently the world's largest producer and consumer of films with 1146 films released in 2007 in 22 Indian languages (FICCI and PwC Report 2008: 100–103). This segment of domestic collections had actually reduced slightly to Rs. 61 billion in 2010 (PwC Report, 2011). The reasons for this are lack of engaging content and closure of some single screen theatres.

The film industry with its earlier connections with unsavoury sources of finance appears to be corporatizing. According to one estimate, a decade ago film producers spent Rs 60–80 million per film on average. This implied a total of about Rs 48 billion per annum. The institutional lending corpus was only a small proportion—Rs 1 billion or about 2.1 per cent of the total industry budget (Puri 2001). In a departure from earlier behaviour, film producers are tapping into corporate sponsorship to fund their capital requirements, as well as going in for IPOs to fund their expansion (*The Economic Times* 2000a).

A recent trend that has emerged from Bollywood is that Hindi films are no longer made primarily for a domestic audience. The foreign markets, especially the 20 million strong Indian diaspora are an important audience to be wooed assiduously. Earnings from film exports in 1999–2000 were Rs 4 billion compared to Rs 2 billion in 1997–1998 (Iyengar 2000: 1). The overseas collections are becoming an important component of revenue and in 2007 were estimated to be Rs 7 billion (FICCI and PwC Report 2008). In 2010, this segment grew to about Rs 7.7 billion (PwC Report 2011).

Even the fate of the money spinning game show on STAR Plus— *Kaun Banega Crorepati* (KBC) rode on the charisma of Bollywood's super icon Amitabh Bachchan who was the celebrity host. The second innings of this show was also anchored by Bollywood superstar Shah Rukh Khan. Zee TV roped in Bollwood celebrities to host its clone game show—*Sawal Dus Crore Ka*—which proved to be very short-lived.

In a further example of the synergy between the television and film industries, television rights have emerged as a significant source of revenue for film producers in India by 2007. For example, Sony Entertainment Television acquired the world satellite rights of popular Yash Raj films such as *Chak De India* and *Tara Rum Pum*. Mukta Arts, a film distribution and production company promoted by Subhash Ghai has sold telecast rights for 12 movies to TV channel Zee Cinema for a reported Rs 220 million. Moser Baer is acquiring IP rights for some films and is selling them to TV Broadcasters such as STAR TV (FICCI and PwC Report 2008). The digital distribution of films, especially via satellite distribution, makes it possible to reach larger audiences more cost-effectively with the smaller release window (PwC Report 2011).

India has one of the largest film audiences in the world, one indicator being an audience of 3 billion viewer admissions a year in 2009 (PwC Report 2010: 59). Popular culture in India has been defined by the vibrant film industry, ever since its inception. One industry watcher describes the Hindi film industry thus:

> The best mirror of Indian society's changing face is the popular Hindi movie. On the face of it, this might seem an absurd proposition. How can a form of expression so utterly removed from reality, so distorted in its depiction of India and so lurid in the escapism it offers be a mirror of anything, let alone Indian society as a whole? The answer lies in the artlessness and complete absence of self-conscious purpose of the popular film (Desai 2000).

Desai (2000) believes that the patterns discernible in popular cinema can be studied and the collective subconscious can be uncovered akin to a Freudian interpretation of dreams. The older Hindi films had a rigid moral formula—any deviations were punished with dire consequences. Poverty was often glorified. The 1990s have seen a marked change in the narrative of popular cinema. There is less fatalism and more optimism. Individual initiative is not frowned upon and the formula has changed from, 'individuals struggling to have a choice in their lives to their struggling with the choices they have' (Desai 2000: 2). The inter-linkages between media and society are illuminated by this change in narrative structure.

As indicated in the preceding section, India's film industry has defined the nation's popular culture for the last five decades. Fare from the film industry has made heavy inroads into the small screen in the last two decades. The Indian film industry is increasingly targeting foreign markets including the Indian diaspora. Many Hindi films are now shot in foreign locales, with non-traditional themes. The statist objectives of promotion of secularism and state led modernization appear to have been jettisoned in favour of rising consumerism. Thus global influences in the last decade have undermined the 'national' values promoted by the Indian film industry for so many years. As indicated earlier, the film industry has a deep influence on television programming. This implies that these changes have also affected the small screen.

A NEW ERA IN INDIAN BROADCASTING POST-1990

Historically there appears to have been a dichotomy in the Indian media. While the print media and the film industry have shown healthy growth and guarded their freedom jealously, the 'electronic media have been possessed, controlled and eventually emasculated by politicians and Government rules' (Reddi 1996: 232). However, developments 1990 onward reflect the de facto liberalization that has occurred in the broadcast sector. The period from 2000, again, is one when private broadcasters both domestic and international have made their presence felt in India.

Trends

Entertainment delivered through the electronic media has spread its tentacles in India with urbanization, rising income levels, and the alignment of Indian media with global trends (Bhandari 2000).

Measured by almost any parameter, television has seen a quantum jump in India in the last two decades. Television has expanded its reach (Figure 5.1a and 5.1b) as well as garnered a larger share of advertising expenditures as compared to the print and other media (Figure 5.2a and 5.2b and Figure 5.3). The estimated TV households have risen from 6.8 million in 1985 to 75.5 million in 2000

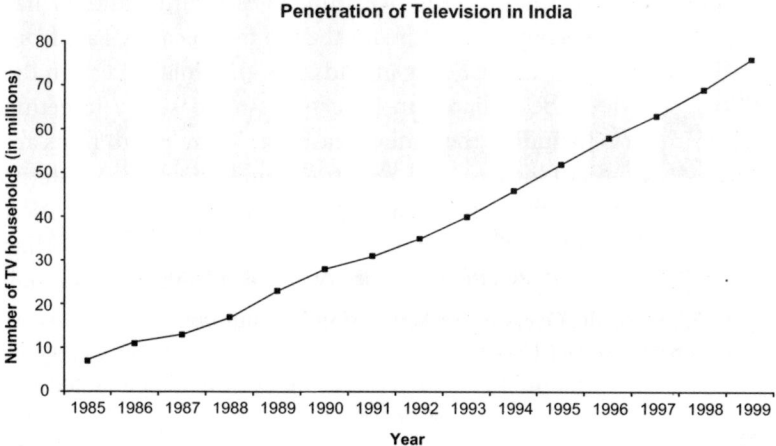

Figure 5.1a   Penetration of Television in India (1985–2000)
Source: Doordarshan (DD) 2000.

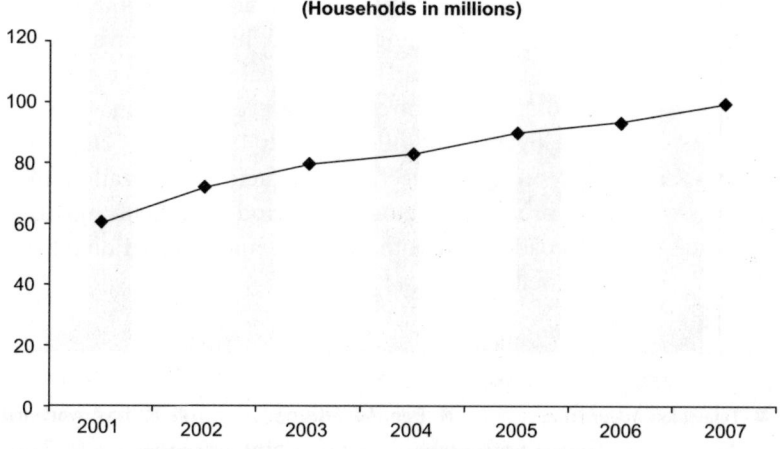

Figure 5.1b   Penetration of Television in India 2001 Onwards
Source: Prasar Bharati Annual Report 2007–2008: 128.

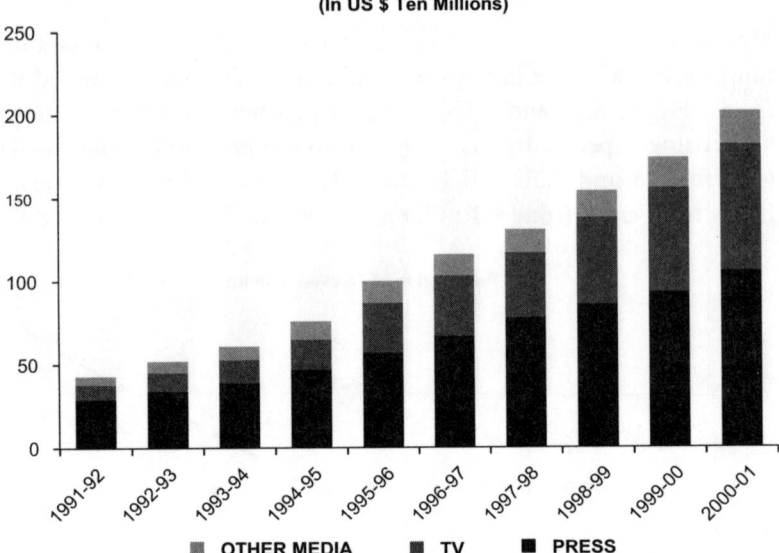

(In US $ Ten Millions)

■ OTHER MEDIA　　■ TV　　■ PRESS

Figure 5.2a Media Overview of Advertising Expenditures
Source: R Bakshi Zee Telefilms.

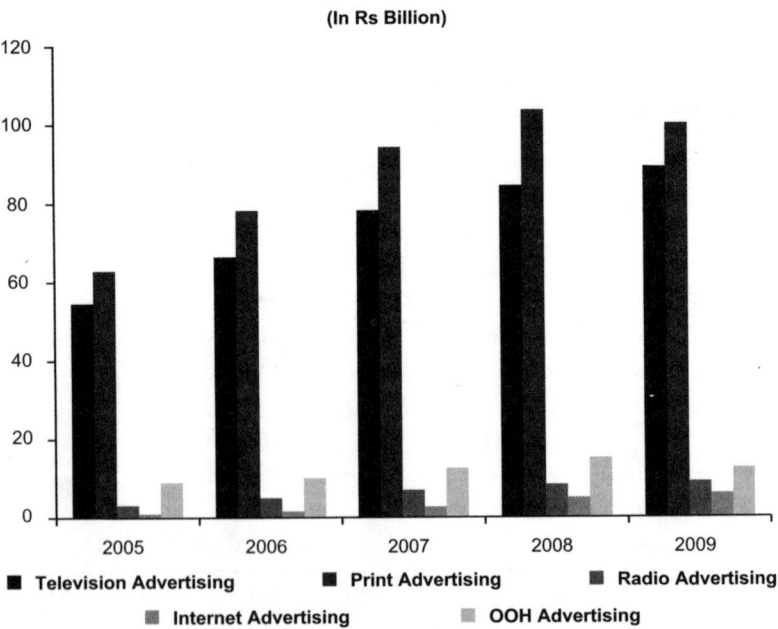

(In Rs Billion)

■ Television Advertising　　■ Print Advertising　　■ Radio Advertising
■ Internet Advertising　　■ OOH Advertising

Figure 5.2b Growth of Indian Advertising Industry (2005–9)
Source: PwC Report, Indian Entertainment and Media Outlook, 2010.

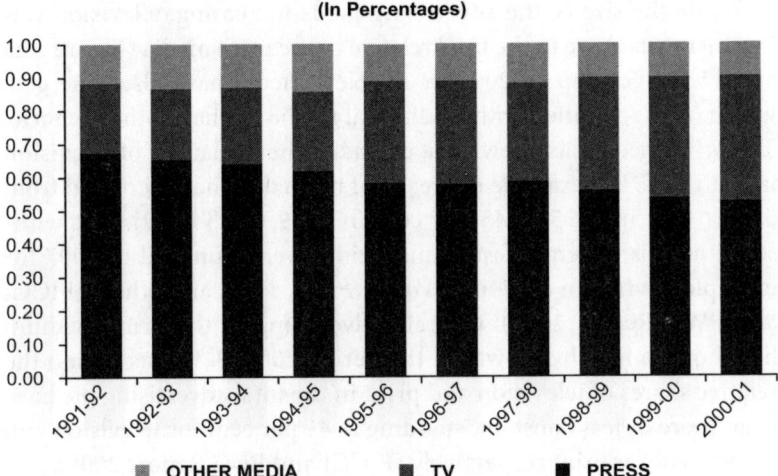

(In Percentages)

■ OTHER MEDIA   ■ TV   ■ PRESS

Figure 5.3:   Shares of Advertising Expenditures across Media
Source: R. Bakshi Zee Telefilms.

(DD 1999: 30; DD 2000: 18). In 2006, the estimated TV households rose to 112 million (FICCI and PwC Report 2008: 53). The cable industry, which is a more recent phenomenon, has increased from negligible penetration in 1990 to an estimated 30 million households in 2000 (Figure 5.1a). This has shown a further increase (Figure 5.1b) and was estimated to be 68 million households in 2006 (FICCI and PwC Report 2008). In 2009, the estimated television households had gone up to 124 million, indicating a penetration of 60 per cent within the country (PwC Report 2010).

There is a differential penetration of television in the rural and urban areas. According to one estimate, in 1999, 73.8 per cent of households in urban areas had television, while only 23.7 per cent of rural households had television. Similarly, while 40.6 per cent of urban households had cable and satellite television, only 6.5 per cent of rural households had cable and satellite television (NRS 1999 in DD 2000: 23). There was a difference across geographic regions as well. While the Northern (104.3 million) and Western (101.3) regions had similar figures for the year 1998 for total TV viewers, the Eastern (84.3) region was lagging behind in terms of total viewers. Conversely, the Southern (113.5) region was ahead with the largest number of TV viewers (DD 2000).

While the size of the advertising pie is increasing, television was increasing its share in the total relative to the print media (Figure 5.2a and Figure 5.3) up to 2000 or so. New media have also emerged, which have combined with traditional media to change the scenario. The print media has shown the effects of the onslaught of television in the 1990s. For example the reach of magazines has decreased from 53 per cent in 1995 to 45 per cent in 1999 (NRS 1999). Not with-standing this, several lifestyle magazines were launched in 2007 for example the Indian edition of *Vogue*, *FHM*, *Dare*, and others (FICCI and PWC Report 2008). Overall, advertising in the print medium has shown a healthy growth in the period 2003–7. In this period the relative shares of television and print in the total advertising pie have been more or less constant, standing at 41 per cent for television and 48 per cent for print respectively (FICCI and PwC Report 2008).

When the television industry is examined in depth, it appears that the share of the cable and satellite channels in advertising expen-diture is growing in comparison to DD (Figure 5.4). In this era of audience fragmentation, the satellite channels as a group are gaining ground. According to Manish Bhandari of Rensearch, a division of Renaissance Securities, cable and satellite television attracted 65 per cent of TV advertising, worth Rs 22 billion in 2000. He also estimates that the cable and satellite TV industry had a compound annual growth rate (CAGR) of 21 per cent in terms of reaching TV homes, and a CAGR of 30 per cent in advertising revenues, reaching 50 per cent of TV households by 2003. These sustained high rates of growth have affected DD adversely (Bhandari 2000).

The large private broadcasters which are in operation currently are STAR TV, Zee TV, and Sony or Sony Entertainment Television (SET), and Network 18 group. The NDTV Group has also gained prominence in the last few years. While STAR and SET are part of global media conglomerates, Zee is a home grown enterprise that has been nursing global aspirations. Besides these three entities, there are many other channels in operation controlled by foreign trans-nationals, as well as Indian entrepreneurs. The number of channels available also expanded from a paltry two aired by DD at the beginning of the decade to over 70 in January 2001 and further increased to over 360 channels by September 2009. Competition for DD has assumed immense propor-tions, even though it still has a monopoly over terrestrial broadcasting.

The arrival of satellite channels in India meant that audiences were exposed to different genres of programming, with different production techniques and styles. The volume of programming in general and entertainment programming in particular has expanded in order to meet the increased demand. In fact, it had been predicted as early as 1994 that within two years many excellent indigenous channels would be created, which would be more localized than foreign programming (Davies 1995). This forecast had been based on the fact that India is a more open market than other Asian countries. In addition, its political and economic structure promotes entrepreneurship. One feature of the new successful programming is that it is mainly in Hindi, Tamil, Malayalam, Bengali, and other regional languages in addition to English. This trend of fragmentation of the television markets is likely to grow in the future. There will also be an emphasis on contemporary Indian cultural themes in the future (Malhotra 1995).

Thus, satellite channels have shown global influences in terms of the ownership of many of the channels and global formats, as well as local influences in terms of ownership, language, and some cultural adaptations.

DD, which was state controlled for most of the 1990s, showed a steady growth in advertising revenue till about 1996–7, then it suffered a set-back subsequently. However, DD, which had seen its ad revenues slip from 1998 onwards, had managed to stem the tide in 2000. This will be discussed at length in the following section.

DOORDARSHAN AND PRASAR BHARATI

After examining some of the broad trends discernible in Indian broadcasting in the last decade, a detailed analysis of some of the major broadcasters is undertaken. Doordarshan with its close links to the state is a major subject of study here.

Doordarshan and All India Radio were brought under the umbrella of the autonomous Prasar Bharati in 1997 (see Table 5.1). Prior to 1997, DD was one of the departments of the Ministry of Information and Broadcasting with the Director General as the head. The Directorate General is responsible for policy formulation, planning and development, marketing, budgetary control, channel management, and audience research, amongst other topics. There

Table 5.1a   Doordarshan Salient Statistics (1982–2000)

Doordarshan Indicators	1982	1987	1992	1997	1999	2000
Program Production Centres	10	17	20	41	46	47
Total Transmitters	19	199	535	921	1,041	1,090
Population Covered (%)	26	70	81	87	87.6	87.9
Area Covered (%)	14	47	61	69	72.9	74.8
Total Program Output (Terrestrial and Satellite) Hours per Week	184	346	478	1,422	1,393	1,485
Home Viewers (Million)	17	74	195	296	362	403
Commercial Revenue (Rupee millions)	172	1376	3010	5719	3999	6106
Personnel	4,918	10714	19975	19576	20451	21464

Source: Doordarshan, 2000, Audience Research Unit.

Table 5.1b   Doordarshan Salient Statistics (2001–7)

Doordarshan Indicators	2001	2002	2003	2004	2005	2006	2007
Program Production Centers	55	56	59	60	64	64	66
Total Transmitters	1236	1358	1396	1403	1400	1399	1403
Television Homes (Millions)	60.6	72.2	79.8	83.1	90.0	93.3	99.6
Number of Viewers (Millions)	261.8	270.2	296.3	307.5	337.9	444.2	460.5

Source: Prasar Bharati Annual Report 2007–2008: 128.

are three main divisions within DD—Program, Engineering, and Administration. The Directorate also controls the programming for the National and International channels. Programming activities at the Directorate include news and current affairs, commercial operations, and audience research. While the officers of the Indian Information Service determine the editorial aspect of the news and current affairs programmes, the other programme activities are managed by personnel of the Indian Broadcasting Service. As in other government organizations, DD is a hierarchical organization, with government bureaucrats in key positions and this has not really changed even after Prasar Bharati was made 'autonomous'.

While one crucial aspect of DD, namely its organizational structure has been touched upon, another aspect—its finances are also of vital importance. DD is provided with funds by the Government of India through annual grants voted by Parliament (see Table 5.2). Another source of income for DD is internal resources generated through commercial operations. This revenue is transferred to a special fund, which is used for the development activities of DD. The Shunu Sen Committee Report (2000) had recommended that Prasar Bharati should aim at generating enough resources internally, so that it became independent of government funding in five years. This suggestion was with a view towards preserving the independence of Prasar Bharati.

Over the years, DD's earnings from advertising revenues have increased manifold (see Figure 5.5). From the relatively small figure of about Rs 43 million in 1977, DD's advertising revenues increased slowly to approximately Rs 344 million in 1984. The rate of growth of revenues accelerated with the appearance of India's first soap opera *Hum Log* in 1984–5 (Figure 5.6). Advertising revenues accelerated till they peaked at Rs 5719 million in 1997. Thenceforth, they slipped down wards. However, DD's earnings from advertising showed a recovery in the year 2000. The period when DD's revenues show a decline is the same period when satellite television was garnering a greater share of the television advertising pie (see Figure 5.4). Thus,

Table 5.2 Plan Expenditure on Doordarshan (In million Rupees)

Year	Revenue and Capital Account
Up to 1980	342.28
1981–1985	1342.89
1986–1990	7162.94
1991–1995	8968.51
1996–2000	17267.94
Total	35085.42

Source: Compiled from Doordarshan 2000, Audience Research Unit.

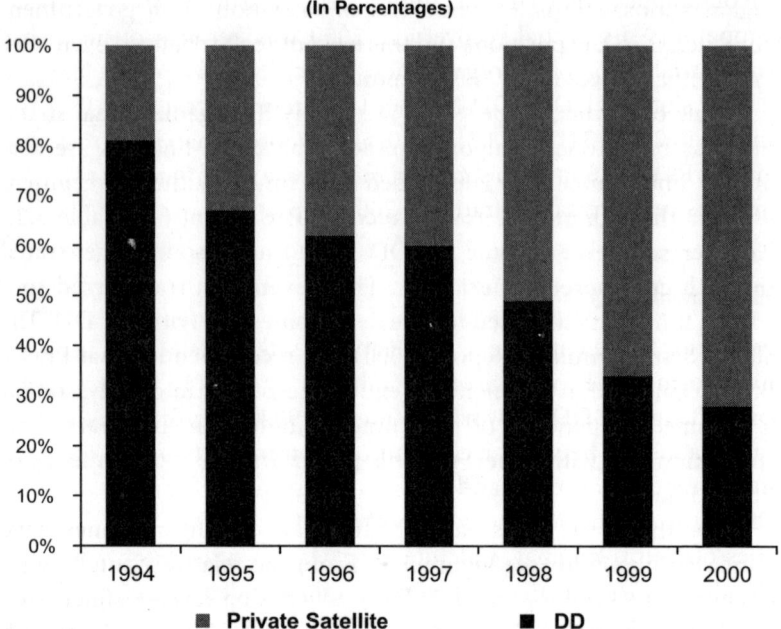

Figure 5.4 Television Advertising Expenditures—Doordarshan versus Private Satellite Channels

Source: Carat Media Services cited in the Shunu Sen Committee Report, 2000.

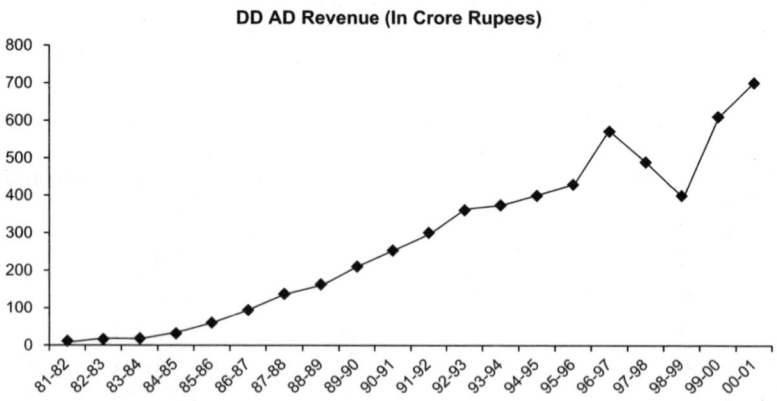

Figure 5.5 Advertising Revenues of Doordarshan

Source: DD Annual Reports of various years.

it would appear that DD was under great pressure from the private competitors. Its partial recovery in 2000 was because of increased commercialization of the organization, especially measures like the sale of time slots on DD 2 (DD Metro). DD's revenues touched Rs 5538 million in 2002–3 (DD 2003). In 2005–6, Doordarshan had gross revenue of Rs 9543.6 million showing an increase of 42 per cent over the previous year (Prasar Bharati, DD 2005–6).

DD Growth

Even prior to the entrance of transnational satellite television in India in the form of the coverage of the Gulf War by CNN in January 1991, some changes in DD are worth noting. In 1982, a regular satellite link was established between Delhi and other transmitters, the national programme was started and colour television was introduced (DD 1999). The second channel was introduced in the four metropolitan cities of Delhi, Bombay, Calcutta, and Madras after 1984. Morning and afternoon transmissions were also introduced by 1989 (Saxena 1997). The decade 1981–90 also saw the number of transmitters

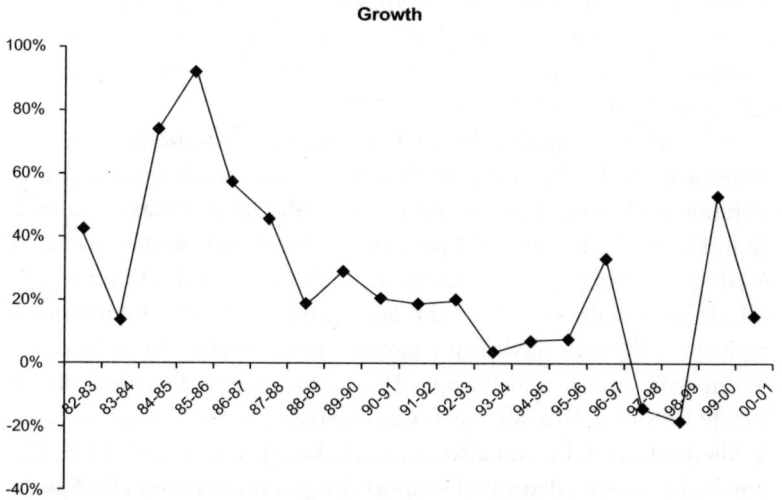

Figure 5.6   Percentage Growth of Advertising Revenues of Doordarshan
Source: DD Annual Reports 1994, 1995, 1997, 1999, 2000.

increase from 19 to 519 (DD 1999: 3). This factor has political significance, which will be examined later.

The 1990s ushered in a bewildering array of options that had heretofore not existed as far as the national broadcaster was concerned. The entry of STAR TV irrevocably changed the equation in India. In 1993, DD took the initiative and linked up the second metro channel with satellite networking, and started regional language satellite channels. The other satellite channels started by DD in 1993 included the business news and current affairs, sports, music, and enrichment channels. Thus, the five satellite channels available in 1995 were DD1 (DD's flagship channel), DD2 (the Metro channel), DD3 (catering to intellectuals), DD-CNNI (news and current affairs), and the Movie Club channel. All these channels started with a transmission of one to three hours each day. DD3 was described as, 'the infotainment channel with programmes on culture and current affairs' (DD 1996: 3). It was available terrestrially in the four metros and elsewhere by satellite. In a marked departure for the national broadcaster, the DD–CNNI venture was set up as a 24-hour current affairs channel with programmes from DD and CNNI. Regional language satellite channels in Assamese, Bengali, Gujarati, Kannada, Kashmiri, Malayalam, Marathi, Oriya, Tamil, and Telugu (Table 5.3) had been introduced by October 1993 (DD 1994). The metro channel (DD-2 Metro) targeted urban viewers, while the regional channels are aimed at particular linguistic groups. The DD-2 Metro channel was available terrestrially in 56 cities by the end of 1999 (DD 1999).

This was the response by DD to increased competition on the domestic front. By the end of 1993, Zee TV had completed one year of operation and it was directly competing with DD as it was broadcasting in Hindi. At this time, 50 per cent of Zee shares were acquired by Murdoch's News Corp. Competition to DD increased. However, DD had global ambitions too, as the launching of the DD International channel in 1995 indicated. This channel initially reached about 50 countries in Asia, Africa, and Europe. This service was re-launched on the satellite PAS-4, so that the reach was expanded to South East Asia, the Middle East, the CIS, and also to North America. In March 1999, DD launched a channel dedicated to sports programmes called DD-Sports.

In terms of infrastructure, DD has expanded until it now has one of the largest terrestrial networks in the world. In late 2009, DD had

Table 5.3   Doordarshan Channels in 2000

DD-1	National Channel
DD-2	Metro Entertainment
DD-4	RLSC - Malayalam
DD-5	RLSC - Tamil: Podigai
DD-6	RLSC -Oriya
DD-7	RLSC - Bengali
DD-8	RLSC - Telugu
DD-9	RLSC - Kannada: Chandana
DD-10	RLSC - Marathi: Sahyadri
DD-11	RLSC - Gujarati
DD-12	RLSC - Kashmiri
DD-13	RLSC - Assamese and Languages of North East
DD-14	SN - Rajasthan
DD-15	SN - Madhya Pradesh
DD-16	SN - Uttar Pradesh
DD-17	SN - Bihar
DD-18	RLSC - Punjabi
DD-India	International Service
DD-Sports	Sports
DD-News	News & Current Affairs
DD-Gyandarshan	Educational TV

(RLSC—Regional Language Satellite Channel; SN—State Network)
Source: Doordarshan, 2000, Audience Research Unit, New Delhi

a massive network with 31 channels, 66 studios, and 1,413 transmitters (Shukla 2009). The emphasis in the last few decades was on hardware and setting up of transmission facilities. This went hand in hand with India's vision of establishing its own space programme (the INSAT satellites) in the 1970s. DD uses transponders on the INSAT and other satellites to support its terrestrial transmitters and to provide additional satellite channels. The total number of transmitters increased from 18 in 1980 to 519 in 1990 and then increased further to 1107 by the year 2000 (for a year-wise breakdown of transmitter installation, see Figure 5.7a and Figure 5.7b). By 2007, the number of transmitters had increased to 1403 (Prasar Bharati Annual Report 2007–8).

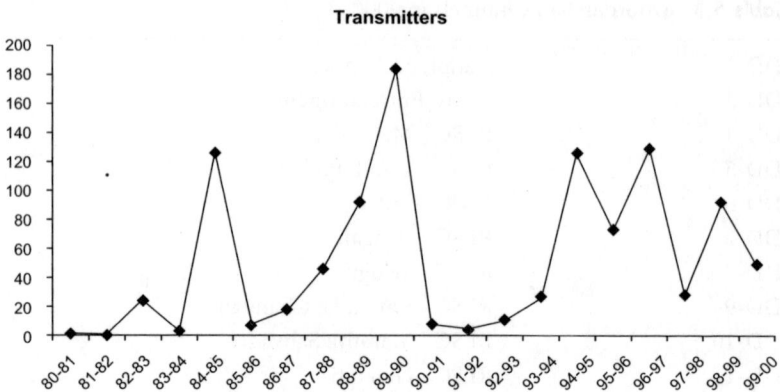

Figure 5.7a Installation of Doordarshan Transmitters (Year-wise)
Source: DD Annual Report 1994, 1995, 1997, 1999, 2000.

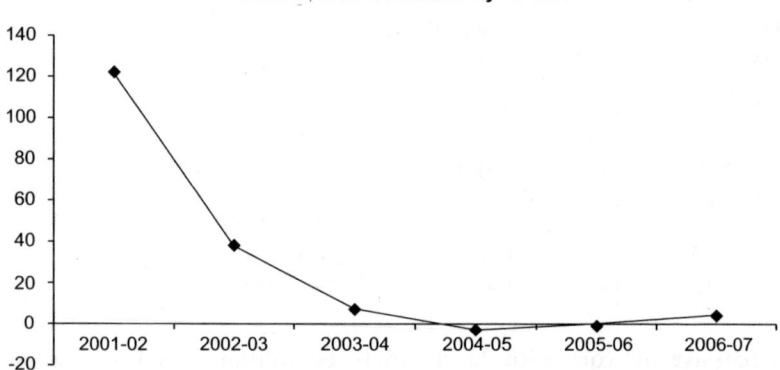

Figure 5.7b Installation of Doordarshan Transmitters 2001 Onwards
Source: Prasar Bharti Annual Report 2007–2008: 128.

The geographical area coverage increased from 13.5 per cent in 1980 to 54.5 per cent in 1990. By the year 2000, the area covered had expanded to 74.8 per cent. The percentage of population covered increased from 25 per cent in 1980 to 76.3 per cent in 1990, and then increased again to 87.9 per cent in 2000 (DD 1994; DD 2000). By 2006, terrestrially DD was covering 79 per cent area and 91.2 per cent of the population of India. At this time, the DD network consisted of

64 DD Kendras or branches. The total channels offered by DD were 24, with four national channels—DD-National, DD News, DD Sports, and DD Bharati. The Regional Language Satellite Channels include DD-Malyalam, DD-Podhigai (Tamil), DD-Oriya, DD-Bangla, DD-Saptagiri (Telugu), DD-Chandana (Kannada), DD-Sahyadri (Marathi), DD-Gujarati, DD-Kashir (Kashmir), DD-North East, and DD-Punjabi. The State Network Service is offered for Rajasthan, Madhya Pradesh, Uttar Pradesh, Bihar, Jharkhand, Chhattisgarh, Himachal Pradesh, and Haryana (Prasar Bharati DD 2005–6). DD also operates an international channel called DD-India. Amongst the newer initiatives, post-2000, DD also has a Direct to Home (DTH) service with a bouquet of 33 TV channels and 12 radio channels.

DD Programming

With regard to programming, DD has attempted to establish a three-tier primary programme service—national, regional, and local. The national programme focuses on, 'events and issues of interest to the whole nation' (DD 1999: 3). The national programme originated from Delhi and all transmitters in the country relay it. It emphasized national integration and communal harmony and the programmes aired under its banner included news, current affairs, cultural magazines, serials, music, dance drama, and feature films (DD 1994; DD 1995). The national programme was introduced in 1982 for a duration of 90 minutes, with two news bulletins—one each in English and Hindi. By the year 1998–9, news bulletins were now telecast in Hindi and English every hour on the national network. National programmes could also reach over 87 per cent of the population through programmes that are aired for about 15 hours daily. These programmes were also available in satellite mode between midnight and 5.30 a.m. (DD 1999).

The regional programmes originated from the state capitals and were relayed by all transmitters in the respective states (Table 5.5). The regional programmes were similar to the national programme in many respects, except that they were in the language of that particular region. They also included programmes on agriculture, health, family planning, and adult education. In 2000, regional programmes of 16 states and one composite zone (Northeast) were telecast for four to six hours each day. The local programmes were specific to a particular area; they covered local issues and featured local people. They were telecast for the people of an ethno-linguistic region. Local programmes of the duration of about an hour were telecast from 30 centres in 1999 (DD 1994; DD 1995; DD 1999).

The programming available over DD's major channels is a mixture of information, education, and entertainment.[16] Information programmes as classified by DD range from news and current affairs to programmes on rural development, family welfare, and special programmes targeting women and children. This category of programmes also includes sports. While the national network airs news bulletins in Hindi and English on the hour, the major TV stations telecast news bulletins in the regional languages in the evenings, where regional events are covered in greater detail. A weekly news magazine in Sanskrit was also introduced on the national network in 1995. DD also telecasts programmes relating to sports.

Educational television (ETV) has been stressed by the state right from the time India gained her Independence in 1947. The educational programmes targeted different viewers, ranging from basic health education for the semi-literates, to the higher education programmes for university students. School TV programmes were produced and telecast from Delhi, Bombay, and Madras stations. ETV programmes were also broadcast from a number of states in different languages. These were produced by the Central Institute of Education Technology in Delhi and State Institutes of Education Technology at different states. The University Grants Commission (UGC), which is the body responsible for university education in India, had a tele-classroom programme broadcast regularly on the national network. This aimed at reaching the students all over India, including the small villages and towns. Distance education is also provided by broadcasting curriculum-related programmes for the Indira Gandhi National Open University (DD 1994; DD 1999). The Consortium for Educational Communication is also continuing the work of broadcasting educational lectures over satellite receivable across India in 2009.

The entertainment programmes aired on DD include serials, sitcoms, soaps, and film-based programmes. A large proportion of the entertainment programmes are broadcast on sponsorship basis. The objective of the entertainment programmes is of 'creating commonality in tastes and preferences' (DD 1999). Programmes on DD channels are garnered from different sources, these include:

- in-house production, or programs produced by DD professionals using DD infrastructure;
- commissioned programs, or programs funded by DD but produced by eminent persons;
- royalty, or programs produced privately which are accepted for telecast and payment made according to a fixed rate structure;
- sponsorship, or programs produced privately, telecast for the payment of a telecast fee against free commercial time;
- film based, or feature films and film based programs;
- acquired, or programs acquired from mostly foreign companies for single or multiple telecasts;
- educational, or ETV programs produced by organizations under the aegis of the Department of Education of the state and central government (DD 1999: 25).

The socialist mores were visible in DD's programmes, right up to the 1980s, but things have changed in the last two decades. Some scholars have accused DD of abandoning its public broadcaster's mantle in the pursuit of commercial revenues in the 1990s (Sinha 1999; Karnik 2001; Singhal and Rogers 2001).

In the last decade, DD has again tried to introduce some new public service elements in its programming. For example the National channel DD Bharati was launched in 2002. This telecasts programmes on health, children, the arts, heritage, and so on. DD Urdu made its appearance in 2006 to cater to the Urdu speakers. Amongst the objectives of the channel are to strengthen democracy, to change the attitude of the Urdu speakers to make them more amenable to modern ideas, and to serve as an instrument of national integration (Prasar Bharati Annual Report, 2007–2008). Thus, it would seem that this channel would be harnessed for propaganda purposes by the State, as a weapon against divisive forces.

CONTENT ANALYSIS OF DD'S PROGRAMMES

A detailed examination of programming content on DD's flagship channel, DD1 is undertaken in the following section. DD's own categories of information, education, and entertainment are utilized to examine changes in these categories over time. Changes in these categories give some indication of whether the statist objectives (emphasizing development programming and education) are being adhered to or not.

In an examination of the programming genres aired by DD1 in the period 1990–2007, it would appear that the broad categories of education, information, and entertainment have shown change over time (Table 5.4). This change is both quantitative, as well as qualitative. For the period 1994–2007, for which data is available, certain trends have emerged. The amount of educational programming as a percentage of total programming has shown a decrease across the board, for the national network, regional services, and the local stations. The decrease is fairly significant for the national network, as education was 28.3 per cent of the total in 1994, decreasing to 18.4 per cent for 1999, slipping still further to 11 per cent in 2003 and 9 per cent in 2006–7.

As expected, the proportion of entertainment in the total programming has increased over the period 1994–2007. While both the national network and the regional services have shown an appreciable

Table 5.4 Programme Composition of DD I

Year	Education			Information			Entertainment		
	NN	RS	LK	NN	RS	LK	NN	RS	LK
1994–1995	28.3	39.3	53.0	34.3	35.5	30.0	37.4	25.2	17.0
1996–1997	23.9	37.5	50	38.2	32.5	40.0	37.9	30.0	10.0
1997–1998	26.0	35.0	40.0	39.0	34.0	50.0	35.0	31.0	10.0
1998–1999	23.0	33.0	50.0	35.0	36.0	40.0	42.0	31.0	10.0
1999*	18.4	32.1	40.0	35.0	31.3	50.0	46.6	36.6	10.0
2003	11			32			57		
2006–2007	9			NA			51		

* Figures for 1999 are up to December 1999. For all other years the figures are from April–March.

NN - National Network, RS - Regional Service, LK - Local *Kendras* (Centres).

Source: Doordarshan 1994; Doordarshan 1995; Doordarshan 1997; Doordarshan 1999; Doordarshan 2000. Doordarshan India 2003; Prasar Bharati, Doordarshan 2006–7.

increase in this segment, the entertainment aired by the local stations has remained constant. The share of entertainment in the total programming aired over the national network was 37.4 per cent in 1994, which increased to 46.6 per cent by 1999, and reached 57 per cent by 2003 (Table 5.4). This implies that by DD's own definitions of education and entertainment, erosion had occurred in the development agenda. If DD1 was airing entertainment for almost half the time on the national network in 1999, this statistic speaks for itself. By 2003, the component of entertainment on DD1 had shot up to 57 per cent (DD 2003). In subsequent years, this figure showed a slight decline to 51 per cent in 2006–7 (DD 2006–7).

The figures for information programming, as a percentage of total programming are somewhat ambiguous. For the period 1994–9, the amount of informational programming in the national network has hovered around 35 per cent (Table 5.4). The comparable figure for the regional service has shown a slight decrease, while only the local stations have recorded an increase in the proportion of informational programming aired. Within the category of information, news, which accounted for 50 per cent of informational programming on the national network in 1995, has decreased to 30 per cent in 1999.

Table 5.5 Doordarshan Terrestrial Reach (2000)

DD-1	National	All transmitters in all parts of the country
	Regional	All transmitters in the respective states
	Local	Single transmitter
DD-2	Metro Network	62 transmitters in larger towns and cities
	Single Metro	Four transmitters in metro cities
RLSC	Regional Service	All transmitters in the respective states
	Additional Programmes	(Not available on terrestrial mode)
SN	Regional Service	All transmitters in the respective states

Doordarshan Terrestrial (only) Services

1. Local Kendras (at 33 places)
2. Kashir Channel (Srinagar)
3. Lok Sabha and Rajya Sabha (Delhi)

Source: Doordarshan, 2000, Audience Research Unit, New Delhi.

Correspondingly, the proportion of sports programming aired on the national network has increased from 7 per cent of informational programming in 1995 to 31 per cent in 1999. The story that these statistics tell is that even within the category of information, 'hard' genres like news are waning in percentage terms, while 'soft' genres like sports are gaining ground (DD 1995: 28; DD 2000: 14).

The component of information programming as a percentage of total programming on the DD1 channel was about 32 per cent in 2003, while that of education was about 11 per cent. The share of educational programming slipped further to 9 per cent by 2006–7 (DD 2003; DD 2006–7).

Another factor that must be taken into account is that the total amount of programming in terms of hours aired by DD1 has increased. The national network was being aired on DD1 for an average of 62 hours per week in 1993. By December 1994, this figure had increased to 70 hours per week. The corresponding figure for 1999 is 168. An implication of this changing base is that the amounts of information, education, and entertainment as percentages are less illustrative than the absolute amounts of the degree of change. For example the share of education in 1994 was 28.3 per cent for the national network, when the base was 70 hours a week. In 1999, this figure had dropped to 18.4 per cent when the base was 168 hours a week. A similar comparison can be made for the category of entertainment education and the increase, both in relative, as well as absolute terms (DD 1994: 8; DD 1995: 28; DD 2000: 13).

The share of foreign programming aired by DD is also a matter of interest. The foreign programmes mainly consisting of serials, films, and sports were 2.3 per cent of the total programmes aired by the national network, DD1, in 1995. In 1999, this figure had gone up to 4.1 per cent. However, this marginal increase in percentage terms concealed a larger increase in absolute terms because of the increase in the base. The regional stations and local stations do not air foreign acquired programming; it is only for the national network.

After sketching out the contours of DD's programming in terms of the broad categories described above, a more detailed analysis was done for some sample television schedules in order to examine the changes within these categories. In other words, an attempt was made to capture some of the finer nuances of the broader changes in programming content. An analysis of the telecast schedules for DD1 for sample weeks in September 1994, March 1996, and March 2001 also reveals the increasing commercialization of DD. The sample schedules for 1994 and 1996 were selected on the criteria of availability and convenience.

For the week commencing on 1 September 1994 and terminating on 7 September 1994, except for Saturday and Sunday, there was mainly one short programme aired in the morning transmission of DD1. On weekdays, the morning transmission consisted of educational documentaries or current affairs discussions. On the weekend, historical serials and animated series for children were aired in the morning transmission. The animated series for children included 'Alice in Wonderland' and 'Disney Adventures'.

The afternoon transmission for this sample period in 1994, for the most part, commenced at 1.00 p.m. and terminated at 5.00 p.m. The afternoon transmission generally commenced with a one-hour educational programme produced by the UGC. Next came news in Hindi and in English. This was followed with serials, educational programmes, and special programmes catering to women and children. For example, some of the programmes aired in the afternoon included *Shanti*, *Stritama*, and *Jagte Raho*. Incidentally all three of these serials stressed empowerment for women. It also included entertaining programmes, either sitcoms or films, based on some weekdays. The educational programmes included a science magazine, a programme on the environment, a programme on literacy, and a developmental programme aired during the weekdays. Sometimes cricket was shown on the weekends.

The national programme was generally aired between 8.30 p.m. and 12.00 p.m. in the evening. This generally commenced with the news in Hindi. Next, primarily, entertaining serials were shown on weekdays. This was followed by the news in English. After the English news, educational/information based programmes were aired such as news magazines, cultural magazines, for example *Surabhi*, and current affairs programmes. Sometimes telefilms with social messages and documentaries such as 'Nehru and Agrarian Reforms' were broadcast. Transmission on most weekdays terminated with programmes showcasing the music and dance of different regions in India. Sometimes, feature films and sports were shown on weekends.

Analysis of the telecast schedule for DD1 for the period 25 March 1996 to 31 March 1996 reveals an increase in the total hours of transmission for the network programme. The morning transmission now commenced at about 6.00 a.m. and delinked at 10.30 a.m. for regional transmission. The morning television broadcast commenced with a one-hour educational programme, which covered different topics such as science, issues in higher education, environmental issues, and others. This was followed by the news in Hindi and short programmes on topics such as health, development, and current affairs. English news came next, with business news and world news following. Morning transmission over the network generally concluded with an interview and a documentary. For the period under examination, afternoon transmission began with a one-hour educational programme, which covered topics ranging from history to medicine. The news came next, in Hindi, then in English. This was followed by some serials, a documentary, and sometimes a programme for children. The national network was delinked at 4.30 p.m. for regional programming.

The national network resumed transmission at 8.30 p.m. with the Hindi news. This was followed by promotional short films for other DD programmes. Next came the news in English. The evening transmission generally showed four or five serials, aired in half-hour slots. These were generally entertaining in nature. Some serials such as *Shanti* and *Junoon*, which had figured in the telecast schedule analysed for 1994, were still being aired in 1996. Sometimes, classical dance or music programmes were also aired in a half-hour slot. Hindi feature films were aired on the weekends.

Lastly, the telecast schedule for DD1 was analysed for the period 25 March to 31 March 2001. In terms of hours of programming, there is a vast difference between the telecast schedules of 1994, 1996, and 2001. DD1 is now a 24-hour channel. In addition to news and educational programmes, the morning transmission now aired a 90-minute long morning show called *Subah Savere*, which was more along the lines of entertainment, although it was also informational. This appears to be a more staid copy of the morning shows aired on STAR TV and Zee TV, which have proven to be fairly popular. This represented a new format as far as DD was concerned. Devotional and classical music was also aired early in the mornings.

In comparison to the telecast schedules examined for earlier years, more entertaining serials were aired in the afternoons in 2001. The telecast schedules for 1994 and 1996 analysed for this project revealed an average of two or three entertaining serials aired on the national network in the afternoon. While the hours of transmission had expanded over the years, this did not mean an expansion in educational programmes. In fact, by 2001, for the week under review, over five entertainment programmes were aired in the afternoons on week-days over the national network. There was also a reduction in documentaries aired in the afternoons as compared to earlier years.

An analysis of the national network evening transmission on DD1 for the sample week in 2001 indicates a slight increase in the number of entertaining serials broadcast as compared to 1996 and 1994. Moreover there was a reduction in classical music and dance programmes. Mythological serials such as *Om Namah Shivay* and *Jai Hanuman* were still proving popular. Serials belonging to the thriller/suspense genre were also aired on most weekdays. While there seems to be a lack of any sitcoms, or even game-shows that were attracting audiences on DD, STAR Plus was having a magnetic effect with programmes such as the popular game show *Kaun Banega Crorepati* and family dramas *Kora Kaghaz* and *Kyonki Saas Bhi Kabhi Bahu Thi*. Thus, not only was DD's fief of public service broadcasting being eroded by reduction in educational programming, but it was not even attracting audiences by pandering to commercial tastes. As Karnik (2001) put it succinctly, 'you name one program that has been aired on DD in the last few years that has quality and that people are talking about—there aren't any'. The issue of commercialization of DD Metro by the auctioning off of half-hour slots is taken up later.

Regarding the genre of children's programming, this also reflects a decrease for the period under review. There was generally one children's programme aired on weekday afternoons, and two children's programs aired on Sunday in 1994. By 1996, for the week under review, this had reduced slightly—only 3 children's programmes were aired on week-day afternoons, while only one short programme was aired for children on Sunday. By 2001, even though the hours of transmission had increased, only 3 programmes which were specifically aimed at children were shown in the entire week, including the week-end. While these figures indicate that one section of the populace—namely children—is being underserved by DD's flagship channel, it must be added that DD Metro had been airing entertaining programmes for children daily. As DD Metro had an urban bias as compared to DD1, this implied that children in rural areas are even more disadvantaged than before. The Sen Committee Report (2000) also examined the issue of DD's public service mandate and the fact that children have been underserved.

DD PAST AND PRESENT

Notwithstanding the dilution of its commitment to educational programming over its primary channels, DD actually launched an educational channel Gyan Darshan in 2000. The educational programmes are drawn from various sources such as the Indira Gandhi National Open University, the University Grants Commission, National Council of Educational Research and Training, and others. DD was also trying to attempt subtle propaganda aimed at Pakistan via the airing of the weekly programme 'Pakistan Reporter' in Urduized Hindi over DD1 in 2000–1. As mentioned earlier, a new channel, DD Urdu, was also introduced in 2006.

The genre of entertainment education which swung into action in the 1980s with the popular soap opera *Hum Log* on DD has failed to make any real impact on audiences in the 1990s, as far as DD is concerned. Entertainment education, as defined by Singhal and Rogers, pioneers in the field in India, 'is the process of purposely designing and implementing a media message to both entertain and educate, in order to increase audience members' knowledge about an educational issue, create favourable attitudes, and change behaviour' (2001: 71). *Hum Log* targeted issues such as gender equality, national integration, and smaller family size.

This path-breaking soap opera was followed by *Buniyaad*, a historical soap opera based on the partition of India and creation of Pakistan in 1947. The Hindu mythological serials Ramayana and Mahabharata were huge hits in 1987–8 and 1988–9 respectively measured in terms of audience response. Mythological/religious serials were still popular on DD in the 1990s, as *Shri Krishna, Jai Hanuman*, and *Om Namah Shivay* were pulling in the audiences and the advertising revenues. Some family serials which did well in the 1990s on

DD were *Shanti, Hum Rahi,* and *Udaan* (Singhal and Rogers 2001). However, none of these ever came close to the earlier hits on DD in terms of popularity.

The problems with India's public broadcasting have been summed up by Singhal and Rogers (2001) as a misplaced focus on quantitative targets, that is, infrastructure, rather than programming, a lack of autonomy for the public service broadcaster, Delhi and Hindi language centric broadcasting, and lastly, a programming bias in favour of urban audiences. The Sen Committee Report (2001) also mentions the lack of focus or identity for many of DD's channels, with special reference to the DD metro channel. In the period following 2000, DD tried to address some of these problems by, for example, introducing an Urdu channel and the Bharati channel with emphasis on health and the arts. The Development Communication Division also launched several major public service campaigns in health, education, sanitation, nutrition, and so on. To cater to the rural audiences, area specific information on agriculture was introduced, called 'narrowcasting' (Prasar Bharati Annual Report 2007–8).

Some of the problems identified by Singhal and Rogers stemmed from the fact that DD had a monopoly over broadcasting up till the early 1990s. Competition from terrestrial television never developed in India, when it did arrive, it was via satellite. DD was never challenged in the courts on the grounds that monopoly in broadcasting was violating the constitutional guarantees of freedom of expression right up to the mid-1990s (Bhatt 1994). It is interesting that DD has decided to join the commercial bandwagon, and join in the race for ratings that satellite television has sparked off.

In terms of the theoretical frame-work adapted from Rosenau, DD has represented the state's interests directly for the greater part of the nineties decade. Thus, it can be categorized as national. By most indicators—organizational structure, finances, reach, and content, it can be considered to be a national broadcaster. Even in the post-1997 'autonomous' avatar as part of Prasar Bharati, DD still has close ties with the Ministry of Information and Broadcasting and it is still the only terrestrial broadcaster in operation.

To reiterate, in terms of the analytical dimensions of ownership, advertisement revenues, and content, the influence of DD, and indirectly the state, has waned. The state had direct control over DD as it was a department controlled by the Ministry of Information and Broadcasting until 1997. Post-1997, Prasar Bharati is officially autonomous and a corporation, although the Ministry of Information and Broadcasting still has influence over DD (this is studied in detail in the next chapter). However, the authority of the state as represented by direct control over DD has decreased with the change in organizational structure. Prasar Bharati now has to, at least, maintain the appearance of being objective.

While DD has been funded by parliamentary grants in the past and it continues to be so, it has also been earning revenues from its commercial operations. These earnings are important for two reasons. Firstly, they are a gauge of the popularity of the broadcaster and reflect viewership figures. This has the implication of control over the audience via dissemination of messages. To elaborate, the greater the viewership and advertisement revenue figures, the greater the potential to influence the audience. Secondly, larger commercial revenues accruing to DD imply a greater degree of independence (from the ministry) for the broadcaster. Though DD's advertisement revenues climbed steadily from 1983 onwards, they declined over the period 1996–7 to 1998–9. This implies that DD's programmes were slipping in terms of viewership and ratings as compared to the satellite channels over the latter period. In terms of the percentage growth rate, DD's advertising revenues show a decline from 1990 to 1999 with the exception of one year 1996–7. The declining share of DD in the total television advertising spends as compared to the private satellite channels over the period 1994–2000 has implications for the state.

From 2001 onwards, DD's fortunes as indicated in the revenues earned have had their share of ups and downs. DD's revenues actually showed a decline from 2001–4. Again, revenues increased from 2004 to 2006. This was followed by a decline in 2006–7. Revenues increased in 2007–8, again followed by a decrease in 2008–9 (Shukla 2009). Thus, there is no clear trend of DD's revenue increase for the decade 2000 onwards. While DD had revenues of Rs 8,180 million in 2008–9, STAR India, with only 19 channels had revenues of Rs 22,000 million for the same year (Shukla 2009). This statistic clearly reveals the relative weakness of DD versus the large private broadcasters in the marketplace.

A weakening hold over audiences by DD as suggested by the slipping advertising revenue figures implies that audiences have been shifting their preferences to other channels—global, as well as local, at the cost of the national broadcaster. The repercussions on the state are a loss of control as a smaller percentage of the audience tune in to the erstwhile monopoly broadcaster. While the advertising revenues of DD made a partial recovery by 1999, the rate of growth slacked off subsequently. In addition, many industry analysts have a poor prognosis for DD's survival in the long run. By the criterion of advertisement revenues also, it is clear that the authority of the state has waned. However, the state still has some control as evidenced by the fact that DD has the largest broadcast network in the world with 31 channels, 66 studios, and 1,413 transmitters. Channels such as DD1 and DD News are available in all 123 million TV households in India as they are available in terrestrial mode, as well as cable and satellite channels (Shukla 2009).

In terms of content also, it would appear that the categories of educational and informational programming on DD's major channels have suffered as compared to entertainment programming. The paternalistic state, with its socialist bias in attempts at modernization and nation-building, has found its voice muffled by an increasingly commercial cacophony. Thus, the statist emphasis on development programming appears to have been diluted over time, again suggesting a reduction of the sphere of control of the state.

NOTES

1. The preamble to the Constitution of India adopted in November 1949 is worded thus, 'we the people of India having solemnly resolved to constitute India into a sovereign socialist secular democratic republic and to secure to all its citizens: justice, social, economic and political; liberty of thought, expression and belief, faith and worship; equality of status and opportunity; and to promote among them all fraternity assuring the dignity of the individual and the unity and integrity of the Nation'; (*Constitution of India*, 1999. Government of India, Ministry of Law, Justice and Company Affairs).

2. The Fundamental Rights enshrined in the Constitution of India mention the prohibition of discrimination on grounds of religion, race, caste, sex

or place of birth, right to equality before law, abolition of "untouchabil-ity", right to freedom and other basic rights applicable to the territory of India (*Constitution of India*, 1999: 6–15, Government of India).

3. Positive discrimination for the 'untouchables' implied job reservation policies for the lowest castes mandated by the state.
4. The emphasis on development planning continued (in theory) even when Prasar Bharati became autonomous. For example, the social objec-tives of Doordarshan as indicated in its Annual Report for 1999, include the following:

- To act as a catalyst of social change.
- To promote National Integration.
- To stimulate a scientific temper in the minds of the people.
- To disseminate the message of family planning as a means of popula-tion control and family welfare.
- To provide essential information and knowledge in order to stimulate greater agricultural production.
- To promote and help preserve environmental and ecological balance.
- To highlight the need for social welfare measures, including welfare of women, children and the less privileged.
- To promote interest in games and sports.
- To create values of appraisal of art and cultural heritage (1999: 15).

5. While the literal meaning of *Hindutva* deriving from Sanskrit means the nature of Hinduism, this term has acquired slightly derogatory over-tones to liberals, over the last decade.
6. A turning point in Hindu–Muslim relations on the Indian sub-continent occurred when the centuries old Babri Masjid (mosque) at Ayodhya in northern India was demolished by Hindu zealots in 1992. The Hindu nationalist Bharatiya Janata Party (BJP) had led the movement for the demolition of the Babri mosque and the establishment of a Ram temple at the same site. The Hindu god Ram is an avatar of Vishnu, one of the major gods in the Hindu pantheon. In fact, Brahma, Vishnu, and Shiva form the holy trinity of Hinduism.
7. The issue of caste has always been present in Indian politics. However, the 1990s witnessed the rise in the rise in importance of caste-based parties, especially the lowest castes or Dalits.
8. While positive discrimination policies such as job reservation quo-tas for the lowest castes were in practice for a long time, the Mandal

Commission's recommendations that these quotas be increased sparked-off unrest among the upper castes.

9. The Congress government of India faced a severe fiscal and balance-of-payments crisis in July 1991. These crises occurred mainly due to expansionary macroeconomic policies on the part of the state, coupled with heavy borrowing from abroad and a sharp decline in remittances from overseas Indian workers in the wake of the Gulf War. The government responded to the economic crisis by ushering in liberalization measures including reforms of industrial policy, trade and exchange rate policies, investment policy, in tandem with reforms in taxation, the financial sector, and the public sector. For an analysis of India's economic liberalization in the early 1990s see Jagdish Bhagwati (1993) and Sachs *et al.* (1999).

10. In 1990, the BJP attempted political mobilization by carrying out *Rath Yatras* (journeys across the nation in the manner of god Ram in a triumphal march by chariot, symbolic of the vanquishment of evil).

11. Available at www.rediff.com/money/2008.

12. Available at www.internetworldstats.com/top20.htm.

13. Some scholars of the political economy of communications have argued that the last two decades till the nineties have witnessed an increased commodification of culture. For a detailed analysis see Bettig (1997) and Jhally (1995). Hence, the methods used in the marketing of consumer products have also been applied for the marketing of media and cultural products.

14. See *Hindustan Times*, 6 September 2010, page 23.

15. See *Hindustan Times*, 6 September 2010.

16. The classification of programmes into these three major categories is undertaken by DD itself, as indicated in the Annual Reports of DD prepared by the Audience Research Unit of DD.

Content Analysis of DD's Programming

A content analysis for the programming broadcast on Doordarshan's flagship channel, DD1 was undertaken for the period 1994–2001. DD's Annual reports published by the Audience Research Unit, DD were utilized for this purpose. They were provided by Mr. B.S. Chandrasekhar, Director Audience Research Unit, Prasar Bharati, New Delhi. The annual amounts of educational, entertainment, and information based programming were calculated as a percentage of total programming. These figures were examined comparatively over time in order to examine long term trends. The total number of hours of broadcast time was also taken into account.

The broad categories of information, education, and entertainment were also broken up into the sub-categories of broadcast over the national network, regional service, and local centres.

A more detailed analysis of some sample television schedules for DD1 was undertaken. The sample weeks selected were 1–7 September 1994, 25–31 March 1996, and 25–31 March 2001. The sample schedules were chosen on the basis of availability and convenience. They could be easily located in the Prasar Bharati's New Delhi office. They were provided by Mr C. Vyas, Assistant Controller of Programs, Prasar Bharati.

Since DD1 was not a 24-hour channel in the earlier period under review, an analysis was done by examining morning, afternoon, and national network/evening transmission as separate categories. An effort was made to examine the kind of programmes aired within the categories of educational, information, and entertainment based programming. Even the broad social/developmental messages (such as women's empowerment) imbedded in the serials broadcast by DD1 were identified to see if these had changed over time.

There was a difference in number of hours of broadcast time on weekdays and weekends in 1994. Morning transmission generally commenced at 8.30 a.m. in 1994. On weekdays it varied in length between 30 minutes to one hour. Weekends had longer morning transmission periods, extending up to 12 a.m. on Sundays. By 1996, morning transmission had been extended from 6.00 a.m. to 11.00 a.m. on weekdays, as well as weekends. By 2001, DD1 was a 24-hour channel.

In 1994, afternoon transmission commenced at 1.00 p.m. and was terminated by 5.00 p.m. In 1996, the network programme aired from 1.00 p.m. to 5.00 p.m. in the afternoons.

CHAPTER SIX

THE RISE OF PRIVATE TELEVISION

The advent of satellite delivery of television programming brought about a sea change in the Indian broadcasting landscape (see Table 6.1 and Table 6.2). The decade of the 1990s saw private television players establish themselves in India, changing the contours of the industry. The provision of television was no longer the monopoly of the state; vibrant competition had grown from both transnational and local media groups.

STAR TV

Satellite Television Asian Region or STAR TV was the new player on the horizon that shot into action in the early 1990s. STAR's footprint covered most of Central and South Asia (Kishore, 1994). The Hong Kong based STAR TV was founded by Li Ka-Shing in 1990. It origi-nally aired a free package of BBC, MTV, Prime Sports, Chinese TV, and other channels. In 1993, Rupert Murdoch's News Corp purchased STAR TV from Hong Kong based Hutchinson Whampoa.

The satellite service that STAR TV offered in India in 1994 consisted of five channels. Four of these channels had English programming, while only one had programming in Hindi. Most of the programming was geared towards providing entertainment. During 1994–5, other satellite based services operating from companies in India as well as abroad came into existence. The new offerings on television proliferated, and in 1996 listings in Delhi included EL TV, Jain TV, three Doordarshan (DD) channels, STAR Sports, and the other STAR TV services (McDowell, 1997). In terms of the number of channels available, the services being offered certainly represented an increase in this period. However, it is necessary to critically examine the content of these new offerings.

STAR TV's ownership changed hands in 1993, when Rupert Murdoch's News Corp acquired the majority interest. STAR TV's footprint covered 53 countries in 1995. It reached about 54 million households in Asia (Kwang 1995). This had relevance for the cable industry as 90 per cent of STAR TV's audience viewed it through some redistribution mechanism. STAR TV's main source of revenue was advertising. Advertisement revenues accounted for 70 per cent of the pie, while subscription revenues accounted for only 30 per cent in 1994–5 (Davies 1995).

In the mid-1990s, STAR had explored the possibility of acquiring equity stakes in cable operations in Asia. STAR TV was pursuing a strategy of 'localism' in Asia. In line with this policy, STAR had entered into partnerships with local broadcasters. Another aspect of STAR's localism was splitting broadcasts into different beams for different markets. For example, the north beam targeted Taiwan and China, and had programming tailored to this region. The Southern beam was aired over the Indian subcontinent, the Middle East, and South East Asia (Davies 1995)

STAR was indeed important in the Indian media firmament. It was a reciprocal relationship, as India had also been first priority for the media mandarins at STAR in 1994–5. This was because India's burgeoning middle class, numbering 250 million, had a voracious appetite for TV programming of all kinds. In 1995, STAR TV was beaming down the following channels over India—Channel V, Prime

Sports, Chinese Channel (Mandarin), STAR Plus, BBC World, Zee TV, and EL TV. These were free channels. STAR TV had a 50 per cent ownership in Zee and EL TV, which were Hindi language channels. These were joint ventures with local programmers. In addition, STAR had launched two paid, encrypted channels—STAR Movies in English and Chinese, and Zee Cinema in Hindi (Kwang 1995).

At the end of the year 2000, STAR was broadcasting several additional channels as compared to 1995. These were (a) STAR Plus, which originally began as an English channel, but was reinvented as a Hindi channel by April 2000; (b) STAR World, an English entertainment channel; (c) STAR Gold, which showed the golden old films of Bollywood; (d) STAR News, a 24-hour news channel; and (e) the National Geographic Channel. STAR TV's agreement with Zee TV

Table 6.1 Satellite Channels: General Entertainment (Excluding Doordarshan), 1998–9.

Hindi	Bengali	Tamil
Zee TV	Alpha Bengali	Sun TV
STAR Plus	ETV Bangla	Vijay TV
Sony TV	Tara Bangla	Raj TV
Sahara TV		Jaya TV
Sab TV		
Telugu	**Malayalam**	**Kannada**
Eenadu TV	Asianet TV	Udaya TV
Gemini TV	Surya TV	Suprabhata TV
		Asianet Kaveri
Marathi	**Punjabi**	**Gujarati**
Alpha Marathi	Alpha Punjabi	Alpha Gujarati
Prabhat	Lashkara	Tara Gujarati
	Tara Punjabi	
Rajasthani	**Bhojpuri**	**Urdu**
		Zee Urdu

Compiled by the author from various sources.

Table 6.2 Satellite Channels: Thematic (Excluding Doordarshan), 1998–9

News/Business (English)	News/Business (Hindi/English)	News (Tamil)
BBC World	STAR News	Sun News
CNN I	Zee News	
CNBC	Aaj Tak	
	Jain TV	

Movie (English)	Movie (Hindi)	Movie (Kannada)
Home Box Office	Zee Cinema	Ushe TV
Hallmark	Set Max	
STAR Movies	STAR Gold	
Zee MGM		
AXN		

Music	Children	Sports
MTV	Cartoon Network	ESPN
Channel [V]	Nickelodeon	STAR Sports
B4U	Kermit	
Zee Music	Animal Planet	
ETC		
MCM		

Religious/Spiritual	Nature	Miscellaneous
Aastha	Discovery	TV5 (French)
Maharishi Ved Vision	National Geographic	DW (German)
Sanskar		RAI (Italian)
		FTV (French)

Compiled by the author from various sources.

was terminated in September 1999, and Zee channel and Zee Cinema were dropped from STAR's bouquet. In fact, STAR TV sold its stake in Zee, which was a 50–50 joint venture for approximately US $300 million, to Zee Telefilms.

The termination of this agreement meant that STAR TV could air Hindi programming and STAR Plus was converted into a vehicle to compete directly with Zee TV, Sony, and DD. Zee was also able to launch new channels in English. When STAR Plus, the flagship channel of STAR TV, converted to Hindi, it was perceived as a major event in the Indian media scene. As one journalist writing about STAR and Zee commented, 'the irony in this image makeover of the two networks couldn't be starker. While the upmarket channel is wooing the masses, the channel of the masses is now targeting the classes' (Joshi 2000). In other words, the two major broadcasters were competing in each other's territories even more closely than before.

STAR World started broadcasting in India in early 1999. In June 2000, it was accessible in 53 countries and covered more than 14 million households in India. This channel aired English language programming. It gained in popularity by airing popular American sitcoms such as *Friends* (Nayak 2000). The news programme, which was aired at nine o'clock on STAR Plus, was also shifted to STAR World in the second half of 2000.

The National Geographic Channel also formed part of STAR's offerings. It started beaming over Asia in 1998. By 2000, it was available to 28 million homes in Asia. It expanded its viewership in India by launching India-specific programmes such as *Wild India, The Great Indian Railways*, and *India Diaries* (Sehgal 2000e).

STAR's fortunes which had been eclipsed somewhat by Zee's meteoric rise in the years 1998–2000, showed a turnaround in 2000. It is interesting that STAR managed its recovery mainly based on a single programme, *Kaun Banega Crorepati?* (KBC), the Indian version of *Who Wants to be a Millionaire?* The original show *Who Wants to be a Millionaire?* aired on ABC network in the US, and was a money-spinner as well, pulling in audiences of 20 million viewers per night in October 2000 (Mozumder 2000). India's aging superstar Amitabh Bachchan was dusted off and pressed into service as a host in the game show KBC, a role he played to perfection. With an estimated cable audience of 100 million viewers, this programme had audience shares and advertisement rates going sky high. In fact this one show made ratings for STAR Plus soar to the detriment of Zee and Sony. KBC catapulted STAR Plus to be the most expensive advertising platform, ahead of DD and Zee. In August 2000, STAR Plus was charging Rs 1 million for a 30 second spot on KBC (Singh 2000a). Zee TV responded by airing a game show in a similar format, but it was a failure and developed problems by late 2000. Subsequently, it died a premature death.

STAR's strategy with KBC and indeed with some of its other programming is 'glocal'. Once again the two categories meet and merge in fascinating ways. The idea is imported; *Who Wants to be a Millionaire?* is clearly a foreign concept, as are the slick sets, and the game-show format. What is Indian is the language, the subject matter, the players, and the larger than life persona of the anchor Amitabh Bachchan. KBC's wooing of the masses is a strategy other channels are sought to emulate. According to an editorial in *The Times of India*:

> The stupendous success of *Kaun Banega Crorepati*, which surely surpasses the wildest expectations of even the producers, has created a new arrangement between middle India and multinationals, one that will finally clear the way to the former's hearts, minds and wallets.... In the final analysis, the success of KBC is the triumph of middle India. Globalisation has come to it and on its own terms. Urban, upper class India, with its polished accents and well cut clothes, has finally had to bow to the logic of numbers (Bhatia, 2000).

The large number of articles devoted to KBC in the print media stand testimony to its hold over the popular imagination.

STAR TV had also allied with the BBC to launch a Hindi serial *Ji Mantriji* based on the classic series *Yes Minister*. The Hindi serial was aired on STAR Plus from April 2001. The label 'glocal' is, again, appropriate for this kind of programming. *Yes Minister* had originally been aired by DD in India. Michael Young, BBC Worldwide's managing director commented, 'It is the first time we are making a programme locally in Hindi, and it is the first time a BBC-made local programme will premiere on a non BBC platform' (quoted in Singh 2000b). This show was an Indian version in Hindi, with Indian actors, and an adapted screenplay. Adaptations had also been made to suit the Indian cultural milieu. Thus, this programme, which aired on STAR Plus, was innovative in many respects.

STAR's programming strategies paid off in the year 2000. In April 2001, 34 of the top rated 50 programmes were from the STAR stable (Sehgal 2001). STAR Plus was also placed as the top Hindi channel in the country, overtaking Zee and Sony. The runaway success of

KBC and family soaps contributed in large measure to the success of this network. Notwithstanding this popularity, an analysis of popular prime-time soaps aired on STAR Plus in 2000–1 reveals a neo-conservative portrayal of women. There is very little emphasis on female empowerment, once a theme encouraged on DD. This global corporation's portrayal of traditional women is at variance with the state's objectives of encouraging modernization and the empowerment of women.

News Corp's strategy for STAR TV in India in the years to come was to substantially expand its base. As Peter Mukerjea, the then CEO of News Television India elaborated, 'At STAR, we want to set the pace for broadband multimedia opportunities in this country' (Mukerjea 2000). STAR TV planned to enter the field of digital media and convergence forthwith. In March 2000, News Corp. announced that it had decided to invest over US $200 million in InfoTech related ventures in India over the next one year (*Times of India* 2000a).

STAR TV entered India with purely foreign programming. At a later date, programming started being dubbed in Hindi. In the new millennium, STAR seeks to position itself as a 'local' entity with popular game shows, soap operas, and indeed the domestically produced programmes on STAR News which are popular. In fact, the news channel STAR News with primarily local content was introduced in 1998 as a partnership with Prannoy Roy's New Delhi Television (NDTV). Thus, a transnational entity had put down roots and exists today as a hybrid 'glocal' presence. NDTV has since cut its moorings to STAR TV and emerged as a media presence in its own right, in the decade since it started on STAR's platform.

As of late 2009, STAR TV, part of the STAR Broadcasting Corporation offers programming, which includes entertainment, sports, films and news. It is a media conglomerate, which offers a range of services from filmed entertainment, television production, cable, direct to home, and wireless and digital services in partnership with various other companies. Among the channels it offers in India are STAR Movies, an English language movie channel, STAR World, an English language entertainment channel, STAR Plus, STAR Utsav, and STAR One, which are Hindi entertainment channels, STAR Gold, a Hindi movie channel, STAR Vijay, a Tamil entertainment channel, STAR News, a Hindi news channel, STAR Ananda, a Bengali news channel, STAR Majha, a Marathi news channel, STAR Jalsha, a Bengali entertainment channel, STAR Pravah, Marathi entertainment, ESPN, STAR Sports, Asianet, a Malayalam entertainment channel, AsianetSitara, a Telugu entertainment channel, and AsianetSuvarna, a Kannada entertainment channel. Some of these are joint ventures.[1]

According to STAR TV's own website in December 2009, the STAR Plus channel claims to be the number one Hindi entertainment channel for the last five years. They claim to have 42 out of 46 top programmes in India, with audiences of over 75 million people every week.[2] The programming on this channel is a mix of films, reality shows, and soap operas. For the past decade, STAR Plus has occupied the number one position in terms of Hindi entertainment channels, except in 2009, when it was briefly overtaken by new entrant Colors channel. In 2010, this channel recovered its premier position again, fuelled by family soaps and serials (Saxena 2010). Unfortunately, through this decade, regressive portrayals of women on family drama serials and soaps continued unabated. STAR Plus is currently expanding its presence outside India, as it has recently launched on Verizon FiOS TV's network in the US.

The STAR World channel airs popular shows from the US, UK, and Australia. Its programming is a mix of drama, comedy and reality shows. Some of its popular shows include *Desperate Housewives* and *American Idol*. While STAR TV is a leader in the category of Hindi entertainment, it has also made inroads into regional entertainment in other languages such as Bengali, Marathi, Malayalam, Telugu, Kannada, and English. It also has a presence in other genres such as news, sports, and music.

In terms of Rosenau's theoretical framework, the ownership of STAR TV is foreign. In fact it is part of Rupert Murdoch's News Corporation—a truly global media conglomerate. While a detailed breakdown of STAR TV's advertising revenues are not available, indications are that it was doing well in terms of viewership and advertisement revenues in 2001.[3] They have maintained healthy revenues even in the following decade as they had an estimated Rs. 22 billion in revenues in 2008–9 (Shukla 2009). In terms of content, STAR TV does not attempt educational programming along the lines of DD. It is mainly an entertainment driven entity. However, it is present in the information category in terms of its news channels. The content of the Hindi and regional channels is largely local. The soap operas currently being aired on STAR are popular, as evidenced by the fact that STAR Plus has retained its number one slot for most of the decade 2000–10. Some of the STAR Plus shows appearing in the top ten programmes in terms of viewership in October 2010 are *Yeh Rishta Kya Kehlata Hai, Bidaai, Tereliye, Mann Ki Awaaz Pratigya,* and *Saath Nibhaana Saathiya.* Interestingly, KBC is making its reappearance on Sony entertainment television channel in October 2010 with Amitabh Bachchan as the host.[4] This is a testament to the show's popularity.

ZEE TV

Zee TV is an enterprise set up by an Indian company Zee Telefilms Ltd. (ZTL), headed by a domestic entrepreneur Subhash Chandra Goel, along with a group of Non Resident Indians. Zee TV started its life by using the sixth STAR TV transponder to broadcast in Hindi in October 1992 (Saxena 1997). Thus, from its inception it competed directly with DD. Zee TV has undoubtedly been a success story from the viewpoint of growth in revenues and market share. According to Subhash Chandra, the chairman of ZTL, by 1999, Zee had achieved 38 per cent penetration of all Indian TV homes. Of the 65 million TV homes in India, 25 million had access to Zee (Zee Telefilms Ltd., 17th Annual Report, 1998–9: 4).

It is also a prime example of a 'glocal' product. Thussu (1998) in a study of Zee TV mentions glocal strategies:

> This localization of the global works at different levels—in employing metropolitan visual codes and conventions, in broadcast language, and in programme formats, such as game- and chat-shows, unknown on television in India before globalization. Zee TV was one of the first Indian channels to understand the value of locally produced entertainment-based television (p. 273).

ZTL describes itself as 'India's first global media conglomerate entering the exclusive billion dollar club' (Zee Telefilms Ltd., 17th Annual Report 1998–99).

Zee TV positioned itself as a family entertainment channel, which relied heavily on popular cultural products, largely derivative of the Hindi film industry. It was a resounding success. The importance of entertainment based on the Hindi film industry cannot be over-emphasized 'in a country whose popular culture has been defined for the past six decades by the hugely successful Hindi film industry' (Thussu 1998: 278). The programming of Hindi films, some recycled DD serials, and some of its own productions may have been old wine in a new bottle, but the packaging worked.

Zee did not have any pretensions of being upmarket or educational when it first set up shop. It broke even in the first year of its operation, and in 1993 Rupert Murdoch's News Corporation acquired 49.9 per cent of Zee TV. This marriage split up in late 1999, leaving STAR free to venture into Hindi programming, while Zee could pursue English language channels. Zee wooed its audience by catering to all kinds of tastes (except perhaps the highbrow). In fact, the range of programmes varies from 'path-breaking talk shows to incisive news analysis, rip-roaring sitcoms to subtler shades of humour, enthralling soaps to spine-chilling thrillers, musical game shows to Bollywood block-busters' (Zee Telefilms Ltd., 17th Annual Report, 1998–9: 10). While Zee's programming may not be all that is claimed by the company, it has definitely broadcast entertaining programmes which have shown high audience ratings such as *Sa-Re-Ga-Ma, Hum Paanch, Amanat, Hasratein,* and *Antakshari*. Zee's performance was good right up to 1999, as evidenced by the fact that in 1998–9, for a period of time 35 out of the top 50 programmes as measured by audience ratings were on Zee TV (Zee Telefilms Ltd., 17th Annual Report, 1998–9: 11). However, in 2000 the tide turned. STAR Plus turned Hindi and aggressively wooed the same audiences with chart topping programmes such as KBC.

In addition to Zee TV, the other channels aired by this group in 2000 included Zee Cinema, Zee News, and the SitiCable channel. Zee Cinema was launched in 1995 as a Hindi language pay channel show-ing movies. Zee Cinema broke even in less than two years and formed an important plank in Zee's bouquet strategy. The programming fare of Bollywood blockbusters and perennial favourites certainly seemed to have won the audiences over. The company claims that Zee Cinema's initial success was due to the policy of encouraging liberal usage of its signal by cable operators (Zee Telefilms Ltd., 17th Annual Report, 1998–9: 13). In this regard, it is appropriate to mention that ZTL owns the SitiCable TV network. Thus Zee had dominance over the airwaves, and exerted muscle power over the distribution on the ground. Zee's vertical integration into production, broadcasting, and distribution via cable paid off as a strategy.

In 1999, SitiCable had a 20 per cent market share of the country's Cable and Satellite homes, making it the largest cable TV network in the country. SitiCable provided city-specific programming. This included a mix of films and live telecasts of local events. A new cable channel—Siti Cinema was launched in April 1999. SitiCable had also launched into convergence media, with the provision of net-over-cable. These issues will be explored at length later in this chapter.

Zee News telecasts news ranging from local, state level news, to national and news with an international focus. While this channel primarily broadcasts in Hindi, it aired a few English language broadcasts a day in 2000. Zee News had been getting a high viewership share in 1999, in comparison with the other private news channels. News channels in general garnered higher viewership figures in 2001, in the wake of the Gujarat earthquake tragedy in January, and the Tehelka expose of graft and corruption in defence deals, which rocked the nation in March.

Although Zee launched its English movie channel Zee Movies in March 2000, it was unable to make any real headway with its audiences, given the stiff competition from STAR Movies and Home Box Office (HBO). Consequently, it entered a joint venture with Hollywood studio Metro-Goldwyn-Meyer which gave the new entity Zee MGM exclusive rights to MGM's library for the South Asian market. The revamped channel was launched in February 2001 as part of Zee's encrypted direct-to-operator (DTO) service (*The Economic Times* 2000c).

In a major effort at restructuring and retrenching, Zee announced that it had decided to merge its news and current affairs divisions with entertainment, in an attempt to cope with the downturn in its fortunes (*The Times of India* 2001a). It also decided to drop the plan of launching a sports channel, which had been on the anvil. The downward slide of Zee had been exacerbated with the poor performance of some programmes such as the KBC clone, *Sawal Dus Crore Ka*

(*The Times of India* 2000j). Ranjan Bakshi (2001), the Vice President, Corporate Communications ZTL indicated that Zee wanted to be at the cutting edge of television, 'our new channels will be TV for the dot com generation, we are not restricted by Zee's home-grown image'. Though Zee appeared to be restructuring and cutting back at the national level, it was venturing into untested waters in terms of its new global channel.

Even though Zee is unashamedly commercial, witness Bakshi's (2001) admission, 'our position is very clear—we have out and out entertainment channels', it is venturing into the field of education. Zee Interactive Learning Systems (ZILS), a fully owned subsidiary of ZTL had drawn up a plan of investing Rs 1000 million for educational activities in its first year of operations. These included deploying a variety of channels, supporting services, and creating zeelearn.com and an interactive centre called Zee Livewire. ZILS also launched a 24-hour learning channel, ZED TV in 2000. The purpose of ZED TV was to disseminate education with entertainment and information (*The Times of India* 2000e). Notwithstanding these grandiose plans, Zee TV's ZED channel did not really take-off in 2000.

The Zee group had plans afoot to launch a novel initiative to take basic education to the rural areas via digital technology. This educational television venture was slated for introduction in April 2001. Zee intended to cover 10,000 villages in the Hindi speaking areas, with educational programmes in association with NGOs and teachers, to provide primary school education (*The Economic Times* 2000b). From these forays into education, especially rural education, it would appear that Zee was entering into territory so far monopolized by the government and DD. In mid-2010, Zee Learn, the education division of ETC Networks Ltd, was to be hived off into a separate entity, and it was planning to invest Rs 5–7 billion in setting up schools as well as a university in India by 2015. Zee Learn currently operates about 55 schools and 700 preparatory schools across India (Ram 2010).

Over the years there have been changes in Zee's programming trajectories, which are discernible in the other broadcaster's fare as well. When Zee first came into existence, it broadcast soap operas and serials with a relatively small number of episodes. Gradually, things changed and Zee started to air family dramas, which could be stretched over a large number of episodes. This was partly in response to audience preferences. In July 2000, the trend changed again. STAR TV was a trendsetter, grabbing the lion's share of the audience by airing KBC and family dramas, which were daily soaps. Zee responded to these new trends by airing daily soaps at prime time in the latter half of 2000.

In terms of content, Zee started by airing popular game shows such as *Saap Sidi* and *Tol Mol ke Bol*. Music-based programmes such as *Antakshari* and *Sa-Re-Ga-Ma* continue to be popular right through Zee's innings. It also aired soap operas that showed strong women characters such as *Tara* and *Hasratein*. Thorny issues such as unwed motherhood (*Tara*) were also dealt with in these soap operas. There has been a change in the depiction of women over the last decade. While the early 1990s showed women rebelling against men (injustice, patriarchy, and so on), post-2000, women are shown as struggling to balance the competing demands of family life and career.

The Zee network took a beating in 2000. STAR Plus overtook Zee with its line-up of popular quiz based shows and soap operas. While stocks of the Zee TV group had crashed in the stock market in 2000, the paradox is that the Zee entertainment channel still continued to enjoy second place in terms of its ratings for its popular prime time soaps (Sehgal 2001). While Zee was riding a high in 1999, Subhash Chandra Goel had global ambitions. In fact he announced in May 2000 that Zee would apply for an American public issue for US $1.5 billion. Ambitious plans for setting up a satellite project and launching a DTH platform were also announced. However, a lot of these projects had to be put on hold or cancelled, as Zee faced a credit crunch in 2000. Thus, though the domestic broadcaster was aiming at a global presence, the plans did not really materialize and in 2001, Zee was struggling to hold its place on the national turf.

In 2001, ZTL converted its flagship channel Zee TV into a pay channel. In another glocal initiative in 2003, the Zee group permitted other international news channels to beam its exclusive footage and programmes for a fee. In a further development, Zee and Turner International expanded their partnership with three new channels— Zee English, Zee MGM, and Trendz. In the same year, the foreign shareholdings in ZTL also increased above the 50 per cent mark. Over 2005–6, ZTL continued its international ventures by joining with Malaysia's Astro to launch a Hindi channel and a new channel in Indonesia. ZTL also acquired a stake in Ten Sports channel. In 2009, the ETC network was merged with the company, and the educational business was spun off into Zee Learn.

Zee TV is an example of how vibrant competition developed domestically. While its major presence is in Hindi language programming, it has also introduced regional language channels in the last few years. Thus, private enterprise has made its presence felt at the sub-national level. Even though Zee is a home-grown enterprise with local roots, it has introduced global programming genres and channels as well. It also has a strong presence in other countries, for example, the Middle East. Subhash Chandra Goel also nursed global ambitions, even though some of these plans were shelved temporarily. Thus, Zee also has 'glocal' dimensions, though in a different manner from STAR TV.

In terms of Rosenau's framework, Zee has been examined along the lines of ownership, advertising revenues, and content. Zee's ownership is majority Indian, but private, as opposed to DD. It had shown a healthy growth rate in terms of advertising revenues over the period 1993–9. Ten years later, it was still showing healthy revenues of Rs 21.77 billion in the financial year 2009. Since Zee's flagship channel is Hindi, its growing popularity over the decade has in part weaned audiences away from DD's major channels, especially in urban areas. Zee's regional channels such as Bengali, Gujarati, and Punjabi are also eating into the audiences for DD's regional channels.

Thus, the phenomenal success of local broadcasters as represented by Zee at a time when advertising revenues for DD have been dwindling again, has implications for the national broadcaster and the state. The advertising revenues of Zee suggest that it has had healthy growth in viewership for most of the decade. Some of this growth has been at the cost of DD. A vibrant domestic voice has appeared as an alternative to DD, and some of the audience has switched allegiance. Again, the state's monopoly over the message has been challenged from within.

Regarding content, Zee's flagship channel Zee TV is entertainment driven. However, this broadcaster does cater to the information needs of the audience through its popular Zee News channel. A news channel is more important than an entertainment channel in setting the agenda. In a significant development, this broadcasting group has undertaken initiatives in education, once the exclusive territory of the national broadcaster. This implies that in comparison with DD, Zee is attracting audiences for its entertainment programming, and also pursuing statist objectives, such as educational initiatives. This development is a watershed for the broadcast industry.

The Zee News channel also represents an alternative voice to DD in the core area of Hindi news. In March 2001, Zee appeared to have adopted an adversarial stance to the government in power at the centre, as it repeatedly aired footage relating to the private media portal Tehelka.com's expose of corruption in defence deals. This scandal rocked the government, as the defence minister and other politicians had to resign in its wake. Zee's repeated broadcast of tapes recorded on spy cams showing attempts at bribery and corruption of important officials emphasized its difference from DD. DD blacked out the broadcast of these tapes in 'public interest'. In this fashion, Zee provided a voice contrary to that of the Central Government. On the basis of ownership, advertisement revenues, and content, Zee's presence seems to have had a negative impact on the authority exercised by the state in the sphere of broadcasting.

While Zee was the first domestic enterprise to compete directly with DD with the launch of its flagship channel Zee TV in October 1992, by late 2009 it claimed to reach 500 million viewers globally in 167 countries.[4] Today, it is a large media group serving the South Asian diaspora in countries including the USA, Canada, Europe, Africa, Middle East, and South East Asia. In order to expand globally, Zee TV was launched in Europe in 1995 and in USA and Africa in 1998. Today, it is available across 5 continents (Sehgal 2001). In 2006, ZTL was renamed Zee Entertainment Enterprises (ZEEL) and split into four companies. ZEEL currently has an integrated range of businesses, ranging from content production to distribution via satellite, cable, and Internet.

While the mainstay of Zee is entertainment, it also has channels offering news, music, and sports. Its portfolio of brands include Zee TV and Zee Smile, which are general entertainment channels, Zee Cinema and Zee Action, which are Hindi movie channels, Zee Studio, which is an English movie channel, Zee Classic for old films, ETC, which is a music channel, ETC Punjabi, which is a Punjabi language channel, Zee Trends, a fashion and style channel, Zee Café with English entertainment programming, Zed which is an educational initiative, and others. Thus, it is evident that the Zee Network is an important player in the field of broadcasting, with a presence in the entertainment and information segments of the market. It has also shown healthy growth in the last decade as is evidenced by the fact that in financial year 2009, this group had revenues of Rs 21.77 billion.[5]

NEW DELHI TELEVISION (NDTV)

NDTV was founded in India in 1988 as a private television company by Dr. Prannoy Roy, an eminent journalist. NDTV started life with a single programme called *The World This Week*. This was a news and current affairs programme which aired on the DD platform, and proved to be very popular. This news programme established NDTV's credibility as a private news producer. It became the content provider for the 24 hour news channel STAR News. In 2003, NDTV launched two 24-hour news channels—NDTV 24/7 in English, and NDTV India in Hindi. NDTV Profit, a business and news oriented channel, was launched in 2005.

NDTV grew to be a market leader in English news and in 2006, NDTV 24/7 had the highest market share among English news channels. NDTV expanded its horizons beyond news and entered the segment of general entertainment with NDTV Imagine in 2007, followed by NDTV Good Times. By 2009, the NDTV group had become a major media group in India, with news channels, a business channel, as well as general entertainment channels. Currently, the group has three major national news channels, that is, NDTV 24/7, NDTV India, and the business oriented NDTV Profit. The newer entertainment channels launched by this group include NDTV Imagine, Good Times, and others.

NDTV is also venturing into new areas with NDTV Convergence, where it is seeking to harness the synergies between TV, the Internet, and mobiles. It has also entered the media software sector with NDTV labs. More recently, NDTV has widened its scope even further with the launch of the world cinema channel NDTV Lumiere, NDTV Hindu, and NDTV Imagine Showbiz.

This media group has made its mark on the news landscape with its path-breaking news and current affairs based talk shows such as *Big Fight, Walk the Talk, We the People,* and others. It has also expanded into entertainment programming in niche segments. In the core area of news, NDTV has emerged as a credible voice, and a popular one. It has been instrumental in the weaning away of audiences (within the news genre) from DD in the urban areas.

SONY

Like STAR TV, Sony was another transnational broadcaster to make its presence felt on the Indian subcontinent. An important contender in the channel sweepstakes in India was the channel aired by Sony, or more precisely Sony Entertainment Television (SET). This channel was owned by the Sony Corporation of Japan. Sony entered India and commenced broadcasting in 1995. In the first three years of its existence, the parent company Columbia Tristar poured a lot of money into SET. It broke even around this time (Dasgupta 2000). It quickly established itself as the second most popular private channel, ahead of STAR TV, but trailing Zee TV (Singhal and Rogers 2001). SET gave DD a run for its money.

The programming mix was largely entertainment in the Hindi medium; it also had a fairly downmarket profile. Some of the popular shows on SET are soap operas, game shows, talk shows, and sitcoms. SET managed to attain a leadership position by promoting live shows, movies, cricket, events, and general entertainment as a whole (Dasgupta 2000). This broadcaster did extremely well in 1999, pulling in revenues of Rs 4 billion according to one estimate (Sehgal 2000a). In 2000, the channels which formed part of SET's bouquet included Sony, a Hindi language general entertainment channel, AXN which focused on English action films, Max which was a mixture of entertainment and sports, and CNBC which concentrated on business related matters. SET Max tried to differentiate itself from SET by focusing on cricket, movies, and sports. It also targeted the 18–35-year old demographic. However, this strategy seemed to have met with uncertain success, as in early 2001, SET Max appeared to be floundering without any clear identity.

Even SET could not be complacent for long. The runaway success of *KBC* on STAR Plus in the latter half of 2000 ate into SET's revenues. According to Kunal Dasgupta, CEO of SET, the *KBC* factor had played havoc with his channels' prospects in 2000. SET was growing at 45–50 per cent per year in the couple of years prior to 2000, but in 2000 its growth had reduced to 10–15 per cent (Dasgupta 2000). As a result, Dasgupta expected the programming budget of SET to increase by 100 per cent.

SET also fought back by expanding its prime time from 7 pm to 11.30 pm. In January 2001, Sony had introduced a game show to compete with STAR's *KBC*. With popular film star Govinda as a host, *Chhapad Phad Ke* was marketed as a game and entertainment show (Singh 2000e). Shows like *Who Wants to Marry a Millionaire?* also debuted on SET. SET was also in the process of developing more channels, in order to have a larger bouquet. Another strategy followed by SET was to build alliances with regional groups.

Like STAR TV, Sony is an important broadcaster in India. The similarity does not end there. It is also owned by a global media conglomerate, the Sony Corporation of Japan. Thus, the ownership of this broadcaster is clearly global. Regarding advertising revenues, Sony had healthy growth in this area till 2000. In terms of viewership, Sony trailed Zee in popularity until they were both overtaken by STAR Plus in 2000. However, Sony is still a popular Hindi entertainment channel vis-à-vis DD.

In the post-2000 decade, Sony Pictures Television International (SPTI) is part of the global Sony Pictures Entertainment company. SPTI backs the Multi Screen Media Private Limited, which is among the region's leading TV channel operators. It comprises Sony (SET), the Hindi general entertainment channel MAX, the premium movies and special events channel SAB, a Hindi entertainment channel, and PIX which shows Hollywood films. AXN channel is also part of the Sony Pictures Entertainment Company. SET claims to have audiences of a total 300 million viewers across the Indian subcontinent, Middle East, and the South Asian diaspora worldwide (www.setindia.com). According to the company's own sources, SET reaches about 42 million households in India. It is available in the US, UK, Africa, the Middle East, Europe, Canada, Australia, New Zealand, Singapore, Nepal, Bangladesh, Maldives, and Malaysia (Singh 2000e).

The programme *Indian Idol* which aired on Sony was very successful in 2004 and 2005. In the financial year 2009, Sony Corp's estimated revenues in India from TV, films, and music business were about Rs. 12 billion (Kohli-Khandekar 2010).

The AXN channel is a popular channel among the youth, having a programming mix of serials, adventure-reality shows, and lifestyle sports programming. AXN is seen in 60 countries across Asia, Latin America, Europe, and the Middle East. It is part of SPTI's portfolio of over 40 global networks. Its popular shows in India include *Caught on Camera, Estate of Panic,* and others. The SAB channel is also part of this group owned by Multi Screen Media Private Limited. This channel's identity is that of a family comedy entertainment channel in Hindi. It has made strides in the category of general entertainment in recent years, competing with other channels in the segment such as STAR One and 9X. Some of the popular shows on this channel include *Tarak Mehta Ka Oltah Chashmah* and *FIR.*

As far as content is concerned, Sony has no pretence of being educational. Unlike Zee it has not made any forays into educational programming. However, this broadcaster is primarily identified by its flagship channel Sony in India, which provides Hindi entertainment programming. Thus, in terms of ownership, advertising revenues, and content, Sony has established itself as a popular broadcaster, which again leaves less room for the state's voice to be heard.

NEWS AND BUSINESS CHANNELS

The major news channels in English and Hindi that Indians tune into apart from DD are NDTV, Cable News Network-Indian Broadcasting Network (CNN-IBN), STAR News, Headlines Today, AajTak, India TV, Zee TV, British Broadcasting Corporation World (BBC), and Cable News Network (CNN) International. In August 2000, Zee News and STAR News were the undisputed market leaders with Zee News having 51 per cent of the total viewership among news channels, and STAR News following with 38 per cent. STAR News set up shop in 1998. Zee News, which came into being as EL TV had a more pedestrian image than STAR (Ninan 2000). CNN-IBN was launched post-2000, and rapidly became a popular English language news channel viewed across India.

The two global brand names in news, CNN and BBC, had a smaller viewership in India in 2000, than STAR News and Zee. BBC Worldwide was however way ahead of CNN with a reach of 8.5 million cable homes, compared to CNN's reach of 4.5 million Indian cable homes in mid-2000 (Vidyasagar 2000e). While STAR News relied heavily on programming from New Delhi Television (NDTV), a home grown venture, CNN still used a large amount of global programming. This has changed in the last few years with NDTV launching its own news channels.

In mid-2000, CNN was beamed to 122 countries on five feeds. There were separate regional feeds in Europe, Latin America, and now South Asia. CNN South Asia was launched in July 2000, catering to India, Pakistan, Nepal, Bangladesh, and Sri Lanka. CNN was wooing regional audiences by putting country specific content on prime time, a strategy pursued from September 1997. It would appear that this strategy has paid off as CNN's viewers had grown from 115 million household to 150 million households from end 1997 to mid-2000 (Rodrigues 2000).

There were different genres of programming on CNN-SA—news and current affairs, business programming, and technology shows. The programme mix had been decided after qualitative research had been carried out in the major cities in India. The CNN viewer profile that emerged in 2000 was young, upwardly mobile, and tech-savvy; the preferences of this group were taken into account. CNN International established several alliances in South Asia for the provision of news content including DD and Eenadu in India, Nepal TV, and Sri Lankan Rupavahini, that allowed reciprocal use of news footage. Increasing use of local content however, is indicated by the fact that CNN South Asia launched two half-hour shows *CNN India dot com* and *Style South Asia* produced by UTV Entertainment, in November 2000 (Singh 2000c). Interactivity is another aspect of localism that appeals to the South Asian market. The weekly question and answer show, originally with Riz Khan focused on a current news story and event, which the viewers could interact with via phone, fax or email (Rodrigues 2000). In fact CNN International executive vice president and general manager Rena Golden forecast increasing local programming, and indicated that India-sourced news programs would be used on CNN channels around the world in greater quantity.

With regard to business channels, NDTV Profit, and CNBC-TV 18 have a major presence in this segment. CNBC-TV 18 is a business news channel broadcast in India. It represents a tie-up between Network 18 and CNBC. Network 18 is one of India's media conglomerates with interests in television, print, the Internet, films, mobile content, and so on. It operates the CNBC-TV 18 and CNBC Awaaz channels through its holding in Television 18. In the 2009 financial year, the Network 18 group had estimated revenues of Rs 19 billion (Kohli-Khandekar 2010).

Network 18 has interests in the Internet through its holdings in Web 18, as well as providing financial information through Newswire 18. Network 18 also has a presence in the general news and entertainment segment through channels CNN-IBN and IBN 7 respectively, which it operates through its holding in IBN 18 Broadcast Ltd. It has recently made a foray into regional news with the launch of IBN Lokmat, a Marathi news channel in partnership with the Lokmat group. Most recently, Network 18 and Sun Network have entered into an alliance to launch Sun 18, a distribution company, with the goal of becoming a major player in the pay-TV subscription market. In a significant development, this alliance also marks the entry of Network 18 into distribution, as Sun 18 aims to distribute 33 channels across all platforms including networks, cable, DTH, IPTV, and so on.[6]

CNBC-TV 18 was launched in 1999. It covers corporate news, financial markets, and investment and management issues. It has audiences across India, ranging from business leaders, professionals, brokers, and self-employed persons, to students. CNBC Awaaz is a Hindi channel focusing on consumer related information. It focuses on information related to investing, saving, making purchases, and career choices.

The CNN-IBN channel is an English language Indian TV news channel. It is the result of a partnership between Cable News Network and the Global Broadcast News, a Network 18 company. The CNN-IBN channel is a 24-hour news channel which uses some of CNN's type of programming models with news and current event based talk programmes. This channel's strategy is to use news from across India, and relevant global news from CNN. It has gained in popularity and uses some novel strategies such as the 'citizen journalist' concept.

The channel is headed by Rajdeep Sardesai, a well-known journalist, formerly with NDTV.

BBC Worldwide had the advantage that it built up on the historic brand acceptance of the BBC in India. The BBC's strategy is innovative in the sense that it is extending its brand by creating content for other broadcasters in India, including DD and STAR TV. The BBC has produced *Teletubbies* and *Tweenies*, children's programmes which have been accepted by DD. STAR Plus aired *JiMantriji*, a programme jointly produced by BBC and NDTV. *Walking with Dinosaurs*, a BBC documentary has already been aired by the Discovery channel in India. An important aspect of BBC's India strategy is the establishment of a local production base in India. Going a step further than dubbed UK programmes, the 'BBC has begun to produce in India, using Indian talent, and specifically aimed at the tastes of Indian TV audiences' (Singh 2000d).

In 2008, BBC World was renamed BBC World News. This global channel claims to have the largest audience in comparison with any other news channel in the world. It was launched in 1991 and it focuses on news and current affairs. This channel airs a mix of news bulletins, documentaries, lifestyle programmes, and interviews. In India, this channel was available free to air till mid-2006, but it is now a pay channel.

The recent entrant in the business of news is the 24-hour news and current affairs channel AajTak, promoted by the India Today group. This channel was a free to air digital channel, which targeted Hindi speaking TV viewing homes. Starting its operations in January 2001, it was the first satellite channel (non-DD) to be up linked from India. It competes directly with Zee News, since it targets a similar demographic. Headlines Today is a premier English news channel belonging to the TV Today Network group launched in 2003. It belongs to the same group as AajTak. Times Now is another 24-hour English news channel; a joint venture between the Times group in India and the Reuters news service.

The Hinduja's media group already operates a fairly popular local cable news channels over its extensive national cable network. The Sahara group intended to utilize the resources it already had in its news division at Sahara TV to spin-off a separate news channel

(Singh 2001a). In fact, a 24-hour national Hindi news channel Sahara Samay was launched by the Sahara India Parivar in 2003.

The impetus for the proliferation of news channels in 2001 had come in part from the high viewership garnered by news channels in the wake of the Gujarat earthquake and the Tehelka expose of the defence scam. Ratings of news channels soared again in the wake of the terrorist attacks on New York and Washington on 11 September 2001. In fact, post-2000, Indian news channels rank among the most viewed channels on Indian television. By the end of this decade, some of the most viewed news channels on Indian television were AajTak, CNN-IBN, NDTV, Headlines Today, Times Now, India TV, and others. While these are national news channels, some regional news channels have also become popular such as Tara News, Asianet, Punjab Today, and others. Both BBC World and CNN International still use programming which is overwhelmingly globally produced. STAR News, on the other hand, primarily uses locally produced programmes.

On the domestic news front, DD's credibility appears to have been eroded in the last decade. Even though DD News—a dedicated news channel—was introduced in 2000, Hindi speaking audiences were showing a preference for Zee news, at least in the urban areas. The new entrant AajTak had emerged a front runner in Hindi news in 2001. While the elites tune in to NDTV, CNN-IBN, BBC World, and to a lesser extent CNN, Zee News and AajTak are proving to be popular with the masses. Even regional broadcasters have introduced news channels such as Sun TV with its Tamil news channel. The proliferation of news channels has implied the entrance of alternative voices in an area which was once the stronghold of the state. News is a vital genre of programming in a democracy. While DD still has a captive audience in rural areas that do not have access to cable, in the urban areas the audiences are tuning in to a range of private news channels. Thus ownership, advertising revenues, and viewership figures suggest a healthy growth for both transnational and sub-national broadcasters during the last decade, negatively impacting DD. In terms of content also, the new breed of broadcasters often adopts an adversarial stance to the government of the day, again adding to a loss of control for the state.

By 2008 there were over 40 news channels on Indian television. Most major media players had at least one news channel as part of their offerings. This is true for groups such as DD, STAR, Zee, TV-18, Eenadu, Sahara, NDTV, TV-Today and INX (Kumar 2008). Most of the National news channels rely on agencies such as Reuters, Associated Press, and Agence France Presse for foreign news footage. In an interesting development, the major print media houses in India have expanded horizontally to own radio and television channels. For example, Bennett Coleman & Co. Ltd., or the *Times of India* Group, has Times Now, a television news channel, Zoom, a lifestyle channel, as well as an FM radio station. Similarly, Living Media, the publisher of *India Today* and other foreign magazines, owns prominent news channels such as Headlines Today in English, and AajTak and Delhi AajTak in Hindi.

Other trends in the news segment include the entry of television production houses into the news genre. An example of this is TV 18 teaming up with CNN to launch various news and business channels. Other major players such as STAR and Zee offer news and business related programming as well as entertainment. Yet another development is the launch of news channels by political parties. These ideological divisions are fairly apparent in the channels being beamed in some South Indian states. This is true of the Marxists in Kerala, the DMK and AIADMK in Tamil Nadu, and others (Kumar 2008). Most of the news channels rely on advertising as a source of revenue. There has also been a proliferation of city centric channels launched by media groups relying on news programming. Examples of this phenomenon are Sahara and AajTak. Apart from news and current affairs based programmes, news channels also show crime shows, documentaries, and spoofs on the news.

In 2009, news channels had lost ground to the Hindi general entertainment channels. Two channels gained in popularity in this year, namely AajTak and Times Now. DD News managed to retain the fourth position with attractive content and higher penetration in areas where cable and satellite penetration is weak. There were an estimated 250 channels approximately in 2009 (PwC Report 2010). This is more than any other country. There are a lot of synergies in terms of content between news channels and general entertainment channels, since many such channels are part of larger media groups, for example the STAR and IBN7 groups. Since there are many news channels, there is fierce competition among them. Content remains a problem since programmes have to be filled in a 24-hour period, and advertisement rates are lower than general entertainment channels.

MUSIC CHANNELS

No analysis of satellite television in the Indian subcontinent is complete without a detour into the territory of music channels. Music programmes in general enjoy great popularity in India. In fact, one of the most popular programmes on DD before satellite TV was a twinkle in anybody's eye was *Chitrahaar*. This programme had a selection of music videos strung together from popular Hindi films. At this juncture, it may be useful to explain that most Hindi films are musicals, and song and dance numbers are an essential element of their appeal. This was the legacy that the music channels exploited when they sought to establish themselves in India. The [V] channel, majority owned by STAR TV, and Music Television (MTV) India were the major music channels to establish a presence in India in the 1990s. Another channel, Bollywood for You (B4U), relying mostly on music and Bollywood fare, has made strides in the last few years.

MTV was the most widely distributed network in the world in 1999, reaching 300 million homes in over 80 territories according to Thomas Freston, Chairman MTV Networks (Freston, 2000). MTV India is a 24-hour music channel targeting young Indians in the 15–24 years demographic. While MTV has been reviled by the custodians of national cultures the world over as being emblematic of globalization, it has in fact succeeded in large measure because of its 'glocal' strategies. Singhal and Rogers (2001), in their study of India's 'communications revolution' are informative about MTV India:

> MTV India represents a fascinating case of how a foreign, private channel transforms itself to create a hybrid identity that appears Indian, but embodies Western traits. MTV India's logo uses the tricolours of the Indian national flag, and its fare comprises 70 per cent Indian film and popular music, and 30 per cent foreign, Western music (Dey, 1999). MTV India employs 10 Indian video jockeys (VJs), and has used music shows including interviews with popular artists, coverage of music

concerts, viewer contests, film countdown shows, and variety, request, and talk shows. Popular MTV programs in India include *MTV House Full, TV Ek Do Teen, MTV India Hit List, MTV Select, MTV Hipshakers, MTV Filmi Fundas, Made in India, MTV Fresh, MTV Bollywood in Control, MTV Cricket in Control, MTV Chill Out and others* (2001: 119).

Research from MTV India suggests that though young people in India have access to different genres of music, they prefer Hindi film music, and this preference spans socio-economic, geographical, and gender categories. It is also significant that only three foreign performers, namely Michael Jackson, Madonna, and the Spice Girls figured in the top 20 favourites of young Indians. The others making the list were all Indians in the decade 1990 onwards (Freston 2000). MTV's strategies mirror those employed by the [V] channel in India. The website of the [V] channel also used the Indian tricolour—an attempt at appealing to nationalist sentiment.

MTV has also been a success in India through its website, and also because it seeks to involve the audience in various contests. According to Vikram Raizada, the Marketing Director of MTV India, each year his channel launched four big interactive contests, as well as 12 local level interactive contests such as *Kaun Banega Kangaal*, the concept being a spoof of KBC (Raizada 2000). While the main MTV channel in India primarily airs Hindi film music and local content, a more international music package was being contemplated for VH 1 on the subcontinent (Singh 2001b).

To reiterate, some of the most popular music channels in India such as MTV India and the [V] channel were jointly owned by transnational entities, News Corp and MTV Networks respectively till the late 1990s. The Network 18 group, through its holding in IBN Broadcast Ltd, has a joint venture with Viacom called Viacom 18 which has been airing MTV, VH1, Nickelodeon India, and Colors in India post-1997. While MTV India was a market leader, [V] had shown improvement in its viewership figures and advertising revenues in the year 2001. Both these channels have been successful in employing 'glocal' strategies to generate India-specific content. The other channel to emerge as popular in this genre is B4U, which is mainly promoted by a group of Non-Resident Indians. Content on this channel is more local; as the name suggests, the emphasis is on Bollywood fare. What is noteworthy is that Network 18 has also made a foray into education, once the preserve of the state, through its topper channel which is an Educomp 18 channel. A genre that has been immensely popular post-2000 is the song and dance reality show format. Programmes such as *Indian Idol* based on the international format of programmes such as *American Idol* have been immensely popular, although they have generally aired on general entertainment channels.

DD has not ventured into the realm of a dedicated music channel. It still airs some music-based programmes—both classical and popular—on its various channels. DD Bharati airs some classical music based programmes. The age demographic of music channels such as [V] and MTV is the youth. Thus DD's hold in the area of youth seems to be slipping.

Many popular music channels rebranded themselves or changed their content in 2009. For example, Zee Music was changed to Zing, MTV dropped Music Television from its name, and VH1 also went in for reprogramming. Many music channels are offering non-music programming aimed at the youth such as 'Roadies' and 'Splitsvilla' on MTV. The VH1 channel also announced that they would air a movie every Sunday with repeat telecasts. The channel 9XM has lost market share, but it still continues to be a market leader in the category of music channels (PwC Report 2010).

REGIONAL CHANNELS

Apart from DD's foray into the vernacular channels, private broadcasters have also established stakes in the large regional language market. The leaders of the pack were the private broadcasters who made their presence felt in the South, broadcasting in languages such as Tamil, Telugu, and Malayalam. Why did regional channels develop? There was a demand emanating from across the country for programming in the vernacular, with sensitivity shown to the diverse culture of each region. One of the factors driving the demand for regional channels is the hunger for news, especially local news and current affairs programmes, as the national channels were remiss in this respect. However, demand for entertainment programming in the regional languages also existed.

On the supply side, programming in regional languages is much cheaper than in Hindi. Well-established content providers in English and Hindi have branched out into production in regional languages. For example, the Prannoy Roy promoted New Delhi Television (NDTV), which earlier supplied much of the content for STAR News, later branched out into programming in Tamil for Vijay TV. STAR TV had entered the regional media via Vijay TV. Other large content providers which were plucking both the national and regional strings were Balaji Telefilms and Nimbus (Thakur and Govardhan 2000).

Unlike national television though, there is no formula for successful programming that can be uniformly implemented across regions. For example, some national channels aired one episode of a soap opera per week,[7] but regional channels like Asianet (Malayalam) and Sun TV (Tamil) aired an episode of various soaps, five days a week. This strategy is in answer to audience demand. When an entertainment channel first starts out, the primary genre of programming it broadcasts is film-based. The reason for this is simply economics; film-based programmes are among the cheapest and easiest to produce as royalties are still not a major issue in India. Over time, as a channel gets established, it moves away from this trend and prefers to use higher quantities of non-film based programmes, especially at prime time (Thakur and Govardhan 2000). Vijaya TV was airing film-based programmes accounting for only 30 per cent of the airtime in October 2000. This is in part due to the fact that TV channel managers had a disagreement with the film industry in 1995–6 as it objected to declining audiences at cinema halls (Subramaniam, 2000). Dubbed programmes have also not proven to be very popular on regional channels. They are rarely used on prime time.

Kalanithi Maran's Sun TV launched in 1993 has been extremely successful. In August 2000, Sun TV's channels had more than 50 per cent viewership share in Tamil Nadu, Andhra Pradesh, and Karnataka with Sun (Tamil), Gemini (Telugu), and Udaya (Kannada) TV respectively. It also had a 50 per cent share in Kerala with Surya TV (Malayalam) (quoted in Question and Answer with Kalanithi Maran, Maran 2000). The other satellite channels broadcasting in Tamil were Vijay TV, Jaya TV, and Raj TV. Both Sun TV and Vijaya TV were estimated to reach 4 million cable households. The cable and satellite advertisement market in Tamil Nadu was estimated to be US $37 million (Rs 1,590 million) in 2000 (Vidyasagar 2000b). The Sun Network set up its own earth station in 2000, a move that implied direct up-linking to satellites, eliminating the middle man of VSNL, the government entity. This group subsequently launched a 24-hour news channel in Tamil, the first of its kind in the South (Subramaniam 2000). In the financial year 2009, the Sun Network had estimated revenues of Rs 10 billion.

Besides Sun TV and Zee TV, ETV and Asianet also have a strong regional presence. The ETV group is part of the Ramoji Group. This network has about 12 regional infotainment channels in languages such as Telugu, Bangla, Marathi, Kannada, Oriya, Gujarati, Urdu, and Hindi. Asianet was the first among the Malayalam channels in the South. Another Malayalam channel backed by the Communist government of Kerala, the CPI (M) was launched in the second half of 2000.

There is also a link between these regional broadcasters and politics. In the words of Subramaniam (2000), 'The networks have also kept their political stands clearly defined. While Sun TV and Jaya TV have, obviously, adopted the political planks of the two major political parties in the state, Raj TV has been trying to woo the audience with the mantra of being apolitical'. Thus, Jaya TV actively supported the ex-chief minister Jayalalitha. It would appear that political influence seeping into the electronic media is not the prerogative of DD. With respect to the regional TV channels in the South, Ray (2000) is of the opinion that:

> In the south, enough pot shots are taken at politicians on the six Tamil channels, but only two—Sun TV, owned by the family of senior Dravida Munnettra Kazhagam (DMK) leader Murasoli Maran, whose son Kalanidhi is its CEO; and Jaya TV, functioning out of Jayalalitha's Poes Garden residence—engage in outright propaganda. While Sun does so subtly, no such rules apply to Jaya TV, the channel for Jaya, by Jaya, and of Jaya. All four daily bulletins are structured unabashedly to include news-items about the lady. Sun, on the other hand, mildly canvasses for the BJP-DMK front in the poll analysis section it's introduced within its main news capsule at 8 pm (Ray 1999: 41).

As already mentioned in the preceding paragraph, even the Marxist government of Kerala has had a hand in promoting a capitalist venture such as a private television channel. Even though Malayalam

Communications, the CPI (M) backed 24-hour Malayalam channel is a public limited company, the list of 25 promoters mainly consists of people with close affiliations with the CPI (M). In fact, opposition leaders have argued that the bulk of the shareholders reveal a left-wing bias (Menon 2000).

One may ask why such vibrant competition first arose from the South. One answer may lie in the South's dislike of the perceived domination of the North and the North Indian languages; dislike of Hindi runs strong in states such as Tamil Nadu. However regional chauvinism only provides part of the answer. Another reason could be the presence of a healthy film industry in the South. This implied that a relatively inexpensive supply of software was readily available (Rao 2001). The existing supply of technical expertise and film studios could also be adapted to suit the needs of television. The South is also taking the lead where the information technology industry (IT) is concerned. Southern cities such as Bangalore, Hyderabad, and Chennai have gained global recognition as centres of excellence. In this context, it is interesting to note that the state governments of Karnataka and Andhra Pradesh have been proactive in encouraging FDI and other forms of joint ventures as a way of encouraging the IT industry.

The regional channels in the South, encouraged by the success of KBC, had introduced game shows in a similar format. Sun TV had *Kodeeswaran* anchored by cine star Sarath Kumar. Raj TV also had plans of launching a big money game show from January 2001. Vijay TV had already aired a game show before the phenomenal success of the Hindi game show (Dey 2000b). Again, amongst the regional channels, the ones from the South have been the quickest to clone KBC type shows, but in their own languages. Thus the global original *Who Wants to be a Millionaire?* was copied successfully in the national language Hindi, and its variants debuted in the local, vernacular languages.

As opposed to the South and the success of private broadcasters in Tamil, Telugu, Kannada, and Malayalam, DD's regional channel in Bengali has been a resounding success. In fact, DD's Bengali channel was so successful from its inception that competition from private broadcasters has only appeared in the period following 1998. Alpha Bengali, part of the Zee group came on the scene in 1999, and

TARA Bengali, part of the Broadcast Worldwide group commenced operations in mid-2000. Rathikant Basu, who headed STAR TV's India operations till early 2000, promoted the Broadcast Worldwide group.

Programming in other languages in the eastern region such as Oriya and Assamese had not shown the kind of growth that Bengali programming has exhibited. Growth in cable penetration has also been low in Assam and Orissa as compared to states in the South and the West. This may have been because Bengali, besides being the *lingua franca* of Bangladesh, is spoken in West Bengal and by a large expatriate population. The film industry in Bengal is also well established and it has strong traditions of theatre. The cultural dominance of Bengal in the eastern region has historical roots in the colonial occupation by the British. Calcutta (Kolkata) was the most important city in the erstwhile Bengal Presidency, while Bombay (Mumbai) and Madras (Chennai) occupied similar positions of importance in the Bombay and Madras Presidencies.

While channels in Bangla were vibrant with DD Bangla paving the way, Oriya channels gained in popularity a little later. The first private TV channel in Orissa was OTV launched in Bhubaneswar and Cuttack in 1997. OTV is a division of Ortel communications, and is telecast through the Sky View Home Cable. This channel is strong in local coverage and local events. Its daily news bulletin is gaining in popularity. Another entertainment channel called OTV Chamatkar which focuses on entertainment and showcases local talent was launched recently. ETV Oriya was launched in January 2002 and it has been growing in popularity. This channel has a mixture of entertainment and news-based programming. In general, cable penetration is lower in Orissa as compared to West and South India. This however represents a good opportunity for growth, as cable growth rates have been high in this region in the last two years.

Regarding the Western part of India, the Zee group launched the channels Alpha Gujarati and Alpha Marathi in 1999–2000. The Broadcast Worldwide group also launched TARA Gujarati in June 2000. There is also the Gurjari channel promoted by the UK based Non Resident Indian (NRI) consortium, Reminiscent Television. Mallika Sarabhai, the CEO of TARA Gujarati had encouraged local talent and coverage of local issues in the programming aired over this new channel (Sehgal 2000d). The challenge for new language channels in Marathi and Gujarati is to wean away audience from DD's regional stations which had gained viewership in the early 1980s (Thakur and Govardhan 2000).

The regional viewers in the West are being seduced by content that is aiming at the lifestyle and ethos of the particular region. The growth in regional channels may have been spurred on by the spurt in cable penetration in the Western states. In the state of Gujarat, 79 per cent of television homes had cable by 2000 (Sehgal 2000d). These states have also shown higher rates of industrial growth as compared to the central and eastern parts of India. The exception is Bihar which has shown high rates of growth over the period 2006–9. These may have translated into higher levels of disposable income, and hence the acquisition of consumer durables such as televisions and subscription to cable television by households.

Large parts of the northern and central parts of India have been catered to by the Hindi channels including those of DD, STAR, Zee, Sony, and others. Punjabi channels have proliferated, including Lashkara promoted by a Non Resident Indian joint venture, Alpha Punjabi from the Zee stable, and TARA Punjabi launched by the Broadcast Worldwide group in mid-2000. The Punjabi channel Lashkara, along with Gurjari is owned by a UK based NRI consortium, Reminiscent Television, distributed by a subsidiary in India. These two channels also target the Gujarati and Punjabi diaspora, because these two communities have the largest section of non-resident Indians. Both these channels claimed to be family entertainment channels, airing sitcoms, soaps, music-based shows, and religious programming (Das 1999).

Again, the dominance of Punjabi channels as compared to other North Indian languages (excluding Hindi) may be explained by a combination of factors; the economy of Punjab had shown healthy growth in the period 1996–2000, and there is also a large expatriate Punjabi population. Think local is the mantra of some entrepreneurs who have promoted sub-regional channels such as Bhojpuri and Rajasthani in India. Zee's new Urdu channel started in 2001 also targets a sub-regional slot.

As this section indicates, vibrant competition has risen from the regional channels across the subcontinent. While DD also airs channels in regional languages, the private broadcasters are enjoying great popularity in most states. The South has seen the emergence of strong domestic broadcasting networks, which is exemplified by the growth of Sun TV. Programming on these channels is largely local in terms of production. However, some global dimensions exist such as in soap opera, news, and game show formats.

Viewership and advertising figures indicate that these private regional channels have made inroads into DD's audience, and in many cases (for example Sun TV) have eclipsed DD's regional language channels. It would appear that in terms of ownership, audiences, and content, the regional language channels are tilting the power balance away from the national broadcaster—towards sub-national private entities.

Regional channels have shown healthy growth in the last few years. In fact, in 2009, the number of regional channels stood at 135 as compared to 114 in 2008. Advertising revenues from regional channels were robust in 2009, as advertisers aimed at winning over local audiences in specific target groups, for example, Malayalam, Tamil, Bengali, Kannada, Telugu, and Marathi had a large viewership share. The regional channels had lower costs of production as compared to Hindi channels. There are also diaspora audiences for regional channels, so these channels can be marketed internationally. For example, the Sun TV network's channels are available in 27 countries from the US and Europe, to Malaysia. Local advertisements on the regional channels also cost less than the Hindi general entertainment channels (PwC Report 2010).

MOVIE CHANNELS

The English movie channels available in India in 2000 were HBO, STAR Movies, Zee Movies, AXN, and the Hallmark Entertainment Network. Zee Movies was revamped and released as the joint venture Zee MGM in mid-2001. In a bid to pull in audiences, Zee English and Zee MGM have been airing some contemporary classics, but they also show some R rated movies in the late night slots (Bamzai 2001). As mentioned in the preceding sections, large broadcasting groups have movie channels in Indian languages such as STAR Gold, which shows older Hindi movies.

According to a survey by Television Asia, an affiliate of Broadcasting and Cable International, HBO had been voted as the most popular channel and also the best value for money by cable operators across Asia in 2000 (Vidyasagar 19 November 2000). The popular Hindi movie channels were Zee Cinema, STAR Gold, B4U, and the local cable channel.

Foreign films are also gaining a foothold in India in the last few years via channels such as NDTV Lumiere, World Movies promoted by the UTV group, and TV5. While the audiences for these channels are small, they do represent an alternative from mainstream Hollywood and Bollywood fare. In the Hollywood dominated segment, HBO, STAR Movies, and WB continue to be popular. According to some estimates, HBO has a 25 per cent market share among English movie channels in India, while Sony PIX has about 21 per cent, and STAR Movies, higher at about 30 per cent (Sharan 2010). As a strategy, PIX has premiered several blockbusters in India such as *Slumdog Millionaire* and *The Hurt Locker*.

The new distribution platform of DTH has meant that companies such as Tata Sky and AirTel can provide films on a pay per view basis. Fairly new Bollywood films have been shown in this medium. Apart from films, programming related to Bollywood, such as film reviews, interviews with actors, and so on, have continued to draw in audiences.

Again in the genre of films, global as well as local broadcasters are represented. DD, which airs popular Hindi films on weekends is facing competition in this area as well. Thus, the dimensions of ownership and viewership suggest growing popularity for the various private movie channels. The global movie channels such as HBO air primarily Hollywood fare. The domestic channels such as Zee Cinema and the local cable channel air Bollywood productions. The changing themes of Indian films from nationalist themes to themes emphasizing consumerism and individualism have already been touched upon in an earlier section.

CHILDREN'S/ANIMATION CHANNELS

The children's channel segment has become increasingly competitive post-2000. The major channels on the subcontinent targeting children are Cartoon Network, Nickelodeon, Disney Channel, Pogo, Hungama TV, and Animal Planet. Cartoon Network and Pogo virtually ruled the children's channel segment till about 2–3 years ago. Disney and Hungama entered the market at this juncture, and caused a subsequent decline in market share for Cartoon Network.

Nickelodeon, one of the popular children's channels in the USA, was introduced in India in November 1999. SitiCable distributed it in India. Not withstanding Nickelodeon's popularity in the US, it had not managed to make appreciable inroads in the Indian market up to May 2001. The exclusive distribution platform of SitiCable may in part have been responsible for Nickelodeon's low performance and penetration. Accordingly, Tom Freston, CEO of MTV Networks announced in May 2001 that MTV India would oversee the distribution of Nickelodeon in India, and it would also be distributed via other cable platforms such as Hathaway Cable and the Hindujas' IN Cable Net. In terms of content, Freston also indicated that more programming would be produced in India. This local programming would be in the form of live action episodes, game shows, and quiz contests. Thus, in 2001, distribution and local content were revamped to popularize Nickelodeon. Animation programmes would continue to be sourced globally (Singh 2001b). In 2002, this channel had about 12 hours of Hindi shows. In a bid to localize further, this channel also showed Bakra, the MTV India produced comedy series.

Kermit was launched in India in June 1999. The 24-hour channel beamed programming in English distributed in India by the Modi Entertainment Network. Kermit aired four hours of educational television every day, anchored by the *Sesame Street* characters. The Disney Channel more recently introduced programming that ranged from films, series, animation, sitcoms, and family dramas, to special programmes. Pogo also airs popular children's programmes. These include programmes such as *Boohbah, Barney and Friends*, and *Tweenies*, aimed at small children. It also screens documentaries and some films like *Harry Potter*. Yet another children's channel introduced recently is CBeeBies from the BBC. This is gaining in popularity among young children, as it targets the 0–6 demographic.

Cartoon Network is popular among Indian children; this channel is the market leader in the children's TV entertainment segment. Cartoon Network had attempted to expand its popularity by using some local programming. The network had examined the possibility of using animation produced in India, and on Indian themes such as *Panchatantra* and *Amar Chitra Katha*. Indian language programming would also be encouraged. Internal research at the network has revealed a clear preference for Hindi programming in the Hindi-speaking areas. There is also a focus on Indian festivals and popular games such as cricket (John 2 May 2001). The animated series *Pandavas*, based on the ancient Indian epic Mahabharata, aired on Cartoon Network in mid-2001. Interestingly, this had both Hindi and English versions, and the animation style was reminiscent of a video game.

In the sphere of children's programming, foreign presence has been dominant. There have been very few Indian broadcasters who have ventured into this field so far, although some children's animated programs are currently in production in India. Even the Animal Planet channel, which was introduced in India in the first quarter of 1999, was a joint venture between Discovery Communications and BBC World (Das 1999). The UTV group launched Hungama TV, an Indian children's channel in the last few years. It was distributed via the STAR Network. However, this was acquired by Disney in 2006. In a glocal combination, the channel retained its own identity, but is an operating unit of Disney Channel Worldwide. Perhaps the only Indian owned channel to operate in the children's segment is Chutti TV. This was launched by the Sun TV network in April, 2007. While it is owned by an Indian group, this channel targets Tamil speaking children all over the world. The target age group is two to fourteen, and the programming is a mix of regional and international flavours, available 24 hours a day. This is again an interesting venture in the sense of combining local and global elements.

The niche area of children's programming is largely being met by transnational broadcasters. Even local broadcasters like Zee have arrangements with Disney and Nickelodeon to air children's channels, largely dubbed in Hindi. Interestingly, even DD has used this route to fill the children's slots. It would appear that while global broadcasters are making some attempts at localizing their products (for example the *Pandavas* on Cartoon Network), the bulk of the programming is overwhelmingly global. At the national level DD does not have a dedicated children's channel. In general, this section of the population is underserved by the national broadcaster, even on channels such as DD1 and DD's regional channels.

SPORTS CHANNELS

The sports channels available in India, around the year 2000, were ESPN, STAR Sports, and DD Sports. The former two channels provide extensive coverage of cricket (a national obsession in India). DD Sports is a public service sports channel, part of the DD group. DD Sports covers cricket matches played in India, as well as international sporting events such as the Olympics, Asian Games, and World Cup football. ESPN is an American cable television network which broadcasts sports and related events twenty-four hours a day. The channel was launched in 1979. ESPN International is a global channel which is available across 150 countries. This channel was launched in India in 1995 with the India–New Zealand cricket series.

STAR Sports and ESPN are private sports channels which air primarily global programming. Their coverage of cricket is very popular. These channels are attempting to introduce some local programming such as sports news in Hindi and talk shows produced in India. Apart from cricket, ESPN in India also airs programmes such as Formula 1, soccer, tennis, golf, boxing, horse racing, news shows, and special shows. STAR Sports has audiences across Asia, and offers coverage of Asian and international sports. The channel has popular commentators such as Geoffrey Boycott, Sunil Gavaskar, and Ravi Shastri.

Other channels dedicated to sports are Zee Sports, Ten Sports, and more recently Neo Sports. Zee Sports was India's first private sports channel. It is part of the ZTL media conglomerate. Zee's programming reflects issues of interest on Indian sports, and showcases Indian sporting talent. Zee Sports has the rights for the Indian Cricket Board's rights for neutral venues. This channel is popular in India, Bangladesh, Middle East, Pakistan, and Sri Lanka. Neo Sports is only dedicated to cricket. The new entrant is Neo Sports plus which offers more diverse content, covering sports like soccer, badminton, motor sports, and others.

TEN (Taj Entertainment Network) Sports is a leading sports channel in India in terms of viewership. It entered India in 2002 before the football World Cup. TEN Sports is jointly owned by Bukhatir Investments Limited and ZTL. This channel has emerged as one of the most popular ones for South Asians spread across the subcontinent, Middle East, Europe, and Asia. TEN Sports has attempted to customize its programming by transmitting three localized beams to India, Middle East, and Pakistan. TEN Sports is available over cable via the One Alliance distribution bouquet, and is carried on Dish TV and Tata Sky DTH platforms. The programming available on this channel covers Test cricket, one-day international cricket, field hockey, and professional wrestling. Sports-related chat shows and sports news are also aired.

While cricket generally garners the highest viewership figures, including events such as the Indian Premier League matches, football recently proved popular in India, with the World Cup in South Africa in 2010 getting high viewership. In the year 2010, there were eight dedicated sports channels available across India, offering a range of sporting content. It was also a year with many mega sporting events such as Indian Premier League 3 (IPL 3), the T20 Cricket World Cup, the Hockey World Cup, FIFA World Cup 2010, Commonwealth Games, Cricket Asia Cup, and others. The advertising volumes were high on IPL 3, Asia Cup, FIFA World Cup, and Wimbledon (Sharan and Vats 2010a). The most popular sports viewed in India over the period 2005–10 turned out to be cricket, followed by wrestling, football, tennis, and golf, according to a study released by TAM Sports in 2010 (quoted in Sharan and Vats 2010a).

NICHE CHANNELS

One index of a broadcast audience's coming of age is the presence of niche channels. These range from documentary channels such as National Geographic, to religious and foreign language centred channels. India has witnessed a growth in this sector in the last five years. Channels such as Discovery, National Geographic, and Fashion Television have been making inroads in the subcontinent of late. Unfortunately, there are no national channels dedicated to documentaries, although Doordarshan and NDTV do show some documentaries. International documentary channels such as National Geographic, History Channel, Animal Planet, Discovery, and Travel and Living have gained in popularity in the niche segment in recent years.

TV5, the international French language channel, which is one of France's biggest in terms of reach and audience share, is targeting French aficionados in India. Fashion Television and MCM International, which airs European music videos are also French channels (Das 1999). German, Japanese, and Italian channels are also receivable over cable systems in large cities. The Australia Network is operated by the Australian Broadcasting Corporation. Its programming includes news, soap operas, documentaries, and sports. It is aimed at the Asia-Pacific and Indian regions. The latest entrant is a Russian news channel RT, airing in English.

The National Geographic channel commenced operations in India in July 1998. Two years later, it claimed to have reached over 12 million homes. Its decision to broadcast some programming in Hindi daily has apparently added to its popularity (*Times of India* 2000c: 8). The National Geographic channel showcases documentaries, expeditions, and so on. The Discovery channel was undoubtedly the market leader in this genre of programming, as it had a penetration of about 21 million cable and satellite homes in April 2001. This channel also airs chunks of programming dubbed in Indian languages, especially Hindi. According to Kiran Karnik, the then Managing Director of Discovery India, very little programming was sourced from India as it was very expensive. The programming at the time was mostly imported (Karnik 2001). Thus localization of these global channels only existed to the degree that their programming was dubbed in Indian languages, and the original programming was not really sourced from India. Discovery has a variety of programmes about popular science, history, and other information based programmes. The History Channel reaches about 70 countries and has exclusively historical programming. This channel is owned by the A&E television networks.

Religious programming has also made an appearance with channels such as Maharishi Ved Vision, Sanskar, Zee Jagran, Jain TV, and Aastha making their presence felt. The Maharishi Ved channel was launched in India in mid-1998. It offered discourses in religion and spirituality, with an emphasis on the Vedas. Some popular channels in this genre are Aastha, Sanskar TV, Jagran TV, and others. Indian religious channels are watched in the country, as well as overseas. Programming includes religious songs such as Bhajans, lectures, programmes on Yoga and Ayurveda, Astrological forecasts, religious films, and health programmes. Some Punjabi channels transmit

'Gurbani'. There are Christian oriented channels such as Jesus Calls, GOD, Miracle, Tamil Christian TV, and Power Vision, as well as those emphasizing Hinduism (Kumar 2010). Again, it is interesting to note that niche channels like the 'global' Discovery and National Geographic channel coexist with 'local' channels such as Aastha.

The preceding sections have explored the broadcast scenario in India in terms of a number of dimensions such as ownership, advertising revenues, and some reference to content. Thus a picture of classic monopoly around 1990 had changed to competition a decade later. There are new broadcasters in the fray, both global and local. In a parallel development, the national broadcaster has undergone changes and is now 'autonomous'. However, the picture presented here is incomplete without some reference to the cable industry, as it is the primary distribution platform for satellite channels.

THE CABLE INDUSTRY

The following section deals with the development of the cable industry in India. The cable industry is important because it is the conduit for satellite channels. The cable systems also have a local channel and carry DD's channels. Thus, this industry spans global, national and local dimensions. The programming on cable channels ranges from Hindi and regional films, local events, regional news, and sports, and so on. Films have been an important element of programming; unfortunately, the local cable channel has often flouted copyright norms and has aired pirated films. Some large cable TV networks have their own branded channels, for example, SitiCable has Siti Cinema.

A vital development in the 1990s in India, which was closely tied to the growth of satellite television services, was the establishment of the domestic cable industry (Figure 6.1a and Figure 6.1b). The predecessor to the cable industry in India was the video industry. The 1990s ushered in a period of change in communications. Saddam Hussein was an unlikely harbinger of change in India. The CNN coverage of the Gulf War in 1991 was received via satellite in India. A few enterprising operators strung up cable from satellite dishes and started providing cable service (Sharma 1993). Some hotels also provided satellite master antenna television systems to relay the

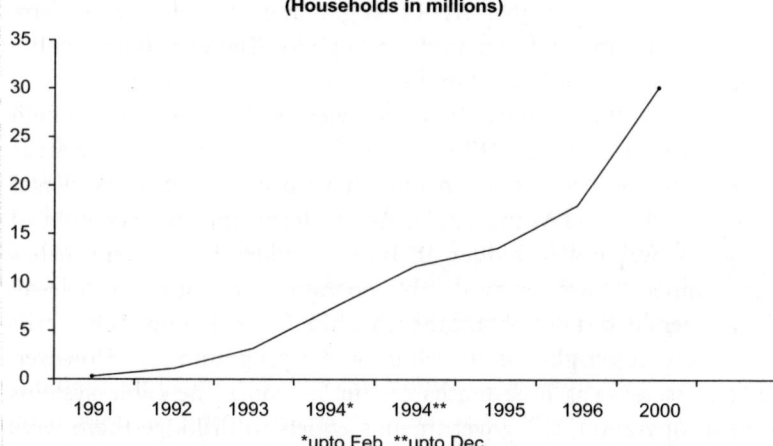

Figure 6.1a Penetration of Cable in India (1991–2000)
Source: Cable Quest 1998, cited in Singhal and Rodgers.

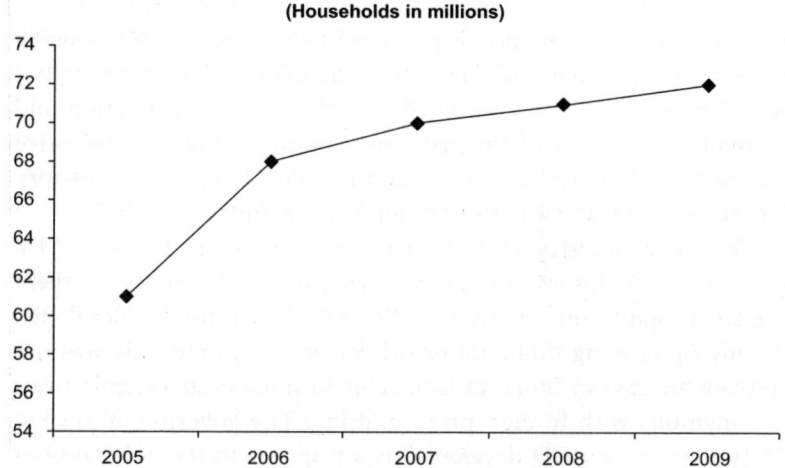

Figure 6.1b Penetration of Cable in India (2005–9)
Source: PwC Report, *Indian Entertainment and Media Outlook*, 2010.

Gulf War coverage. Cable mainly germinated in the metropolitan cities in India.

The development of cable in India in its early phase is inextricably linked to the STAR TV in Asia. Cable operations, which can be classified as Cable Antenna Television or CATV systems, mushroomed in India.

In fact it would appear that STAR's programming was the raison d'être of the Indian cable industry in its early phase. The voracious appetite of the entertainment starved middle class drove this demand.

Cable was the obvious choice for viewers because it was much cheaper than installing a DBS system. The reception of satellite feeds in India like the STAR down-links have been classified as 'illegal openness' (Lee and Wang 1995). As the term implies, reception of STAR TV was not forbidden in India, unlike China where dishes were banned. However, most cable operators were not strictly legal. They generally did not obtain the franchise for wiring up their localities or the copyright for distributing the programming. However, since possession is nine-tenths of the law, once the cable systems were in operation, the government's efforts to dislodge them were met with stiff resistance. The government did improve the state-run Doordarshan as a result of competition from STAR. On the domestic plane, the government did attempt to control cable operations somewhat belatedly as personified by the Cable Act of 1995. However, the Indian government did not respond to STAR's trans-border invasion by applying international law. The principles of international law would have taken into account the right of prior consultation and consent on the part of the receiving country. Another alternative for India could have been to try and establish a regional regulatory structure. This route was also not followed by India.

The cable industry in India has some similarity to the CATV phase of the industry in the U.S. during the 1960s. However, there are some significant differences. While CATV in the US developed mainly by relaying domestic broadcast programming, this was not initially the case in India. In fact, cable in India in its inception was synonymous with foreign programming. The government owned Metro channel on DD developed as a response to the popularity of STAR. Another point of difference worth noting is that cable TV in its early phase in the US was a rural phenomenon, an attempt to overcome poor quality reception in areas where reception of the terrestrial television signal was often unsatisfactory. India, on the other hand, gave birth to a cable industry which started in the metropolitan cities of Mumbai and Delhi, and then spread to smaller areas.

Cable started with small family operators in India. In fact, many video rental stores owned by small proprietors were hastily converted into local cable systems. The hardware used was primitive, and residences were wired up in a haphazard fashion. In fact, the cable was slung from rooftop to rooftop, with no thought of violation of municipal regulations. Service was often poor, and outages a common occurrence (Sharma 1995).

The golden days of small family owned outfits in cable are fast fading, making way for large cable operators. By the end of the 1990s, the presence of Multi System Operators (MSOs) like SitiCable of the ZEE TV Network, INCABLENET of the Hinduja Group, and Hathway and Sumangli Cable of the Sun Network implied that most cable operators had to join an MSO as a survival strategy (Kumar 2010). SitiCable launched its cable operations in 1994. This was a 100 per cent subsidiary of ZTL. SitiCable tied up with local cable operators for provision of services. While SitiCable invested in headends and trunk cable networks, the local cable operators owned and operated the network to the subscribers. SitiCable secured a rapid market penetration through this innovative model. New players also entered the fray, catering to regional audiences. For example Sun TV launched a private channel in South India in 1992. The Raj Television Network was also started in South India in 1994.

The 1990s decade has seen a substantial concentration in ownership of cable systems. In 1995, India's cabled households were estimated to be between 12–16 million (Sharma 1995). When compared to India's total TV households of 45 million, it showed the scope for growth. Big operators banked on this and moved into the cable stakes. For example, the London based Hindujas put in a large investment and controlled about 40 per cent of Bombay's total subscribers in 1995. Zee TV's cable company, SitiCable claimed to have five per cent of India's total cable subscribers in 1995. The India Information Technology Limited (IITL) company—a joint venture with the U.S. company Falcon—also claimed to have about five per cent of Delhi's subscribers in 1995 (Aggarwal 1995).

There was some consolidation taking place among the medium sized cable systems. In 1995, the medium sized operators United Cable Networks and Space Vision came together to form a combined base of 100,000 subscribers in Bombay. This trend was also evident in other metropolises such as Delhi, where six cable operators formed the Forum of Independent Cable Operators, with a total of 30,000 subscribers. However, it seems a foregone conclusion that large companies will absorb small and medium cable operators in the long run. This is partly due to the fact that cable operations are becoming more capital intensive. As the number of channels available increase, the cable companies require more complex hardware, which the smaller ones cannot afford. Another problem, which surfaced in the mid-1990s, is that in order to develop the market for pay channels, the cable operators had to invest in addressable systems. Most operators could not invest in this technology which was expensive and not locally manufactured (Aggarwal 1995).

Some major regulatory hurdles also had to be crossed for many cable operators to get into business. The Indian Cable TV Act of 1994 legalized cable operators. This Act stated that it was the responsibility of each state government to evolve a policy regarding the laying of cables in their jurisdiction. This was partly due to the fact that cable operations had become more capital intensive. In reality things are still in a state of flux, as it is extremely difficult to enforce copyright laws.

Some other trends which are worthy of note, concerned programming. In 1995, most small and medium sized cable operators did not have the hardware required to carry all the channels that were then available. One of the problems faced by broadcasters and programmers then was that there were only 14–16 channels available on the prime band. Unless carriage on these channels was provided, most of the subscribers would not receive the channels (*Times of India* 1995). In 1995, cable operators were also consolidating; hence, they were developing bargaining power. In fact, some cable operators had started demanding carriage fees to carry a certain channel on their system. As late as 1997, most cable networks used and have a bandwidth of 300 MHz. By mid-2000, cable networks in major metros could transmit signals up to 550 MHz (Bamzai 2000b).

How did cable expand from nought to between 30 million and 40 million (depending on which estimate you believe) households over a period of less than a decade (Fig. 6.1a)? The answer lies in the entrepreneurship of the local cable *wallah*, the affordability of cable, and the fact that there were no state imposed barriers to entry (*Times of India* 2000h: 9). This is in contrast to the licensing requirements required to enter telephony. While these are supply-side factors, one cannot ignore the voracious demand of the middle class for television programming.

In August 2000, the statistics for cable were impressive in absolute numbers, if not in terms of percentages. Indian cable households at this point in time were about 32 million households, controlled by about 40,000 cable operators through 6000 head-ends (Vidyasagar 2000c). There was consolidation taking place, as the business of providing net-over-cable was capital intensive, and some of the small operators were being bought out or nudged into strategic alliances by big broadcasters and Internet Service Providers (ISPs).

Why is the cable industry a player in the convergence sweepstakes? The answer may lie in the fact that in mid-2000, there were only 22 million telephone connections in India, as compared to 30 million cable connections. A hurdle in the growth of the cable industry is the presence of many small operators. The unorganized nature of this segment implies that it is hard to tap into institutional sources of funding. Another obstacle to the growth of the cable industry is that it is largely coaxial cable, and not fibre-optic (Mukherjee and Gairola 2000).

The big players like STAR and Zee were eager to get into the net-over-cable business. In mid-2000, SitiCable was present in 43 cities, with a total of 73 million head-ends. Plans were underway for converting their network to a Hybrid Fibre Coaxial (HFC) system, with broadband facility. According to their plans, all head-ends in each city would be connected through an optical fibre ring. Each ring would have branches connecting to nodes. In essence, the fibre would be extended to the nodes, from there on till the drop it would be coaxial cable. The optical fibre ring would also be connected to international gateways either in the same city, or in other cities through leased lines. This architecture would enable the provision of net-over-cable.

The Hinduja-owned InCable Network also claimed to have upgraded its infrastructure to an HFC system by laying fibre optic trunks and upgrading its system from 550 MHz to 860 MHz (Mukherjee and Gairola 2000). The Hindujas were also expanding from controlling the conduit into content.

STAR TV acquired a 26 per cent stake in Hathway Cable and Data com Private Ltd. in September 2000, with a view to launch a fully interactive television and broadband Internet business in early 2001

(*The Economic Times* 2000d: 15). Intel had also acquired a 3.3 per cent equity stake in Indus Ind, a Hinduja company. It is not really surprising that broadcasters such as Zee or STAR were investing in distribution companies, as these held the key to market power.

A new entrant in the field, Atul Punj's Spectranet, which had laid a fibre optic network covering Delhi and Gurgaon, launched its net-over-cable service in September 2000. At the time it had tied up with 150 cable operators in Delhi to offer its services to subscribers to a subscriber base of 65, 000 cable homes (Chatterjee 2000).

MSO's like InCablenet, SitiCable, Asianet, and Hathway hold the reins of the television distribution business. The ISP's that have signed deals with cable operators to provide net-over-cable are Satyam Infoway, Bharati's Mantra Online, Punj's Spectranet, Dishnet, Reliance, and BPL (Kulkarni 2000). At the end of 2000, the big cable operators were a handful—Zee TV's SitiCable, the Hinduja group's InCablenet, and Hathway promoted by the Raheja group. In early 2000, out of a total 24 million cable TV viewers, approximately 8 million were InCable Network subscribers, while another 8 million owed their allegiance to SitiCable. Hathway provided services to the remaining 4 million viewers, mainly in the southern and western states (Sehgal 2000b). The shakedown that has taken place in the cable industry implies that the industry is tending towards oligopoly, with the large cable operators having interests in broadcasting and/or telecommunications.

One factor that has contributed to the growth of the cable industry is the advertising revenue accruing from the local cable channel. The advertisers range from the neighbourhood grocer to large corporate entities. Advertising revenue from the local cable channel accounted for as much as one-third of total revenue generation, while the rest flowed from subscriptions, according to S. N. Sharma of Hathway Cable and Datacom, one of the large cable players (Anand 2000).

The winds of change have blown across the broadcasting and cable landscape in India. Macro factors like technology, regulation, and the economy have undergone many changes in the last decade. Cable is well entrenched in India's major cities, in the southern states of Kerala, Karnataka and Tamil Nadu and the western states of Maharashtra and Gujarat. A study undertaken by Arthur Anderson on the Indian entertainment industry in 2001 predicted high levels of growth and consolidation for the cable industry from a value of US $558 million (Rs 24,000 million) in 2001 to US $1628 (Rs 70,000 million) in 2005.

The trend of consolidation and incorporation with the MSOs has continued with the number of cable operators reducing from 60 thousand to 26 thousand over the period 2002–4 (Kumar 2010). By 2010 India had about 134 million households with television, of which 103 million had access to cable, satellite, or DTH, according to the Television Audience Measurement (TAM) Annual Universe Update. It is interesting to note that approximately 85 per cent of all urban households have a TV and 70 per cent of urban households have access to satellite, cable, or DTH services. Regarding the total number of households with access to cable and satellite, it is probably not representative of total viewership, since many rural families watch TV with their relatives and friends. Secondly, some unregistered cable networks continue to provide service.

In the year 2009, there was continued interest from private equity investors and the capital markets in the television distribution industry. Apollo Management, a US based private equity fund invested US $100 million in an 11 per cent equity stake in Dish TV. Recently, Reliance Communications, ADAG group announced a merger with Digicable, a large MSO in India. This is a mammoth deal, estimated to be in the region of Rs 45 billion (PwC Report 2010). There is also likely to be an increase in investment in the cable industry with the continued acquisition of local cable operators by multi system operators. This would show up in the form of upgradation of infrastructure, and acquisition of new subscribers over the next few years. Another interesting development has been the tapping of the capital market for cable television distributors. Some examples of this are the Initial Public Offering (IPO) of DEN Networks Limited, a leading cable television distributor in October 2009 for Rs 20 million equity, as well as the IPO of Hathway Cable and Datacom Limited in February 2010 to raise an expected amount of Rs 6,660–7,370 million from the market (PwC Report 2010: 37).

The television distribution segment comprising cable and DTH showed healthy growth in 2010 (PwC Report, 2011). This sector continues to be fragmented with an estimated 50,000 plus local cable operators, 7000 MSOs, and about six DTH service providers.

The top five MSOs account for less than 30 per cent of the revenues (PwC Report 2010: 23). In future, digitization and addressable digitization has emerged as an important issue for the television distribution industry.

To reiterate, the cable industry is inextricably linked to the birth and the subsequent growth of satellite television in India. In late 2001, the cable was still the only platform for the distribution of satellite channels. The central government has mandated 'must-carry' provisions for a number of DD channels on all cable systems. The governmental provisions seeking to regulate content on cable have been difficult to enforce. Cable has expanded from being a metropolitan phenomenon to penetrating the smaller towns and cities throughout India.

Small operators started cable systems in India analogous to the 'mom and pop outfits' in the early years of the United States cable industry. Today, this situation is different. A large amount of consolidation has taken place. What is interesting is the manner in which this has occurred. Large satellite broadcasters such as STAR and Zee have stakes in this business. In fact the Zee TV owned cable company SitiCable was one of the largest cable operating systems in 2000.

The implications are that these broadcasters are seeking to control the distribution mechanism on the ground in their battle for audiences. The independent operators will be under increased pressure as cable systems are upgrading and introducing new interactive services which are capital intensive. This implies that consolidation in the cable industry leads to the emergence of large cable systems, many of which are partially or wholly owned by satellite broadcasters—transnational such as STAR, and local such as Zee.

Cable is expanding fast in India—another source of pressure for DD—as audiences in towns across India are opting for cable. The number of viewers watching DD's direct terrestrial broadcast is being negatively impacted by this. The satellite broadcaster's stakes in distribution networks on the ground imply greater leverage for them vis-à-vis the national broadcaster. Apart from expansion into rural areas, the cable industry is also tapping into the revenue stream from the introduction of pay channels.

The ownership of cable systems is skewed in favour of large broadcasters which are competing with DD on the satellite channel front. Secondly, advertising revenues seem to be growing at a healthy rate for the cable industry as a whole. While carriage of certain DD channels is mandated on cable systems, operators have the freedom to air their own packages of channels. The local cable channels are also fairly popular, but to date they carry very little original programming.

The entrance and expansion of the cable industry implied that the national broadcaster had to take cognizance of a new entity, which grew in importance over the last two decades. The state responded by seeking to regulate the mushrooming cable industry (discussed at length in the next chapter). The cable industry represented yet another area where the marriage of the global and the local dimensions were working towards tilting authority away from the state.

Television viewership was impacted by the fact that mandatory conditional access was introduced in January, 2007. Initially, it was introduced in leading metros of Delhi, Mumbai, and Kolkata. The government tried to put various safeguards in place to protect the interests of the Indian consumers (FICCI and PwC Report 2008).

The newest delivery platform to impact the Indian broadcasting sector has been the Direct to Home (DTH) sector. As the term implies, the programmes are delivered directly to the consumers via a pizza sized dish, without the intervention of the cable operator. DTH television is interactive and digital, offering free, as well as subscription packages. This has shown some growth in the last few years with players such as Tata Sky, Airtel, Dish TV, Sun Direct, and DD Direct Plus, and so on, competing. As of late 2010, there are at least six players in the DTH segment, connecting over 20 million subscriber households. They are offering various innovations and discount packages to attract audiences. Cable operators are likely to see some erosion of their audiences in future, as they have been slow to upgrade their systems to digital. The consumers are also getting more demanding, wanting new options offered by digital DTH (Dilip Kumar 2010). The Internet Protocol Television or IPTV was another delivery platform launched in some cities in 2006–7. However it has had hardly any impact in the market.

Analysis of Current Trends

The Indian Entertainment and Media industry is estimated to reach Rupees 580 billion in 2009. It is also estimated to grow at a compound annual growth rate of 12.4 per cent for the next five years, to reach Rs 1040 billion in 2014. The television industry has been forecast to continue to be a major contributor to the overall industry revenues, as it is estimated to grow at 13 per cent cumulatively over the next five years. The television industry revenues are expected to grow from an estimated Rs 265.5 billion in 2009, to Rs 488 billion in 2014. Television distribution is projected to have the lion's share in television revenues, that is, 60 per cent by 2014. The other segments are forecast to be 35 per cent share for television advertising, and five per cent share for television content. In terms of the total advertising industry, television advertising is projected to increase from 41 per cent in 2009 to 46 per cent in 2014 (PwC Report 2010).

As the broadcasting and cable industries evolve, certain trends are emerging in India. In general, it has been suggested that the liberalization of television that has occurred in India in the last two decades has helped to establish a consumer culture. As mentioned earlier, the economic liberalization pursued by the Indian government in the 1990s implied that a lot of global brands such as McDonalds, Nike, Puma, and others entered India. Television helped to popularize them, and rising incomes for urban professionals meant that the disposable income existed for their purchase (Singhal and Rogers 2001).

Table 6.3   Growth of Indian Entertainment and Media Industry (2005–9)

Rs. Billion	2005	2006	2007	2008	2009	CAGR
Television	158.5	191.2	223.9	244.7	265.5	13.8%
Film	68.1	84.5	96.0	107.0	95.0	8.7%
Print	109.5	128.0	149.0	162.0	161.5	10.2%
Radio Advertising	3.2	5.0	6.9	8.3	9.0	29.5%
Internet Advertising	1.0	1.6	2.7	5.0	6.0	56.5%
OOH	9.0	10.0	12.5	15.0	12.5	8.6%
Animation, Gaming & VFX	–	12.6	15.7	19.6	23.8	–
Music	7.2	7.3	7.6	6.9	7.5	1.2%
Total	356.5	440.2	514.3	568.5	580.8	13.0%

Source: PwC Report, Indian Entertainment and Media Outlook 2010: 8.

The number of channels available is proliferating (Tables 6.1 and 6.2). This is going to lead to fragmentation of the TV audience. However, the advertising supported growth of the past few years may not be tenable in the years to come. The television advertising pie may not be sufficient to support the growth of all kinds of channels in the future. The surviving channels would need to have staying power, and this implies deep pockets (Dasgupta 2000) and shifting into pay services. According to one estimate, the number of channels grew from 389 in 2008 to 461 in 2009. Regional channels marked a large increase from 114 in 2008 to 135 in 2009. New channels introduced in 2009–10 include Colors, 9X, Real, and Imagine in the general entertainment category (GEC), and UTV Action movies, Discovery Turbo, and Discovery Science in the non-GEC genres (PwC Report 2010). As channels become paid, they can also go in for more expensive productions. Hence, the nature of the content changes.

In 2000, it was predicted that content would become a key element in the survival of a channel, as the TV audiences get further fragmented. Kunal Dasgupta, the CEO of SET had commented that KBC had really raised the stakes as far as production costs and programme impact was concerned. He described the post KBC period as the 'redefining moment' in Indian television. In his words, 'future prime time is going to be big budget, big promotion, big prizes, big energy and big stars' (Dasgupta 2000). Content continues to be a crucial issue even in 2010. The Indian audience has shown its preference for new content, as is evidenced by the rise in popularity of the new channel Colors which has differentiated entertainment programming. Other Hindi as well as regional entertainment channels have also seen in 2009–10 that the way to attract viewers is to have quality content (PwC Report 2010). Talent costs have also been increasing.

As in other countries, when the industry matures, channels are increasingly being provided in pay mode. In the future, the free channels will veer towards being pay channels, while the existing pay channels will hike their fees. For example, STAR TV had already done so (Kulkarni 2000). One strategy being followed by the three big private broadcasters—namely Zee, STAR, and Sony—is to form bouquets of channels, with which leverage can be exerted vis-à-vis the cable operators. The growth in pay revenues may tip the balance, and in future, a consumer driven market will probably emerge, but the time frame of this occurrence is uncertain. In a significant development, Zee decided to launch digital pay channels from 1 June 2001. STAR TV and Discovery had already forayed into the pay channel territory. However these price hikes were being resisted by independent cable operators (Anand 2001b). The future also seems to have a Darwinian tinge, where single channels that do not have a clearly differentiated product fall by the wayside.

Stiff competition for eyeballs is pushing up prices in the broadcast media. On the flip side, certain brands are chasing the super-hit programmes on Indian television. When a show proves to be successful, more brands are desirous of latching on. The implication is that advertising rates will inflate for those programmes. Media planning is getting more complex. According to some industry analysts:

> By the looks of it, India is headed the same way as most mature TV markets. Media options will get polarized between the high cost, high impact and the low cost, low impact options on the so-called mass channels. Media planning on TV will thus need to constantly juggle efficiency with impact (*Economic Times*, Brand Equity-Madison Advertising 13–19 September 2000).

Though efficiency versus impact is not a new dilemma, post KBC the options have become more polarized than ever before.

As the broadcast and cable industries evolve, the distribution aspect grows in importance. In India, the cable network has emerged as the main platform for the distribution of satellite channels. The penetration of cable was taking place at double-digit rates around 2000. As the business becomes more capital intensive, there is a shakedown taking place. Convergence has added a new dimension to the cable stakes. Consolidation has taken place, and large operators like SitiCable, In Cablenet, Hathway, and Asianet have emerged in urban areas (*The Economic Times* 2000a). The next decade has seen a continuation of this trend with increased penetration and consolidation of cable in rural areas as well. The television distribution segment continued to increase in importance in 2009, with increasing subscription revenues (PwC Report 2010). Distribution issues linked to addressable systems hold the key to future growth in the television distribution segment.

The entry of DTH has again changed the power equation. While it is still perceived to be a relatively expensive option, the quality of service is also substantially better than the friendly neighbourhood cable operator. The digitization of delivery platforms has impacted the distribution network, as is evident from the fact that in 2007, DTH had shown a growth up to 3.5 million subscribers (FICCI and PwC Report 2008). By 2009, the number of DTH subscribers had increased to 14 million (PwC Report 2010.)

Another sign of the coming of age of the entertainment industry in India is the fact that this sector is showing signs of corporatizing. Many media companies have recently raised money from the primary market by going in for IPOs. In the past, the field of entertainment, particularly the film industry, relied on financing with dubious connections. The underworld had links with Bollywood, and it was spurned by the capital market. That is slowly changing, as legitimate sources of finance such as equity and bank finance step in to fill the void. Only six issues were raised from the entertainment sector in the period from March 1996 to March 1999. This figure accelerated to 12 issues over the period April 1999 to October 2000. As many as 40 more issues were planned in the near future (Chopra 2000).

Yet another broad trend that has emerged in 2000 is that as the urban, metropolitan market nears saturation, the growth areas that are emerging are in various regions and specifically in small towns across the country. Hence the spate of regional channels aimed at this slot. This is one aspect of the local, where channels are built around ideas of linguistic and cultural affinity. Even though the regional channels launched are satellite channels, on the subcontinent they have contributed to the resurgence of local and regional identities. Some of these satellite channels have been aimed at the Indian diasporas in different parts of the globe. For example, Lashkara Punjabi and TARA Gujarati in the UK. This strategy may fall under the rubric of 'glocal' for analytical purposes. Many major broadcasters are also targeting regional customers via new channels and content. Zee and STAR have a dominant presence in this segment. Sony Pictures Television International recently acquired Channel 8, a Bengali language film channel. STAR also made its foray into the vibrant TV space of South India by acquiring a controlling stake in Asianet, which has four channels in Kerala, Karnataka, and Andhra Pradesh (PwC Report 2010).

Regional channels are increasing their share in television advertising. Regional channels are also focusing on the children's channel segment (PwC Report 2011).

Localization is being actively pursued as a programming strategy by niche channels to expand their base. MTV and [V] channels have successfully followed this route in India. The MTV format is such that it is a unique combination of the global and local. The formats and ideas are often global, while the programming has symbolic local inserts. Cartoon Network had gone local by providing nine hours of Hindi programming and two hours of Tamil programming every day a decade ago (Kulkarni 2000). Cartoon Network is currently trying to increase Indian content on its feed in an attempt to increase viewership. This trend has been followed by other children's channels in 2010. A new programme based on Indian characters had been aired from January 2001(Vidyasagar 2000a). Even Discovery and National Geographic channels are dubbing some programmes in Hindi. In June 2000, National Geographic started beaming in Hindi for initially 4 hours a day, which was subsequently increased to 7 hours a day. The channel's stated aim in transmitting in Hindi was to bring the latest programming to Hindi audiences (*The Times of India* 2000c: 8).

Yet another aspect of localized content is the continued emphasis on and the popularity of Bollywood fare on TV. In 2009–10 at least 10 channels emerged with predominantly Bollywood related content, for example, Mastii and Zing. Even though these channels have lower viewership ratings than the general entertainment channels, they are able to attract advertising (Vats 2010). A typical Bollywood channel has programmes such as music, fillers, Bollywood related shows, and movies. These include channels such as Zoom, Zing, NDTV Imagine, Showbiz, and others. A decade ago, Bollywood meant just films. Bollywood music gained popularity with the expansion of satellite TV and FM radio. Even largely music oriented channels such as MTV and Channel V have expanded their programming beyond music to include Hindi movies. Adding films to the programming is helping these niche channels to widen their audiences. Advertising in the music genre has increased over the period 2005–10. The Hindi movie and music genre have shown high Television Rating Points (TRPs) (Vats 2010). Hence the boom in Bollywood theme programming in the last few years. The Shri Adhikari Brothers have launched a new channel called Mastii recently, which has predominantly Bollywood music content, with some comedy programming. The expansion of satellite, cable, and DTH delivery modes implies that there will be a greater demand for niche channels in the future. Yet another aspect of glocalization is the dubbing of Hollywood and Bollywood films in local and regional languages in the last few years. For example *Toy Story 3* and *Shrek Forever After* were dubbed in Hindi, *Avatar*, and *Ninja Assassin* were dubbed in Hindi, Tamil and Telugu (PwC Report 2010).

The period after 2000 has shown the emergence of media conglomerates in the Indian market. This is in tune with trends in more developed markets. Many media groups expanded beyond their traditional domains either attempting vertical or horizontal integration. Some of the large and influential media groups in 2007 were Network 18, UTV group, NDTV group, and STAR group. Network 18 is a leading media conglomerate in India, with a presence in television, Internet, films, mobile content, and related areas. Network 18 operates through its holding in TV 18, a listed company. As mentioned earlier, Network 18 operates business channels, news, and entertainment channels, as well as an Internet company, and an on-line and on-air retail venture. This group has a strong presence in the TV news and business segment. (FICCI and PwC Report 2008: 19)

The UTV group is present over the range of film production, film distribution, TV production, broadcasting, and animation and allied businesses. In 2007, the group launched the entertainment channel called Bindass, targeting the youth. The World Movie channel was also launched, showcasing films from around the world. The group also diversified into Telugu films by signing on Telugu star Mahesh Babu for two films (FICCI and PwC Report 2008: 19). While this group is dominant in the entertainment segment, harnessing synergies across film and television, it has more recently ventured into the business news segment via a tie-up between Bloomberg and UTV. The NDTV group, while having a dominant presence in the news and business segments, diversified into entertainment and lifestyle programming in 2007. Thus, we see a trend of diversification into different media segments, as well as different programme genres.

Regarding programming content, one sign of a mature television market is that non-fiction programming is popular and gets high ratings. The phenomenal success story of *KBC* on STAR TV and the clones that it has spawned on other channels points in this direction. Reality TV has come of age. Another trend discernible from the second half of 2000 onwards is that the fiction genre of 'daily soaps' which air at the same time at least 4–5 times a week are gaining in popularity. This is especially true for the Hindi soaps aired on STAR Plus at prime-time. Zee is also following suit with this genre of daily soaps, according to a spokesperson for the company (Zee marketing official April 2001).

Post-2000, small and independent producers have lost ground to large production houses. A few production houses such as Balaji Telefilms, United Television (UTV), TV 18, Cinevista, and others have been dominating prime-time entertainment. The small producers have been marginalized because of changing business realities, emphasis on TRPs, and preference for daily soaps. The earlier practice would be for the channels to give advance for commissioned programmes. Now channels pay producers after the telecast of the first episode. Thus, large investments are required. Available slots for telecast were also reduced by the decision of some channels such as B4U not to air serials, and the closure of other channels such as Channel 9 Gold. Some other channels also started telecasting their own programmes at the cost of commissioned programmes (Walia 31 January 2003).

While non-fiction and reality television programming have proved to be popular, in 2009–10, fiction still continued to be the staple diet for Indian viewers. Hindi general entertainment channels have also targeted regional language channels. The regional general entertainment channels are also showing high viewership figures in 2009. The genre of news has also lost ground to the Hindi general entertainment channels in the race for ratings in this year (PwC Report 2010).

Another trend discernible in entertainment programming in 2010 is that viewership volumes are now coming from middle and small town India, as a result of the demography of television becoming more heterogeneous (Sharan 2010). Out of 134 million television owning households, 70 million are in rural areas, according to the TAM Annual Universe update in 2010. Rural India is embracing new technologies such as DTH and mobile telephones. As a reflection of these newer audiences, characters are sometimes being portrayed in a more realistic fashion, themes are including social issues such as female infanticide, and child marriage, and so on, and many of the stories are set in non-metro India. Viewership ratings suggest that programmes which have more progressive aspirational characters are finding a resonance with the audience. It is predicted that in the next decade, rural audiences for television will be truly large (Sharan 2010).

A lot of daily soaps have lead female characters. In general, the portrayal of women has changed over the decade 1990–2000. Sadly, the emergence of private broadcasters had not led to a more emancipated portrayal of women on television in this decade. While serials such as *Tara* on Zee in 1993 permitted a more realistic portrayal of Indian women in the 1990s, things changed for the worse in 2000. In spite of having female lead characters, one media analyst commented that the spate of soaps especially on the Hindi channels had actually been regressive:

> In the 1980s tele-woman was striving to break traditional moulds, new millennium television is hell-bent on taking the big leap backwards and transforming the country into a nation of *bahus* (daughters-in-law) where marriage is the *raison d'être* of a girl's existence. Getting married or staying married: these are the only motivations for the female species on the small screen…. The success of the extended *parivar* (family) series seems to have totally blocked the path for avantgardism and slice-of-life realism (Kazmi 6 May 2001).

The tradition-bound, stereotypical roles that women have been playing in soaps (especially on the Hindi channels) have recently lead to a convergence in the image of the Indian woman in the new millennium: she is one-dimensional, wears Indian clothes, sports Hindu symbols of marriage such as the *bindi* and the *mangal-sutra*, aspires to be a home-maker, and embraces traditional values including patriarchy and the preservation of the extended family and marriage. The high TRPs garnered by soaps which portrayed women in this fashion, implied that the MNCs and advertisers were backing these programmes in the year 2000. Peter Mukerjea, the CEO of STAR in India commented on the current spate of mother-in-law and daughter-in-law portrayals of women on STAR Plus, 'We are transiting from an English channel to a local channel, so there are some basic ingredients that go into making a channel successful. And quite honestly for us, to go into something radical, in the first instance, would be much too risky' (quoted in Chatterjee 2001).

It would appear that the consumerist imperatives ensured that realism and experimentation took a back-seat to saccharine and neo-conservatism in the portrayal of women in Indian soaps. Is it a contradiction that the liberalization of broadcast media has turned full circle where the portrayal of women on Hindi soaps is concerned? Have audiences voted for the neo-conservative portrayal of women on television in 2000 in part fueiled by renewed family values Hindu style? Is it just a marketing strategy that the family image with a subservient woman character is currently selling well? One suspects that this portrayal of women is a phase that will pass as others have done before it.

While the regressive portrayal of women in soaps has been particularly marked on Hindi channels such as STAR Plus and Sony, regional channels still permit some different portrayals of their female characters. For example, the Marathi serial *Damini* had a female protagonist—an investigative journalist who exposes corruption in high places. This serial had the ability to pull in high TRPs even after airing over 700 episodes (Bannerjee 6 May 2001). Women characters had also dominated Kannada serials in the previous decade. While many serials portrayed women as being employed outside the home, they were simultaneously shown as still endorsing the traditional values of marriage and motherhood. Some portrayals of women have been different, for example, S Narayan's *Parvati* and T N Seethram's *Mayamriga* which won critical acclaim (Hiremath 2001).

It is indeed interesting that a domestic broadcaster, namely Zee has been associated with a popular soap (*Tara*) which portrayed women in a more progressive and nuanced fashion in the early 1990s. In a surprising volte-face, the global players STAR and Sony have been associated with a spate of soaps such as *Kyunki Saas Bhi Kabhi Bahu Thi* in the latter half of 2000, which have reverted to an unrealistic and conservative portrayal of female characters. In fact, many of these serials, aired on different channels such as STAR Plus and Sony, have been produced by the same local content provider—Balaji Telefilms. This company has been very successful in producing soaps for television, with many of them being woman oriented. According to one estimate, Ekta Kapoor the head of Balaji Telefilms was associated with over 20 serials in four languages, airing over 10 channels in April 2001 (Kapoor 2001). Thus global channels, which are competing with each other as well as the national channels, are utilising programming from a common local source projecting similar values. This is yet another example of the surprising ways in which the global/local dimensions of broadcasting can be configured.

A decade later in 2010, STAR Plus has regained its premier position in terms of ratings. STAR Plus still has many women dominated serials, but two of them namely *Pratigya* and *Sasural Genda Phool* show female characters that are relatively more empowered than their earlier avatars (Saxena 2010). However, channels such as Colors and Zee TV have threatened STAR's pre-eminent position in 2009. The end of this decade has seen some new programming trajectories. While daily soap operas in general entertainment channels still remained high at 60 per cent in 2009, there was a huge surge in reality content in the overall GEC programming. In terms of content, audiences preferred more realistic and issue based themes in soap operas. Some new films such as *Delhi 6* and *Dil Bole Hadippa* were also aired on general entertainment channels, adding to their popularity.

Yet another aspect of localization is programming on the local cable operators channel. Currently most operators show videos of Bollywood films on the local channel, many of them with poor quality prints. There has been a crackdown in this area, as cable operators would often show pirated Bollywood films on this channel, sometimes even before they were officially released. Now, the film industry and the policing agencies have become more aware of copyright violations. Spectranet, which commenced its services of net-over-cable in Delhi in September 2000, had started a cable channel. This channel was showing some original programming—mostly local events around the capital—as well as some videos of films.

Another trend that is discernible is the hunt for international markets for India based channels. This is another example of the coming together of the global and the local. The expatriate Indian community is the target. Many Hindi general entertainment channels actively pursued overseas markets in 2009–10, targeting the global diaspora. This is true of channels such as Colors, Zee Group, as well as STAR India (PwC Report 2010). In 2000, Indians in the

US could receive Zee, TV Asia, and SET on the Echostar DTH system for approximately US $35 per month. Two Hindi film based channels B4U and Zee Gold were also available as an option for US $20 per month. The Scandinavian DTH broadcaster Telnor had also tied up with Sony to give SET a platform for satellite access across Europe. Apparently, another agreement had been signed with South African DTH operator Multi-Choice, so that SET would now be available across Africa (Kulkarni 2000). The South India based SUN TV had covered areas ranging from the Middle East, to Singapore-Malaysia. Coverage had been extended to Europe, America, and Australia as well—yet another instance of the local going global (Maran 2000).

Along with stepped up export earnings from Bollywood abroad, there is an expanding overseas market for Indian television content. Whereas the earlier focus had been on the Indian diaspora, the newer developments in the industry were targeting other markets worldwide. Amongst the new markets for Indian content dubbed into the local languages are Sri Lanka, Indonesia, Israel, Malaysia, and the Algerian population in France. The SAB TV network, which had entered into a joint venture with the Sri Lanka based Maharaja TV network, provided programming where popular Indian serials were re-created in the local language, with Sri Lankan artists playing the characters. The story line and the directors were the same as in the original programmes (Vidyasagar 2000d).

The Ronnie Screwvala promoted United TV (UTV) enterprise is also following a strategy where it is aggressively marketing its products in Asian countries. In mid-2000, it had 104 shows in seven languages, beamed across 19 countries. In terms of duration, this works out to about 6000 hours in multiple Asian languages, in addition to 9000 hours in dubbed languages. Screwvala estimated that one of the UTV serials, *Shanti*, had attracted over 2 billion eyeballs, the same as *Baywatch* (Vidyasagar 2000d). In an interesting development, it appears that India may emerge as a regional hub for TV programming, maybe along the lines of Egypt in the Arab world.

Multi-media has also become the name of the game, with broadcasting, cable, telephony, Internet, and DTH converging in a compressed time frame in India. The growth of net-over-cable has already been touched upon in the preceding section. Distribution becomes vital in the process of channel penetration and growth. It is quite possible that the preferred delivery platform of the future will be cable with broadband facility, or DTH providing diverse services. Regulation is struggling to keep up with the runaway growth of technology in the industry.

*   *   *

In examining developments in the broadcast and cable industry in India in the last two decades, the quantum of change is phenomenal. From being a complete monopoly, DD has been relegated to being one of the many broadcasters operating in India. The volume of programming and the choices available to consumers have increased manifold. The entrance of satellite television marks a watershed event in the development of this industry. For much of the decade 1990–2000, the national broadcaster DD was formally under control of the Ministry of Information and Broadcasting. In 1997, while autonomy was granted formally, the Prasar Bharati Corporation has in many ways been unable to cut the umbilical cord with the Ministry of Information and Broadcasting. These issues are explored in depth in the next chapter.

In summing up, while interpreting the developments in the light of Rosenau's framework, certain salient points emerge. The emergence of competition from private broadcasters (both transnational and local) and the cable industry has added new dimensions to the broadcast space. Keeping in pace with the liberalized economy, the entire media industry appears to have become increasingly commercial in the last decade. Competition has brought in its wake new dimensions such as ratings, novel programming genres, and corporate structures for media companies. While some of the competition is from transnationals, media conglomerates such as Sony and the Murdoch-controlled STAR TV, some of the large broadcasters are domestic such as Zee and Sun.

In the year 2001, DD still had a megalithic broadcasting infrastructure but the last few years have shown a decline in audience shares and revenues, with only some improvements. It is losing out in the sense that its content is increasingly being perceived as dull and unattractive as compared to the private channels. One of DD's initial responses was to attract higher advertisement revenues via an increased commercialization especially of the DD metro channel. The drawback of this strategy is that this channel was perceived as having no distinct identity as timeslots were auctioned off to the highest bidder, without keeping some overall programming theme in mind. Thus, one may conclude that power as represented by control over advertising revenues and audiences is getting eroded for the erstwhile national broadcaster, even though these showed an upward trend at times. As explored in the next chapter, no distinct strategy has been adopted which will preserve DDs revenues and audiences in the long run.

However, power is not being redistributed in any simplistic global/local dichotomized manner. Rather, complex combinations of global and local have arisen which pertain to the transnational, as well as the private domestic broadcasters in India. These 'glocal' strategies pursued by broadcasters competing with DD and by the cable industry span programming genres, the language factor, advertising and distribution, culminating in the birth of hybrid cultural products. While 'global' companies such as Sony and News Corp. have pursued 'local' strategies in the last decade as a survival tactic, 'local' enterprises such as Zee Telefilms have nursed 'global' ambitions in their race for survival.

Kiran Karnik (2001), one of the authors of the Shunu Sen Committee Report, is of the opinion that globalization as represented by the foreign invasion of broadcasting has occurred not only in terms of channels and programmes, but more insidiously in terms of the appearance of foreign themes and values. This applies to channels such as STAR Plus, Sony, and others. Speaking more in sociological terms, Karnik believes that the presence of transnational broadcasters has contributed to the rise of consumerism in India. The traditional Indian family and its concern with its progeny is being eroded by the instant gratification culture as purveyed by satellite television (Karnik 2001).

The argument has been made here that authority as represented by control has been redistributed away from the nation-state towards global/local levels. As described earlier, the dimensions of this control are many. They range from straightforward ownership and revenue share, to regulation and content. To revert to the primary research question, this study has undertaken an analysis of these dimensions. To elucidate:

Ownership

At the beginning of the 1990s there was only one broadcaster, with one or two major channels being viewed nationwide. A decade later, there were over 70 channels receivable over an average urban cable system. Global broadcasters had entered the fray. The major transnational ones included STAR, Sony, BBC, CNN, Discovery, and a host of lesser ones. Local enterprise was represented by the rise of broadcasters such as Zee, Sun, Tara, and others. In comparison to 1990, there is a cacophony of voices on air today. Ownership has tilted away from monopoly for DD, towards competition.

DD has also formally become 'autonomous' as part of Prasar Bharati. This implies ownership is no longer a clear cut issue, as compared to the state's direct control prior to 1997. Therefore, in terms of ownership the state's hold definitely seems to have receded. From owning the only electronic voice in 1990, the state now has only an indirect hold over the industry. The proliferation of the cable industry has also meant increased power to the global satellite channels, private local channels, and operators, at the cost of DD.

Advertising revenue

This is another dimension along which the shift in control to supra and sub-national levels have been considered in the light of Rosenau's theoretical framework. As indicated in the earlier sections, advertising revenue for the satellite channels has increased steadily over the last two decades, while DD's has declined in relative terms (with the exception of one or two years). By this index it would appear that DD's hold over the audience is weakening, as viewership figures are being impacted by the satellite channels. This again has the implication that the state's sphere of influence has been rolled back by the advances in private broadcasters, both transnational and local.

Content

The 1990s mark a boom in entertainment programming for the subcontinent. In fact, this area has been the driver of growth for the satellite broadcasting and the cable industry during the last two decades. It would appear that statist objectives such as pursuing developmental programming, particularly educational themes, have fallen by the way side. While private broadcasters are unashamedly commercial, and have actively broadcast entertainment programming, even DD has grown increasingly commercial over the last two decades. This represents a dilution in the state's agenda. To sum up, all the dimensions considered here suggest a dilution in the state's objectives and a reduction in the state's sphere of control.

However there is yet another dimension of control through ideology, which has only been explored peripherally through the medium of content in this study. Suffice to say that the encouragement of consumerism and an emphasis on the individual, which may be an indirect consequence of globalization in the broadcast media, may serve to weaken the hold of the state in India.

If the self-conscious 'national consciousness' as purveyed by DD is giving way to a Western liberal ideology of freedom and the ascendance of the individual, what happens to the nation-state? If consumers are replacing citizens, what happens to a democracy with low standards of living and literacy for many? A uniquely Indian layer—the propagation of cultural nationalism by the rise of *Hindutva*—has to be added to the analysis. It seems likely that the state would have to redefine its notions of' national consciousness' in the new millennium. This redefinition would paradoxically be more universal and more parochial.

Throughout the 1990s, however, the Indian state in the form of the Ministry of Information and Broadcasting has been loath to having its sphere of influence reduced. Successive governments failed to either grant autonomy to the state-run broadcaster, or to legislate to allow domestic terrestrial competition to DD and AIR. When autonomy was finally granted, the 1990s were limping to a close, and the issue appeared to be irrelevant to many, as satellite television and the cable industry provided an alternative view to DD. Prasar Bharati, though supposedly autonomous, still has close links with the ministry. The state has also chosen to exercise its influence through regulation in the last decade, which is the subject of the next chapter.

NOTES

1. Available at www.Star.co.in.
2. Available at www.Star.co.in.

3. Since STAR TV is not a publicly listed company in India, annual reports are not a matter of public record. Many attempts at eliciting this information from STAR TV failed. Ultimately, estimates published by other sources were used.

4. See *Hindustan Times*, 4 October 2010, page 25.

5. Available at www.zeetelevision.com.

6. See *Hindustan Times*, 19 July 2010, page 23.

7. This trend has changed for Hindi channels in 2001, and many of them have now started airing soaps which show 4–5 episodes per week.

CHAPTER SEVEN

REGULATION OF THE BROADCAST AND CABLE MEDIA

....

FOUNDATION OF REGULATION

Regulation of the broadcast media in India till the mid-1990s revolved around two major pieces of legislation. These were the Indian Telegraph Act of 1885, which assigned power over wireless broadcasting to the Central Government, and Article 19 of the Indian Constitution, which guaranteed freedom of speech, subject to certain restrictions (Ninan 1998). As in other countries, regulation of broadcasting represented an attempt to balance the rights of the individual, or those of the audience with the rights of the broadcaster, (in this case the state broadcaster) or the speaker.

It is interesting to note that until the mid-1990s, laws that were not specific to the industry governed broadcasting. Broadcasting was technically subsumed under the Wireless Act even though it was archaic and ill-suited to governance of non-telephony subjects. However, it clearly reflected the state's attempt to control the electronic medium.

The independent Indian government took over from the colonial masters, and used the nascent broadcasting medium as a means of furthering its own agenda.

Certain events occurred in the 1990s, which forced a re-examination of the regulation of television, radio, and telephony. Changes in technology have fuelled a kind of backdoor liberalization and globalization of television through the vehicle of satellite television. Doordarshan (DD) no longer has a de facto monopoly over television; in fact, India witnessed explosive growth in television in the last two decades. The de jure has finally begun to catch up with the de facto. The Cable Act of 1995 represented an attempt by the Central Government to clamp down on the anarchy in the satellite broadcasting and cable industry. Judicial activism on the part of the Supreme Court of India in the mid-1990s helped to bring the rights of the public (as opposed to the government) to the forefront. The Broadcast Bill of 1997, the Prasar Bharati Act of 1997, and the draft Information, Communications, and Entertainment Bill introduced in Parliament in 2000 reflect the vast changes that have occurred in broadcasting and telecommunications in the last two decades. These attempts at legislation also reflect the state's response to unprecedented changes in this arena.

To understand current attempts at regulation by the Central Government, it is necessary to delve into the Indian Telegraph Act of 1885, which is the cornerstone for understanding the government's monopoly of the industry. This Act explicitly stated that 'within India, the Central Government shall have the exclusive privilege of establishing, maintaining, and working telegraphs' (Indian Telegraph Act 1885 pt. II, cited in Ninan 1998). This Act has been amended on five occasions. In 1957, a significant amendment to this Act stretched the term telegraph to include telegraph lines, appliances, or apparatus used for telegraphic communications. Thus, broadcasting was covered in the telegraph net and made subservient to the Central Government.

Unlike the First Amendment in the United States, the Indian Constitution does not make explicit a provision for freedom of the press. While the United Kingdom does not have an explicit 'First Amendment' type of clause in its Constitution, disallowing the government from abridging the freedom of the press, it has a long history of independence of its media. In fact, the social and cultural factors discouraging political interference in the press go back at least to Milton's *Areopagitica* published in 1644, which was a strident defence of the free press in Britain (Knowlton and Parsons 1994).

In India, Article 19 (a) guarantees citizens a fundamental right to freedom of speech and expression. The Right to Freedom, Article 19 is expressed thus:

> Protection of certain rights regarding freedom of speech, etc.-
> (1) All citizens shall have the right–
>   (a) to freedom of speech and expression;
>   (b) to assemble peaceably and without arms;
>   (c) to form associations or unions;
>   (d) to move freely throughout the territory of India;
>   (e) to reside and settle in any part of the territory of India; and
>   (f) to practice any profession and to carry on any occupation, trade or business.
> (2) Nothing in sub-clause (a) of clause (1) shall affect the operation of any existing law, or prevent the State from making any law, in so far as such law imposes reasonable restrictions on the exercise of the right conferred by the said sub-clause in the interests of the sovereignty and integrity of India, the security of the State, friendly relations with foreign States, public order, decency or morality, or in relation to contempt of court, defamation or incitement to an offence (Constitution of India 2000: 8).

Media are thus included, but the Constitution also declares that India is sovereign, secular, socialist, and democratic. It is interesting to note that the provisions of sub-clause (a) do not imply that the rights of the individual override the interests of the State with regard to issues of sovereignty, integrity, security, decency, and other vital issues (as expressed in sub-clause (2) above). Whereas, a whole body of law has evolved around the First Amendment and freedom of speech and the press in the US, these issues are still relatively new where broadcasting in India is concerned; any debate about the rights of the individual versus the rights of the broadcaster is still in its infancy. Issues pertaining to the freedom of press for the printed medium in India are another matter.

Broadcast media also fall within the purview of Article 246 of the Indian Constitution by which Parliament has exclusive powers to make laws with respect to 'post and telegraphs, telephones, wireless broadcasts, and other like forms of communications' (Constitution of India 2000: 216). Broadcasting is thus lumped together with telephony, both figuring on the Union List of Article 246 of the Constitution of India. The implication is that broadcasting is subject to regulation by the Central Government. In addition, broadcasting in India has been regulated by the archaic Telegraphic Act of 1885, by which the Government of India has the exclusive right to establish, maintain, and run 'wireless apparatus' (Reddi 1996). Therefore, the monopoly of broadcasting by the Central Government is explained by this Act which came into existence as an imperial tool of command and control.

The broadcasting sector is also reined in by the Ministry of Information and Broadcasting (MIB), which is the main policy making entity. It is headed by the minister who is a political appointee and a secretary to the Government of India, who is a senior civil servant from the Indian Administrative Service. The post of Director General may also be held by civil servants, rather than specialized media professionals (Reddi 1996).

All India Radio (AIR) and DD were departments directly controlled by the MIB until Prasar Bharati was granted its autonomy in 1997. Until such time, AIR and DD accounted for nearly two-thirds of the ministry's budget. Prasar Bharati, like the DD and AIR of old, continues to be financed by the government, although DD and AIR do earn some commercial revenues. Regarding financing, Reddi (1996) writing about the pre-autonomous AIR and DD informs:

> The budget is prepared, presented, and operated in accordance with the norms and procedures laid down by the Government for its departments, and the Government maintains a tight control on the expenditure of AIR and DD and the powers of the Director General. While the heads of AIR and DD have substantial power to incur expenditure on the purchase of equipment, recruitment of staff and other day-to-day management decisions, the full powers required for the specialized nature of broadcasting are denied to them (Reddi 1996: 233).

Even though Prasar Bharati gained autonomy in 1997 and it earns some commercial revenues, it is still dependent on the government for the greater part of its funding.

The Indian mixed economy structure, although devised for industry, percolated down to the media as well. Telecommunications systems and broadcasting were actively developed by the state, whereas private companies provided telecommunications equipment and some television programmes. Television programmes were produced in-house at DD's stations, and also by private producers (Reddi 1996).

The role of radio and television in India was a topic of political debate right from the time India gained Independence in 1947. Many governments have established expert committees to review the structure and functioning of television. These include the Chanda Committee 1966, the Verghese Committee 1978, the Joshi Committee 1985, the Varadan Committee 1991, and the Sen Committee Report of 2000. Various committees had been appointed with laudable motives such as, 'Working Groups and Expert Committees have a very important function in a democracy of involving people from outside in generating ideas and insights for shaping and influencing policy' (Joshi Committee Report 1985: 7). While the appointment of the Committees has been set in motion by different governments, implementation of their recommendations is another story altogether. Despite the repeated recommendations of various committees suggesting autonomy and increased efficiency for DD, it suffered from the evils of arbitrariness and politicization right through the 1990s (Ninan 1992; Reddi 1996; Sen 2001).

The State has exerted control over broadcasting in India via overt and covert means.[1] The financial provisions for DD and AIR have already been mentioned. Bhatt (1994), a long-time employee of DD, suggests that the MIB has directly influenced the contents of news bulletins and policies governing the dissemination of other programmes, through the functioning of the Director General of AIR and Director General of DD. The method of control is via 'word-of-mouth orders conveyed in official briefings of the top brass of the medium, or on the telephone when urgent instructions are required to be passed on' (Bhatt 1994: 13).

Control of the electronic media in India has existed at many levels and is reflected in different facets. The question of autonomy for

DD and AIR has surfaced at regular intervals, but it was sidelined or sabotaged until it gained impetus in the late 1990s. The fact that DD and AIR were used for political ends is revealed by the fact that political parties ask for autonomy for the broadcasting entities when they are in the Opposition, but the desire for autonomy dissipates rapidly when they come to power (Rao 2001).

The following sections will examine at length the major committee reports which had a bearing on the formulation of policy with respect to the broadcasting sector. Subsequent sections deal with milestones in the field of broadcast regulation. These include the Prasar Bharati Act (1990), the Cable Television Networks Regulation Act (1995), the landmark Hero Cup case (1995), the Broadcasting Bill (1997) and the Communications Draft Bill (2000), as well as subsequent developments. The linkages between broadcasting and politics, as well as the state's role with respect to broadcasting are then examined at length.

SALIENT COMMITTEE REPORTS

The Chanda Committee Report (1964)

Indian television was first reviewed in 1964 by the Committee on Broadcasting and Information Media, popularly called the Chanda Committee. The Chanda Committee recommended that DD be separated from *Akashvani*. It is significant that it also recommended that autonomous corporations be formed to run both. The first recommendation was accepted, and it was implemented fairly soon. The second recommendation, however, ran into rough weather. In fact, in April 1970, the government stated in Parliament that 'the time was not opportune for considering autonomy for the broadcast media' (cited in the Joshi Committee Report 1985: 31). This was one in a series of skirmishes on the autonomy issue. While the Chanda Committee raised important issues, the political opposition to autonomy for the state broadcaster was so strong that it could not be set in motion.

The Verghese Committee Report (1978)

The second review of broadcasting in India was undertaken by the Working Group on Autonomy for Akashvani and Doordarshan,

popularly known as the Verghese Committee in 1977–8. The appointment of the Verghese Committee grew directly out of the imposition
of the Emergency[2] by Indira Gandhi in 1975. During the period
1975–7, the Congress government overtly used broadcast media for
its own purposes. As soon as it assumed office, the Janata government
set up the Verghese group to examine the possibility of freeing AIR
and DD from the government's stranglehold (Gill 1991). The report
of the Verghese Committee proposed some radical changes, including the establishment of an independent National Broadcasting Trust.
Again, while important issues such as use of the broadcast media for
propaganda and suppression of freedom of the press were raised,
no action was taken because of a lack of political will.

The Joshi Committee Report (1985)

The Joshi Committee examined the role of DD and of television
programming in a development context at length. This committee
expressed the opinion that DD's expansion had emphasized hardware, while software or programming was given the short shrift.
The committee report stressed the need for developing indigenous
programming which was more local and participatory. The language
of the Joshi Committee Report is replete with references to 'cultural
sovereignty' and 'cultural domination', which arise in the context
of television in developing countries. The following quotation is
illustrative:

> It is clear that the main source of danger to national cultural identity
> arises from the neglect of software planning by a developing country. To
> meet this threat at its source, developing nations must not allow the gap
> to widen between hardware and software, between programme-trans-
> mitting and programme-making capacities, between the media and the
> message. Restriction of imported programmes is necessary, but not suf-
> ficient. Positive software planning is the most effective way of strength-
> ening the foundations of cultural independence and of national culture
> (Joshi Committee Report 1985: 4)

This report explored the threat faced by the developing nations from
the influx of foreign programming, even before satellite television
had appeared on India's horizon.

The Joshi Committee Report delivered a scathing indictment of the state of affairs at AIR and DD. Referring to the period 1970–85, it maintained:

> During this period the development potential of television has remained largely untapped because of the continuing underdevelopment of software. The growth of installed capacity for transmitting programmes has been utilised more and more for non-developmental purposes. There has emerged in this dismal background a growing hiatus between profession and practice, between official policy pronouncements emphasizing use of television for development and education, and the progressive drift and departure from them in actual practice. The result was what some called a 'credibility gap', finding expression in sharp comments in the press, in the parliament, and in several formal and informal forums all over the country (Joshi Committee Report 1985: 6).

This is even before competition from private broadcasters forced AIR and DD to commercialize in their bid to keep audiences. The committee also emphasized that 'planning' should imply something else in the context of software. The recommendations of the Joshi Committee, like the committees before it, were swept under the rug. Centralization and a lack of 'localism' at DD continued to be the order of the day.

These committee reports indicate that the role of the state-controlled broadcaster was a matter for public debate from as early as 1964, and surfaced at intervals over the subsequent decades. However, even though these issues were on the public agenda at different points in time, the demand for autonomy was repeatedly silenced by the Central Government. The freedom of the press reached an all-time low during the Emergency imposed by Indira Gandhi's Congress government in 1975–7. The Janata government that followed set up the Verghese Committee to examine broadcasting, but its recommendations were not implemented for the most part, and the government fell again. Subsequent Congress governments again suppressed the issue of autonomy for AIR and DD. These actions of the state as represented by the Central Government suggest that it resented any measures that would lead to autonomy for DD, right up to the end of the 1980s.

THE PRASAR BHARATI ACT (1990)

In a significant development, the non-Congress minority government, which won the general election in 1989, decided to act upon its campaign promise of autonomy for the official media (Ninan 1998). The influential Verghese Committee Report resurfaced, but in a new avatar, the Prasar Bharati Bill was born. The Prasar Bharati (Broadcasting Corporation of India) Act, 1990 came into existence, 'to provide for the establishment of a Broadcasting Corporation for India to be known as Prasar Bharati, to define its composition, functions, and powers, and to provide for matters connected therewith or incidental there to' (Prasar Bharati Act, DAVP, Ministry of Information and Broadcasting, Government of India July 1999: 1). The chronology of events pertaining to the Prasar Bharati Act are such that even though the draft bill was introduced in Parliament in 1989, and it was passed in 1990, it only became an Act when it was officially notified, bringing the statute into force in 1997.

This Act decreed that the management of the affairs of the Corporation should be vested in the Prasar Bharati Board. The composition of this Board was specified as follows:

(a)   a Chairman;
(b)   one Executive Member;
(c)   one Member (Finance);
(d)   one Member (Personnel);
(e)   six part-time Members;
(f)   Director- General (Akashvani), *ex-officio;*
(g)   Director- General (Doordarshan), *ex-officio;*
(h)   one representative of the Union Ministry of Information and Broadcasting, to be nominated by that ministry; and
(i)   two representatives of the employees of the corporation, of whom one shall be elected by the engineering staff from amongst themselves, and one shall be elected by the other employees from amongst themselves (Prasar Bharati Act, DAVP, Ministry of Information and Broadcasting, Government of India July 1999: 4).

The Act also laid down the conditions for the appointment of the Chairman and the other members. While the Chairman and the part-time members should be 'persons of eminence in public life', the Executive Member, Member Finance, and Member Personnel should have special knowledge or practical experience in their various fields. The appointment of key board members was mandated as follows:

(1) The Chairman and the other Members, except the *ex-officio* Members, The Nominated Member and the elected Members shall be appointed by the President of India on the recommendation of a committee consisting of—

   (a) the Chairman of the Council of States, who shall be the Chairman of the Committee;

   (b) the Chairman of the Press Council of India established under section 4 of the Press Council Act, 1978; and

   (c) one nominee of the President of India (Prasar Bharati Act, DAVP, Ministry of Information and Broadcasting, Government of India July 1999: 5).

The Executive Member was also designated to be the Chief Executive of the Corporation, exercising powers and discharging functions subject to the control of the Board. The Prasar Bharati Act also made explicit details pertaining to the term of office of the Chairman and Members, the meetings of the Board, the transfer of service of existing employees to the Corporation, the functions and powers of the Corporation, and other subjects.

In the subsection pertaining to functions and powers of the Corporation in the Prasar Bharati Act, it was stated that the primary duty of the Corporation was to 'organize and conduct public broadcasting services to inform, educate, and entertain the public, and to ensure a balanced development on radio and television' (Prasar Bharati Act, DAVP, Ministry of Information and Broadcasting, Government of India July 1999: 12). It was further clarified that the provisions of this section were in addition to the existing Indian Telegraph Act of 1885. Furthermore, in discharging its functions, the Corporation should have the objective of 'upholding the unity and integrity of the country and the values enshrined in the Constitution' (Prasar Bharati Act, DAVP, Ministry of Information and Broadcasting, Government of India July 1999: 12). The stress on development was reiterated through emphasis on education, rural development, health, women and children's issues, as well as the special needs of minorities and tribal communities.

It is interesting to note that though this document professed to safeguard the citizen's 'right to be informed freely, truthfully, and objectively on all matters of public interest, national or international, and presenting a fair and balanced flow of information including contrasting views without advocating any opinion or ideology of its own', it also stated the power of the Central Government to give directions (Prasar Bharati Act, DAVP, Ministry of Information and Broadcasting, Government of India July 1999: 12). In fact, even though the whole of the Prasar Bharati Act revolved around the notion of autonomy, the heavy hand of the Central Government is evident from the following extract:

> 23.
>
> (1) The Central Government may, from time to time, as and when occasion arises, issue to the Corporation such directions as it may think necessary in the interests of the sovereignty, unity, and integrity of India or the security of the State or preservation of public order, requiring it not to make a broadcast on a matter specified in the direction, or to make a broadcast on any matter of public importance specified in the direction (Prasar Bharati Act, DAVP, Ministry of Information and Broadcasting, Government of India July 1999: 20)

However, seen in historical perspective, these provisions appear milder than the original wording of the Akash Bharati Bill of 1978 that was moved in Parliament by the then Minister of Information and Broadcasting, L.K. Advani. The relevant clause stated that: 'The Central Government may from time to time, issue to the Corporation such directions as it may think necessary for the efficient administration of this Act, and a copy thereof shall be laid before each house of Parliament'(Akash Bharati Bill, Clause 23, Ministry of Information and Broadcasting 1979). The 1990 version of the Bill, though still crippling, at least limited the power and specified the reasons for governmental interference. The Verghese Committee appointed by Advani in 1977 submitted its report in February 1978, but the Bill was moved in the Lok Sabha only a year later. This delay may indicate the reluctance of the minister to act upon the Verghese Committee Report's recommendations.

In a regressive step, the degree of autonomy finally conferred to DD and AIR in 1990 was reduced as compared to the more liberal provisions of the Verghese Committee Report in 1978. A comparison between the Akash Bharati Bill of 1978 and the Prasar Bharati Bill of 1989 is instructive. As Ninan (1998) informs us:

> The first was envisaged as a trust, the second as a corporation. Akash Bharati provided for trustees, Prasar Bharati for a board of governors. The first did not envisage any representative of the Union Ministry of Information and Broadcasting on the Trust, the second provides for such a person. The earlier structure talked of granting broadcast franchise licenses to stations or *Kendras* through its Licensing Board, the subsequent one neither provided for granting franchises nor for the constitution of a licensing board.
>
> The charter of the Trust and the objective of the Corporation were very similar, but there were three conspicuous omissions in the latter. The draft Prasar Bharati Bill dropped the clause promising to, 'uphold the fundamental right to freedom of speech and expression guaranteed under Article 19 (1) (a) of the Constitution'. It also dropped the clause pledging to 'uphold the impartiality, integrity, and autonomy of broadcasting in the country'. In addition, Akash Bharati spells out the Trust's relations with the Government, while Prasar Bharati says nothing on the subject (Ninan 1998: 10).

The points of similarity between the two draft Bills worth noting are that both stressed national integration, the need for educational and developmental programming, similar financial provisions, and provision of an entity to receive complaints. While the degree of autonomy conferred on Prasar Bharati in 1990 was generally perceived to be diluted as compared to 1978, there was a major change introduced in the Bill that was passed in 1990 as compared to the draft Bill introduced in 1989. This was the inclusion of a Parliamentary committee to oversee the functioning of the Corporation and submit a report to Parliament. The composition of this committee was 15 members from the Lok Sabha and seven from the Rajya Sabha, bringing the total up to 22 members. The provision of this Parliamentary committee was seen as yet another attempt by the government to reduce the effective measure of autonomy granted to the Prasar Bharati (Ninan 1998). Some other changes in the draft bill of 1989 perceived to be controversial were the reduction of the Chairman from whole time to part time, the addition of two representatives of employees on the Board of the Corporation, and the inclusion of four members of Parliament on the Broadcasting Council (Ninan 1998).

The Prasar Bharati Bill was finally passed by Parliament in 1990, but it was not officially notified because of the change in government. In fact, the Congress Government, contrary to its election promise of granting freedom to the electronic media, mothballed the Prasar Bharati Bill. It was finally notified by a non-Congress coalition government in 1997.

At the risk of being repetitive, it is important to stress that the Prasar Bharati Bill implying autonomy for DD was laid to rest for the greater part of the 1990s. The culprit appears to be the Congress government, which was loath to let go of the reins. Even when the Bill was eventually introduced in Parliament by a non-Congress government, its provisions were diluted. This reluctance on the part of the state to allow independence for the broadcast media implies that it was jealously guarding its turf.

THE CABLE TELEVISION NETWORKS (REGULATION) ACT (1995)

The Cable Television Networks (Regulation) Act, 1995, as the name suggests, came into existence in September 1994 to regulate the cable television industry. According to this Act, all cable operators were required to be registered with the 'registering authority' specified by the Central Government. The registering authority was specified to be the Head Post Master of a Head Post Office of the area within whose territorial jurisdiction the office of the cable operator was situated. The verdict of the registering authority was seen to be crucial as:

> On receipt of the application, the registering authority shall satisfy itself that the applicant has furnished all the required information and on being so satisfied, register the applicant as a cable operator and grant to him a certificate of such registration: Provided that the registering authority may, for reasons to be recorded in writing and communicated

to the applicant, refuse to grant registration to him if it is satisfied that he does not fulfil the conditions specified in clause 0 of section 2 [Cable Television Networks (Regulation) Act, clause 4. (c)1995].

Other than the requirement of being registered by an authority specified by the Central Government, all cable operators were also required to adhere to a programme code, an advertisement code, and to maintain a register of programmes transmitted. The programme code and advertising code were those existing for DD and AIR. Exemptions from the programme and advertising code were 'programmes of foreign satellite channels which can be received without the use of any specialized gadgets or decoder' [Cable Television Networks (Regulation) Act, clauses 5, 6 1995]. A must-carry provision for DD channels was also stipulated as, 'every cable operator using a dish antenna or TVRO shall, from the commencement of this Act, re-transmit at least two Doordarshan channels of his choice through the cable service' [Cable Television Networks (Regulation) Act, clause 8 1995]. The specifications of the programme code are fairly stringent as is evident from the following excerpt:

6. Programme Code:
No programme should be carried in the cable service which:
 (a) Offends against good taste and decency;
 (b) Contains criticism of friendly countries;
 (c) Contains attack on religions, or communities, or visuals or words contemptuous of religious groups, or which promote communal attitudes;
 (d) Contains anything obscene, defamatory, deliberate, false, and suggestive innuendos and half-truths;
 (e) Is likely to encourage or incite violence or contains anything against maintenance of law and order or which promotes anti-national attitudes;
 (f) Contains anything amounting to contempt of court;
 (g) Contains aspersions against the President or the Judiciary;
 (h) Contains anything affecting the integrity of the Nation;
 (i) Criticizes, maligns, or slanders any individual in person or certain groups, segments, or social, public, and moral life of the country;
 (j) Encourages superstition or blind belief;

(k) Denigrates women through the depiction in any manner of the figure of a woman, her form or body, or any part thereof in such a way as to have the effect of being indecent, or derogatory to women, or is likely to deprave, corrupt, or injure the public morality or morals;

(l) Denigrates children;

(m) Contains visuals or words which reflect a slandering, ironical, and snobbish attitude in the portrayal of certain ethnic, linguistic, and regional groups;

(n) Contravenes the provisions of the Cinematograph Act, 1952 (Cable Television Networks (Regulation) Act 1995; Notification in the Gazette of India, Part II, Section 3, Sub-Section (1), No. 6).

The advertising code has similar stipulations about safeguarding the rights of women and children, and not violating any constitutional provisions. In addition, the advertising code mentions that advertisements must not be directed towards any religious or political end.

The registration requirements, must-carry provisions, and adherence to a strict programme and advertising code were all attempts by the government to regulate a hitherto anarchic and rapidly proliferating industry. These requirements can be interpreted to mean that the state was seeking to re-establish its dominance in the broadcast arena, as they pertained to issues of ownership and content. The issues of indecent programming and liquor and tobacco advertisements on the foreign satellite channels relayed by the cable industry have surfaced at regular intervals and will be discussed later.

THE HERO CUP CASE (1995)

In 1995, the Government's exclusive right to the airwaves was challenged by the Supreme Court decision in the Secretary, Ministry of Information and Broadcasting versus Cricket Association of Bengal (1995) case, popularly referred to as the Hero Cup case. The judicial activism displayed in the Hero Cup judgment helped to reduce the State's de jure stranglehold over domestic television. In 1993, the Board for Cricket Control of India and Transworld International (TWI) a foreign sports television entity had a contract whereby TWI was given the right to telecast the international Hero Cup Cricket tournament.

TWI had provided the highest bid in a global tender, including DD, amongst the rival bidders. The Ministry of Information and DD attempted to stop TWI from telecasting the match from Calcutta, and tried to prevent it from up-linking live to its satellite. DD accused TWI of transgressing India's foreign exchange rules, and the Cricket Board of disloyalty to the nation by preferring TWI to DD (Sinha 1998).

The Supreme Court ruled that 'airwaves constitute public property and must be utilized for advancing public good'. (Justice Reddy, concurring). In a separate concurring judgement, Justice Sawant noted that:

(i) The airwaves or frequencies are a public property. Their use has to be controlled and regulated by a public authority in the interests of the public, and to prevent the invasion of their rights. Since the electronic media involves the use of the airwaves, this factor creates an inbuilt restriction on its use, as in the case of any other public property.

(ii) The right to impart and receive information is a species of the right to freedom of speech and expression guaranteed by Article 19 (1) (a) of the Constitution. A citizen has a fundamental right to use the best means of imparting and receiving information, and as such to have an access to telecasting for the purpose. However, this right to have an access to telecasting has limitations on account of the use of public property, viz., the airwaves, involved in the exercise of the right, and can be controlled and regulated by the public authority. This limitation imposed by the nature of the public property involved in the use of the electronic media is in addition to the restrictions imposed on the right to freedom of speech and expression under Article 19 (2) of the Constitution.

(iii) The Central Government shall take immediate steps to establish an independent autonomous public authority representative of all sections and interests in the society to control, and regulate the use of airwaves (Secretary, Ministry of Information and Broadcasting versus Cricket Association of Bengal (1995) 2 S. C. C.: 251–2).

Justice Sawant's judgement emphasized that airwaves are a *public* property. Accordingly, he stated the need for an autonomous public authority to regulate the use of the airwaves.

In a concurring judgement Justice Reddy noted that, 'airwaves being public property, it is the duty of the State to see that airwaves are so utilized as to advance the free speech right of the citizens which is served by ensuring plurality and diversity of views, opinions, and ideas' (Secretary, Ministry of Infomation Broadcasting versus Cricket Association of Bengal (1995) 2 S. C. C.: 251–2). However, he clarified that the free speech right guaranteed to every citizen of India did not encompass the right to use the airwaves in a restricted manner, as this would be detrimental to the body of citizens since only a few powerful economic, commercial, and political interests would be dominant.

The vital issue of the right to operate a private TV station was touched upon in this landmark judgement. Justice Reddy opined that this right, 'does not flow from Article 19 (1) (a); that such a right is not implicit in it' (Secretary, Ministry of Information and Broadcasting versus Cricket Association of Bengal (1995) 2 S. C. C.). He went on to say this was a matter of policy for Parliament. If Parliament conferred such a right, it could only be done by an Act made by Parliament. Commenting on the nature of such an Act, Justice Reddy said it should be consistent with the right of free speech of the citizens and should have strict programme and other controls. It is interesting to note that the judge referred to the Broadcasting Act of 1991 in the United Kingdom as an example.

Echoing Justice Sawant's sentiments, Justice Reddy emphasized that, 'monopoly of this medium (broadcasting media), whether by Government or by an individual, body, or organization is unacceptable...the broadcasting media should be under the control of the public as distinct from government' (Secretary, Ministry of Information and Broadcasting versus Cricket Association of Bengal (1995) 2 S. C. C.). Thus, this Supreme Court judgement opened up the Pandora's Box of domestic competition to DD. It succeeded in prominently placing on the agenda, the issue of competition rather than mere autonomy for Prasar Bharati. It also indicated that the archaic Indian Telegraph Act of 1885 was inadequate to govern broadcasting media. The law had not kept pace with changes in communications technology. Comparing India to other democracies, Justice Reddy observed, 'while all the leading democratic countries have enacted laws specifically governing the broadcasting media, the law in this has stood still, rooted in the Telegraph Act of 1885...It is, therefore, imperative that the Parliament makes a law placing the broadcasting media in the hands of a public/statutory corporate or the corporations, as the case may be' (Secretary, Ministry of Information and Broadcasting versus Cricket Association of Bengal (1995) 2 S. C. C.: 298–301). The ball was, thus, placed in Parliament's court.

The views of these two judges seem to be veering towards a public trustee model for broadcasting, which lies at the heart of many broadcasting issues in the US. The notion that the airwaves were public property in India as opposed to governmental property was popularized by this Supreme Court judgement. It had important repercussions. This judgement increased the salience of the question of autonomy for DD, and put it on the public agenda. Thus, the issue gradually started acquiring momentum, even though the state was not encouraging public debate on this issue. At the same time, this judgement did not take cognizance of the cable television industry, which is not constrained by limited spectrum as it is a closed circuit medium.

THE BROADCASTING BILL (1997)

After the Hero Cup Case decision of 1995 and some other cases involving programmes on private television channels in 1995 and 1996, the issue of reform in the broadcasting sector gained prominence in the public agenda. During this period, satellite and cable television was expanding rapidly in India. STAR TV's plans regarding introduction of direct-to-home (DTH) services in late 1996 acted as a spur to the government. The government did not allow STAR TV to provide DTH because of the fear of monopoly and difficulty in regulation. Permission was finally granted for DTH in 1999, initially only to DD (Page and Crawley 2001). The Prasar Bharati Act of 1990 barely dealt with a plethora of new issues. Even though it was officially notified in 1997, it was already recognized to be defunct. The urgent need for new broadcast legislation was felt.

In a note prepared on the Broadcasting Bill by the MIB (Broadcasting Bill: Issues and Perspectives 1996), it was reiterated that the airwaves were public property, and should be used for the larger public good. The fear of monopoly was expressed with respect to the airwaves as, 'these cannot be a source of merely a commercial venture in the hands of a few affluent people and, therefore, cannot be left to market forces'

(Broadcasting Bill: Issues and Perspectives 1996: 223). The note stated the following objectives of the proposed broadcasting law:

  (i)   Preserve our national identity and give a direction and shape to our national vision.
 (ii)   Give voice to the local and regional aspirations and needs.
(iii)   Provide plurality of news and views.
 (iv)   Promote and groom the indigenous private broadcasters to thwart the invasion from satellite broadcasters.
  (v)   Ensure wide dispersal of media ownership and source of information to avoid monopoly.
 (vi)   Make efficient use of airwaves, a public property, in the larger public interest (Broadcasting Bill: Issues and Perspectives 1996: 224).

It was further stated that the basic framework of the broadcasting law should be based on existing models from democratic countries. Broadcasting systems from USA, UK, France, Germany, Italy, and Australia were subjected to close scrutiny. Finally it was decided that the broadcasting law should be modelled on the UK pattern as it, 'has much more elaborate rules and regulations on broadcasting, which have been tried and tested for at least six to seven years' (Broadcasting Bill: Issues and Perspectives 1996: 225). Another point stressed in this ministerial note was that India did not want to follow the restrictive route of countries like Singapore, China, and Malaysia. The reasons given were pragmatic as well as ideological:

> Policing of individual dish antennas in a vast country like ours is extremely difficult, and would result in hardship and harassment to individual viewers. In any case, India would not like to join the club of close societies and deny its citizens access to information, knowledge, and healthy entertainment. The only effective alternative is to develop our own indigenous private broadcasters who can provide to our people an alternative to the foreign satellite channels. In the absence of indigenous private broadcasters, the public service broadcasters alone (DD&AIR) may not be able to meet the aspirations of the people in terms of variety and plurality of programmes demanded/required in different regions by different sections of society in this vast country known for its diversity (Broadcasting Bill: Issues and Perspectives 1996: 225).

It is significant that these views about the inadequacies of AIR and DD were acknowledged only after the foreign satellite channels had presented the policy makers with a *fait accompli*. As discussed earlier, private terrestrial competition to the national broadcaster was never seriously contemplated right up till the mid-1990s. Even the decision to licence independent FM radio stations was held up till 1999.

The note quoted at length from the Hero Cup Supreme Court decision reiterated that the airwaves were public property. Interestingly, this document also refers to the classic judicial decision in the Red Lion Broadcasting Co. vs. FCC[3] case when it expresses the opinion that broadcasters' rights may be regulated, notwithstanding the fact that they were public property. Thus the note states that, 'the broadcasting media needs to be regulated and such a regulation is not in conflict with the freedom of speech and expression as enshrined in Article 19 (1) (a) of the Constitution of India...'.

The views of senior bureaucrats in the MIB as expressed in this ministerial note are important. There is still a preoccupation with preserving 'national identity' and the shaping of 'national vision' on the part of the Central Government (Mishra 2001). The domestic private broadcasters were to be encouraged as a countervailing balance to the transnational broadcasters, whose power was beginning to be a matter of concern to the Ministry mandarins.

The Broadcasting Bill, 1997, was introduced in Parliament, 'to provide for the establishment of an independent authority to be known as the Broadcasting Authority of India, for the purposes of facilitating and regulating broadcast services in India, and to provide for matters connected therewith or incidental thereto' (The Broadcasting Bill, Bill No. 71 1997: 1). This Bill was finally drafted in the wake of the realization that an independent regulator was the need of the hour. In a parallel development, the Telecommunications Regulatory Authority of India (TRAI) had also been set up as an independent regulatory body to oversee the functioning of the telecommunications sector.

According to this Bill, the Authority would consist of the following Members:

(a) a Chairperson;
(b) not more than eleven Part-time Members to be appointed by the Central Government in consultation with the Chairperson;

(c)   Secretary to the Government of India in charge of Ministry of Information and Broadcasting, *ex officio;*

(d)   Secretary to the Government of India in charge of Department of Telecommunications, *ex officio*;

(e)   Secretary-General, *ex officio.* (The Broadcasting Bill, Bill No. 71 clause 3, 1997: 5)

The President of India would appoint the Chairperson on the recommendation of a Committee. The Chairman of the Committee would be the Chairman of the Council of States (Rajya Sabha). The other Committee members would be the Minister in charge of the MIB to the Government of India, and the Chairman of the Press Council of India established under section 4 of the Press Council Act, 1978.

Amongst the functions of the Authority, the following are salient; frequency planning for the purposes of broadcasting services, granting licenses for broadcasting services (including terrestrial radio and TV, satellite radio and TV, Direct to Home, local delivery, and other services), ensuring fair competition in the provision of broadcasting services, ensuring that a wide range of broadcasting services are available throughout India, determining by regulations the programme code and standard, and receiving complaints for violation of the code. In other words, the Authority was to be given a wide range of powers. However, these powers could be limited by the Central Government as is evident from the following extract:

25.

(1)   In the event of war or a natural calamity of national magnitude, the Central Government may, in public interest, take over the control and management of any broadcasting service or any facility connected therewith, suspend its operation or entrust the public service broadcaster to manage it in the manner directed by the government for such period as it deems fit.

(2)   the Central Government may if it appears necessary or expedient to do so, may, in public interest, at any time require the Authority to direct any licensee to–

(a)   transmit in his broadcasting service such announcements in such a manner as may be considered necessary;

(b)   stop any broadcasting service which is considered prejudicial to friendly relations with a foreign country, public order, security of state, or communal harmony.

(3) The Central Government may, in public interest, issue such other directions, to the Authority, from time to time as considered necessary (The Broadcasting Bill, Bill No. 71 Clause 25, 1997: 15)

The Broadcasting Bill (1997) represents an attempt by the Central Government to grapple with broadcast related issues, which had finally become prominent on the public agenda. Again a non-Congress government was in power at this time. The proposal in the Bill for an independent regulatory body for broadcasting sought to bring satellite broadcasters under the umbrella of regulation. However, the caveat that the Central Government could still take over control of any broadcasting service for a number of specific reasons such as security of the state and communal harmony implied that the state still had its hand on the tiller.

While the TRAI is functioning fairly effectively, the establishment of an independent broadcast regulator is still in the doldrums. Thus, the unhealthy scenario of the state as represented by the MIB acting as a policing agent for the broadcast industry, while it still has influence over the 'autonomous' Prasar Bharati, continues into the present. This is despite the fact that there have been some recent initiatives towards self-regulation.

THE SHUNU SEN COMMITTEE REPORT (2000)

The Shunu Sen Committee was appointed to examine the working of the Prasar Bharati, with special reference to its public service broadcasting mission. The crucial issues affecting the Prasar Bharati as identified by this committee were the identity, funding, and functioning of the organization. The Sen Committee Report reiterated the view that the structure, financing, and personnel policies of the public service broadcaster 'should be such that it must not be at the mercy of or amenable to pressures from the government of the day' (2000: 4.1). To achieve this goal, the Committee's view was that the Prasar Bharati should aim at financial independence within a five-year time frame. This could be accomplished with a mix of advertising revenues and commercial revenues garnered through the marketing of premium products and services. Furthermore, deputation of government employees to Prasar Bharati should be disallowed in future.

The Committee also recommended that each channel should have a well-defined identity and positioning, so that they attracted their target audience and did not cannibalise viewership from other Prasar Bharati channels. A strong case was also made for decentralization of decision-making, and of increasing regional and local programming. The newly launched education channel called Gyan Darshan would also be given strong support by the parent entity.

THE COMMUNICATIONS BILL (DRAFT, 2000)

The Broadcasting Bill of 1997 appeared to be defunct even before it could be notified in order to become an Act. As N. Murali (2000), the joint managing director of *The Hindu* group of media companies said, 'right now, there is no regulation in the electronic medium except the Cable Networks Regulation Act'. Various drafts of a new bill had been under consideration in the year 2000. According to some press reports, this was initially labelled the Information, Communications, and Entertainment Bill (ICE) draft 2000, but as the year 2000 entered its last quarter, the bill was increasingly referred to as the Communications Bill Draft (2000).

In some quarters, this broadcasting bill was being referred to as the Convergence Bill (Sehgal 2000f; Murali 2000). The semantic confusion only reflects the real state of affairs as far as the bill is concerned; can it be all things to all people? A committee headed by noted jurist F. S. Nariman had prepared the Communication Bill. The law was meant to supersede the existing Indian Telegraph Act, the Information Technology Act, the Broadcasting law, as well as the Cable Network Television Act (Mukul 2000).

While there had been speculation of a supra-national regulatory body replacing the current TRAI and the proposed Broadcasting Authority of India, there had even been talk in the press of combining the information and broadcasting ministry, the communications ministry, and the ministry of information technology. The Communications Minister Ram Vilas Paswan indicated that the government may accept the controversial proposal to merge the three ministries mentioned (*Times of India* 2000i: 1). However, the Information and Broadcasting Minister at the time, Sushma Swaraj, seemed to think a convergence of ministries was unnecessary. If her statement was to be believed, 'convergence can take place under one central regulator, but that does not mean that all the ministries should be made one. Convergence is just one of the issues being overseen by the I&B ministry. I&B looks after many other areas as well' (Sehgal 2000f). It appeared that the Cabinet decision, while being a product of politics, would have far-reaching political ramifications as well.

Fali Nariman, the architect of the draft bill, implied that the recent legislation was attempting to be pro-active in a period of rapid technological change. Writing an editorial in the *Economic Times*, he believed that 'the impact of convergence upon regulation will probably far exceed the impact of regulation upon convergence' (Nariman 2000: 12). Nariman explained the need for a new regulator, as well as a new form of regulation:

> The idea should be to develop new forms of 'reflexive' law. Self-regulation or co-regulation is more effective than 'command and control' regulation. That implies the State requires an industry to set its own standards if it is to avoid harsher, and less appropriate, standards set by the State. We have attempted to weave this into the new Bill. Also, we have deliberately left matters of regulation and censorship to the Communications Commission—a lynch-pin of the Communications Bill (Nariman 2000).

The proposed Communications Commission would have the authority to issue licenses for telecasting, broadcasting, Internet, FM, and related fields (Mukul 2000). It would also be vested with the authority to manage spectrum, resolve disputes, and determine the conditions for fair, equitable, and non-discriminatory access to network facilities and services. Nariman had proposed that the chairperson and the seven members of the CCI be appointed by the President on the recommendation of a committee consisting of the Prime Minister, leaders of the Opposition of both houses, House leader of the Rajya Sabha, and the ministers of Information and Broadcasting, Telecommunications, and IT (Nagaraj 2000). Furthermore, he suggested that two members should have international experience in the functioning of similar Commissions as, 'the Commission cannot function like the Monopolies Commission or any other statutory commission, it is *sui generis*, it requires breadth and vision' (quoted in Nagaraj 2000).

It is an interesting historical fact that while the Broadcast Bill (1997) drew on the UK experience as a source of inspiration, the Communications Bill (2000) Draft talked about the establishment of a Communications Commission along the lines of the Federal Communications Commission of the US. The rhetoric of 'convergence' also seemed to be the magic mantra of the policy makers from Sushma Swaraj (quoted in Sehgal 2000) to Fali Nariman (2000). The purpose of the Bill quoted in the preamble is as follows:

(a)   to facilitate the development of national infrastructure for an information based society, and to enable access thereto;

(b)   to provide a choice of services to the people with a view to promoting plurality of views, news and information, and

(c)   to establish a regulatory framework for carriage and content of information in the scenario of convergence of telecommunication, broadcasting, data communication, multimedia, and other related technologies and services (quoted in Nariman 2000).

While the expressed purposes of the Draft Bill are unexceptionable, the matter has been in cold storage for the better part of the last decade.

AMENDMENTS TO THE CABLE ACT (1994)

The BJP led government announced some important amendments to the existing Cable Act in September 2000. The salient points of these amendments were:

(1)   a complete ban on the telecast of alcohol, tobacco, and synthetic baby food advertisements;

(2)   deletion of the clause enabling telecast of 'adult' programs between 11 p.m. and 6 a.m.;

(3)   prohibition of advertisements that contain references that may be injurious to religious sentiments;

(4) addition of a clause which controls cable piracy by making it mandatory for cable operators to secure copyrights for all the programs they telecast (*Times of India* 2000f: 1).

While the clause seeking to prevent cable piracy was lauded by the film industry, the cable operators opposed these amendments as being unfair. In fact, they protested that even though they do not create the content, the new rules provide for penal action against them. The general complaint from the cable industry was that the satellite broadcasters operated unfettered, even though they were the real creators of content (*Times of India* 2000g: 8).

BROADCAST REGULATION BILL DRAFT (2007)

This Bill reiterated the ideas that the airwaves are public property and that the use of airwaves should be regulated in the national and public interest. The proposed Broadcasting Regulation Bill suggested the establishment of a Broadcast Regulatory Authority of India along the lines of the TRAI. This would imply delegation of the regulatory functions presently being undertaken by the MIB. The provisions of the Cable Television Networks (Regulations) Act 1995 would have to be adhered to in terms of mandatory registration for cable operators (Thomas 2010). All television channels, whether Indian or foreign, would also be expected to comply with the Programme and Advertising Code specified in the Act of 1995. However, the government retained control as is evident from the fact that the registration or licence of the channels, could be revoked by the Central Government if it felt that content was threatening public order, communal harmony, security of the state, or friendly relations with a foreign country (Kumar 2010: 338).

The proposed Bill also specified obligations for all channels regarding public service broadcasting and domestically sourced content, and laid out cross media ownership restrictions in order to encourage competition and plurality of views as well. It was also mandatory for broadcast channels to transmit at least two DD channels and one regional channel of a state in the prime band, the Lok Sabha and Rajya Sabha channels, as well as to carry certain sports-related content available with DD (Kumar 2010: 338). This Draft Bill has been criticized by both the civil society and the market. The practical difficulties encountered in implementing retroactive sanctions against economic interests enjoying political backing also seem insurmountable (Thomas 2010: 107).

NEWS BROADCASTERS CODE OF ETHICS (2008)

As a response to the Draft Broadcasting Bill, the News Broadcasters Association (NBA), a group of twelve Indian broadcasters which operate 25 channels, formalized a Code in 2008. The NBA group includes NDTV, TV Today Network, Times Global Broadcasting, TV 18 Group, and the Sun TV Network. This Code of Ethics and Broadcasting Standards stressed self-regulation, as it was opposed to the idea of regulation of news channels' content by the MIB, as proposed in the Draft Broadcasting Bill. The Code stresses that journalists should operate as trustees of the public, and restricts the depiction of sex, nudity, pornography, violence, and even superstition, and so on. However, this Code did not have much of an impact on television content, firstly because the NBA did not include many broadcasters and secondly, even the NBA members flouted many of their own norms in the period following the publicizing of the Code in April 2008 (Kumar 2010: 341). It is important to recognize the fact that the satellite channels are not subject to government regulation. While advertisements for liquor and tobacco are banned on Indian networks, the satellite channels show 'surrogate' advertisements for the same products, defeating the purpose of restrictions on such advertising. Satellite channels also have different attitudes to the depiction of nudity, sex, and violence as compared to Indian media networks.

BROADCASTING AND POLITICS

From Imperial times right up to the present, the state has actively controlled the broadcast medium on the Indian subcontinent. The four major South Asian countries of India, Pakistan, Bangladesh, and Sri Lanka exhibit some similarities in the functioning of the broadcasting sector, particularly the role of the national broadcaster. Satellite television has had a fierce impact on all these nations, and the initial response of the state to this perceived threat has often not been a coherent one. India's case is particularly complex because of its greater size, cultural and linguistic diversity, and strong secular and democratic traditions.

Throughout the last two decades, the government's response to new developments in broadcasting has often been a defensive one as it seeks to safeguard its territory in the face of a perceived threat. As Usha Reddi (1996), an academic, expresses herself with respect to the former State controlled broadcaster, 'every milestone in DD's growth has been dogged by ad hocism' (1996: 232). While the Indian government has been fairly pro-active in encouraging the information-technology sector, especially the production of software, the same cannot be said of the broadcasting sector. In spite of the plethora of committees set up in the last four decades to examine various aspects of broadcasting and cable, an independent regulator is yet to be established to oversee the sector. The MIB was still acting as the policing authority for the industry in the year 2010.

It is significant to note that though the monopolist national broadcaster was suddenly facing stiff competition on its home turf, the legal provision of banning the reception of satellite television was never resorted to by the Indian government. This is in direct contrast to the Chinese government. In studying the political economy of communications in India during 1990–2000, it would appear that this openness in television was permitted as part of the new *glasnost* strategy of the Indian state. Sinha (1998) believes that adopting a *laissez-faire* policy towards trans-national broadcasters actually sent out the right signal as far as the Indian government was concerned.

In this regard Sinha (1998) is of the opinion that:

> The cornerstone of the Government's new economic policy was globalization. In the Indian context, globalization involved opening up international trade and foreign investment to one of the most tightly closed economies in the world.... Foreign investors, however were not easily convinced of the Government's newfound commitment to liberalization. Despite the policy and legal actions taken to implement the new economic measures, foreign investors remained wary of investing in India during the first year-and-a-half of reforms. FDI flowed in very slowly, much slower than the government needed to ensure the

success of the reforms. By the middle of 1992, only $240 million had been committed by foreign investors, and a mere one-third of that had actually been invested.

As foreign investors watched the economic developments unfolding in the country, the government's attitude toward the new satellite-distributed television services became a barometer of its commitment to reforms. Any attempt to restrict foreign broadcasters would have been construed as evidence of the government's lack of commitment to opening up the economy. Consequently, the government chose to ignore the foreign television services, despite complaints from a number of political and social organizations of the cultural threat posed by these services. The government clearly recognized that television is a highly visible cultural product that functions as the best marketing tool for the liberalization of the Indian economy (1998: 26–7).

Sinha (1998) further suggests that the government was committed to an aggressive strategy of capitalist consumerism. For the market to function as an engine of economic growth, it would be fuelled in part by the expansion of marketing allowed by massive television expansion. Thus, it would appear by Sinha's reasoning that the old dualism of state versus market is defunct, and the state is actively engaged in using the market as a survival tactic. However, things may not be as clear-cut as Sinha suggests. The truth lies somewhere between a sapient state wilfully ignoring satellite television as a plank of its liberalization platform, and a befuddled state reacting to each new impetus in Pavlovian fashion. According to R. C. Mishra (2001), a senior bureaucrat in the MIB during the time the Broadcasting Bill of 1997 was being drafted; the state did not impose a ban on satellite broadcasting because it was felt that alternative voices were in the public interest. This was especially so for a democracy which encouraged the freedom of the press. Thus, his reading of the actions of the state would categorise it as being paternalistic.

However, the political arena itself has grown more diverse in the last two decades, which may have impacted broadcasting policy. The problems stem in part from the political process in India. The second last decade has seen as many as four general elections. Coalition and confessional politics have also become a force to reckon with.

The Bharatiya Janata Party (BJP) had grown in importance in this period. The BJP in the decade 1990–2000 has developed as the second pole in the emergence of a bipolar national polity. In fact it became the largest single party in 1996 (Joshi 1999). The 13th general elections in 1999 brought the BJP as the leader of a centrist coalition of over 22 parties to power. While there was talk about the emergence of bipolarity with the BJP and the Congress as the two major players, the nature of the BJP itself had changed from encouraging the Hindu right-wing, to endorsing a more moderate point of view (Joshi 1999).

The relative decline of the Congress party in this decade implied an increase in the importance of regional factors. The situation today is vastly different from 1989 when the Congress party had a majority, and the Prime Minister's Office (PMO) wielded a lot of clout. Roy (2000) explains how the power structure has changed during 1990–2000, as compared to the situation in 1989:

> Those were the last days of the Congress Empire. The party had 400-odd seats in the Lok Sabha and governments in most of the states. The Prime Minister's Office had a domineering role, overlooking the functioning of every ministry. It would often intervene, pulling up ministers for work not done. Ministers were overawed by the omnipresent PMO.... In just about a decade; the country's power structure has indeed undergone a metamorphosis with centrifugal forces replacing centripetal tendencies. A Karunanidhi in Chennai, a Bal Thackeray in Mumbai, and a Chandrababu Naidu in Hyderabad, control the government as much as the BJP leadership. The over-centralized approach—often with an authoritarian streak—of the one-party era has given way to decentralization (2000: 1)

The PMO under Vajpayee could not adopt a bullying tone because the government was a coalition one where ministers from constituent parties often held allegiance to state capitals and regional parties. Katyal (2000) writing on the state of coalition politics in recent years has noted:

> By its very nature, a coalition is not suited for the build-up of a single individual, with an aura of indispensability. That is because power-sharing entails an effective say for the leaders of the constituents who

choose their nominees for the Cabinet posts, and influence policy decisions in keeping with their programmes and ideologies (4 September 2000: 10)

In fact the government under the leadership of Mr. Vajpayee had united over 22 parties and groups.

The days of mammoth electoral majorities seem to be over. In the words of Sachs, Varshney, and Bajpai (1999), 'the formation and continuance of governments in Delhi increasingly depend on the bargains struck between national and regional political parties. No national party has been strong enough to make a government on its own since 1989. The rise of regional forces has important implications for reforms' (1999: 17). Some of the policies that affect the course of economic reforms in India are on the state list rather than the Central Government list.

An increase in the importance of regional identities and regional parties within India has implied diffusion of power at the centre. The caste factor can never be left out of any analysis of politics in India; the last two decades has seen the rise of the Dalits or the 'backward castes'. In fact, the caste factor appears to be waxing in political importance. In pre-reform days, traditional lobbies of trade unions, farmers, traders, industrialists, and government servants were wooed by fixers of political parties. Aiyer (2000) reports that the period 1990–2000 has seen the caste factor become predominant. In his opinion, 'the old fixers are anti-reform since it reduces the power of their traditional constituents. But the new caste warriors care little for the traditional lobbies, and that is a big change'. The old lobbies of industrialists and bureaucrats were often composed overwhelmingly of upper castes.

Religion-based politics has also come into its own in this period. The Bharatiya Janata Party (BJP) and the Rashtriya Swayamsevak Sangh (RSS) have gained power contributing to the rise of Hindu nationalism, at the cost of secular politics practised by the Congress party. These entities in the political equation have had an impact in the formulation and implementation of broadcasting policies.

Varshney (1999) has addressed the issue of why India's minority government was successful in introducing wide-ranging economic reforms in 1991, when a government with a three-fourths majority in

Parliament failed to do so in 1985. He also speculates about why the post-1991 reforms have succeeded in certain areas and not in others. In doing so, Varshney differentiates between mass politics and elite politics. Following Varshney's line of argument, it would appear that reform in the broadcasting sector was stymied because it was largely a subject of elite politics.

The linkages between politics and broadcasting are many. There are the influences from the nature of the ruling party, direct interference from the PMO, the making of laws pertaining to broadcasting, the appointment of the Minister for Information and Broadcasting, the bureaucrats appointed to key positions, the appointment of various committees, and financial controls exerted over the broadcasters. There is also the political culture; a legacy of interference in the electronic media by the union government, which has been tolerated by the public to varying degrees.

One area in which the linkage between politics and broadcasting is fairly visible is in the expansion of DD's infrastructure. Television in India was born in 1959, but it grew fairly slowly for the next 15 years. India's satellite programme, pioneered by the visionary Vikram Sarabhai, meant that the technological constraints on television were somewhat eased. The communications satellite INSAT launched in 1983 helped to expand access to television. It is significant that Indira Gandhi, who was the Prime Minister in the early 1980s, had previously been Minister for Information and Broadcasting. While supporters of her policies insist that television was actively encouraged as a developmental tool, cynics and critics contend that propaganda was her real objective (Singhal and Rogers 2001: 56). Rudolph and Rudolph (1987) have commented on Indira and Rajiv's use of the broadcast media:

> In an era in which media politics is displacing organizational politics, Rajiv Gandhi is even better equipped than his mother was to fight elections. Both were concerned to extend television coverage prior to the eighth parliamentary elections in December 1984, so as to better exploit their incumbent government's monopoly over the electronic media. Rajiv has a natural and attractive television presence. In an era in which the cassette recorder is replacing the local notability and vote banks, Rajiv's technological bent gives him an advantage (1987: 150).

While the age of satellite television is now upon us, political control (albeit covert) over terrestrial broadcasting is still of value because of the immense audiences that DD still commands, especially in the rural areas.

The government's emphasis on the expansion of the reach of television is apparent in the increase in the number of television transmitters from 20 in 1982 to 564 in 1994. In Arbind Sinha's (1996) opinion, this expansion was politically motivated, 'the expansion of TV technology in terms of its reach by installing transmitters has not been haphazard, or unplanned. The government wanted it to serve the decision-makers or policy planners sitting in Delhi to communicate their views to large numbers of the population' (1996: 304). It is no accident that the number of transmitters installed per annum reached record proportions in 1984 and in 1989, when India was preparing for its Lok Sabha (parliamentary) election to form its federal government (see Figure 5.7a).

Another aspect of the government's preoccupation with broadcasting infrastructure is the installation of transmitters along the western and northern borders that separate India from Pakistan. It may be argued that this stems from the classic use of propaganda by a nation-state. In this regard, the then Information and Broadcasting Minister Arun Jaitley revealed future plans for DD, 'we are planning to set up a chain of high power transmitters along the border so that our transmission can directly reach Lahore, Karachi, Islamabad, and Pakistan occupied Kashmir, barring Gilgit and some high reach areas of Pakistan. Some of these will become operational from June' (*The Times of India* 2000k: 14). Altruism can hardly be the reason for the Indian government's expenditure on broadcasting infrastructure that would mostly be of benefit (a debatable point) to Pakistan.

In the wake of the Kargil conflict between India and Pakistan, there is more awareness of the role of the media in a war. The ministry had also proposed to set up a chain of high-powered transmitters in the North East. These areas have suffered from insurgency from Bangladesh and Myanmar in the last few decades. In this context, Jaitely emphasized the importance of the extension of the broadcasting infrastructure, 'the war against insurgency is a war of information. We have to gear up to fight it' (quoted in Sehgal 2000c: 8).

The political influence on broadcasting is also visible in the programming choices of DD. The Kashir channel targeting the Kashmiri population was launched on 26 January (Republic Day) 2000 amidst much fanfare and trumpeting. According to one estimate, the estimated cost of this channel is Rs 900 million (Bamzai, 2000a: 4). It is another matter altogether that the commercial viability of this venture is dubious.

Government interference or influence in content of programmes being aired is another area where one can discern political influence. Speaking on the issue of autonomy for AIR and DD, the Minister of Information and Broadcasting, P. Upendra commented on political interference in DD's functioning:

> ...right now Doordarshan and Radio are still government organizations. They are not autonomous as on today. Myself or my Ministry cannot abdicate our responsibility about proper functioning of these media. As far as interference is concerned, the persons working there came to me and told how hotline telephones were kept there, how instructions were going on from the Prime Minister's Office and the Minister's Office, how news was tailored and so on. Thus, they lost their power of functioning independently and today this has become the biggest handicap for me (Lok Sabha Debates, 9th series, V. 3, No. 18, 1990: 5)

Upendra was referring to the work culture prevalent at DD. This reference was before DD gained autonomy in 1997. However, the PMO is not the only one that has been accused of interfering with DD and AIR. The rural development minister, Venkaiah Naidu, speaking at a workshop for senior officials of the rural development ministry and producers of AIR and DD in May 2001 said, 'make the Prime Minister your focal point. As a public service broadcaster of a democracy, your concern is the elected government and the symbol of this is the Prime Minister' (quoted in *The Economic Times* 2001h: 3). It is interesting that the minister held this view and expressed it so blatantly in a scenario where Prasar Bharati is meant to be autonomous. At the very least, his notion of public service broadcasting is open to questioning.

Political pressure may also be discerned from what DD abstains from showing. In March 2001, a private media organization,

Tehelka.com revealed an extensive sting operation wherein it had proof on camera of senior army personnel, bureaucrats, and even ministers involved in alleged financial corruption regarding defence deals. The Defence Minister George Fernandes, the Samata Party president Jaya Jaitley, and the BJP president Bangaru Laxman, who were all members of the ruling government's National Democratic Alliance, were all forced to resign from their posts in the wake of this scandal. Private news channels such as Zee News and STAR News extensively aired this footage, while their ratings soared. DD, however, with its 'conservative' news sense blacked out the Tehelka tapes.

The Minister for Information and Broadcasting, Sushma Swaraj, defended DD on the grounds that as a public service broadcaster it had to show more 'responsibility' than the private channels. In fact, she remarked, 'the public service broadcaster has to show some restraint' (quoted in Roy 4 April 2001). However, Swaraj denied that her ministry had influenced Prasar Bharati in the black-out of the Tehelka tapes. In Karnik's (2001) opinion, what is even sadder is the lack of any public hue and cry, or even extensive debate in the print media about DD's lack of coverage on this vital issue that rocked the government. In his opinion it points to the lack of credibility that the public broadcaster suffers from.

However, the personality of the Information and Broadcasting Minister also has to be factored into the equation. While Arun Jaitley, who took over the Information and Broadcasting Ministry in November 2000, was open to the idea of making Prasar Bharati a viable corporation and set up a committee to examine this, his predecessor Pramod Mahajan had a vastly different style of functioning. Sahgal (2000) comments on Mahajan's handling of the Prasar Bharati:

> Mahajan made no bones about the fact that the national network was essentially a government channel and should function as such. And this is something that has been appreciated by his party colleagues. "Mahajan changed the entire nation's perception during the Kargil war and made the government look like a winner...." says a senior party leader. While Jaitely is bothered about his image, his rival is not. For Mahajan, the ends often justify the means. His ability to play the numbers game and woo enemies and fence-sitters has been one of his plus

points, but has also earned him the reputation of being a crafty manipulator. And when it comes to promoting party interests, he does not mind a few knocks from the press for endlessly repeating clips of Advani and Vajpayee on Doordarshan.... Mahajan had turned his fight against the Prasar Bharati board into something of a personal crusade and announced he wanted to do away with autonomy and Prasar Bharati and planned to bring Doordarshan back under government control.

What is interesting is Mahajan's blatant expression of the view that Prasar Bharati was to be used for the government's own purposes.

Another area of influence of the government in the broadcasting sector is via the posting of government bureaucrats on deputation, in Prasar Bharati. In fact, the CEO of Prasar Bharati, Rajeev Ratna Shah, who was in office till early 2001, was a civil servant on deputation. His successor, Anil Baijal, was also a civil servant on deputation. The Vajpayee government had been criticised by former Union Information and Broadcasting Minister Jaipal Reddy, for not letting the Prasar Bharati grow. In fact, he demanded immediate appointments to the Prasar Bharati Board posts of chairman, chief executive officer, director general (DD), director general (AIR), member (personnel), and member (finance). It is a telling fact that all six posts were currently being held by a government officer on deputation. Jaipal Reddy also felt that there had been a rapid turnover of ministers in the Information and Broadcasting Ministry, and inaction of the government with regard to the Prasar Bharati (*Times of India* 2000h: 9).

The government had been criticized because the post of chairman of Prasar Bharati had been lying vacant after Nikhil Chakraborty died. This implies that Prasar Bharati had been functioning with the civil servant CEO as its head without the chairman for the past two years. As mentioned earlier, the CEO of Prasar Bharati has mostly been appointed from the Indian Administrative Service, a Central Government cadre. On another occasion, Jaipal Reddy, who is now a member of the Congress party, expressed the opinion that there was nothing in the Prasar Bharati Act which gave the government powers to appoint an acting CEO as it has been doing recently (*Times of India* 2001c).

The Prasar Bharati board has been a controversial arena as far as the MIB is concerned. This was highlighted by the brouhaha over the 'retirement' of two members from the board, soon after the new BJP led government came into power in 1999. The two members dismissed from the Prasar Bharati board were Romila Thapar, an eminent social scientist, and Rajendra Yadav, a Hindi writer–editor, both of whom were considered to be liberals. According to the Prasar Bharati Act, two members have to be retired at the end of every two years. The question that needs to be asked however, is why these two board members? Romila Thapar expressed the opinion that when the BJP came to power, she was told by various people that her days were numbered. She felt that the government did not understand autonomy or public broadcasting, it was only interested in control. She also was of the view that accountability was not to a body of MPs, or even to Parliament, it was to the people if you are a public service broadcaster.

Romila Thapar, in an interview in the *Outlook*, a magazine, commented:

> Accountability is not even to Parliament; it is to the people, if you are a public service broadcaster. And those on the board are representing the people. As for the legality (of the government action), they keep on saying under clause so-and-so endlessly, and they've checked with the attorney general which obviously indicates they were worried about the legal position. Jaipal Reddy (who has since asserted that the government action is 'outrageously improper and clearly illegal') rang me up to say this was totally illegal and that the government was playing games…. But now, with the BJP in power, the trend seems to be to try and push everybody aside except for the hard-core, those who are committed to the Sangh parivar ideology. Look at what's happening to the educational institutions, school textbooks, Indian Council of Historical Research, Indian Council of Social Scientific Research, NCERT…(in conversation with Ishan Joshi, 6 December: 10–12)

Romila Thapar expressed the opinion that their functioning on the board was limited from the start. In fact, she had been instrumental in planning a series of educational programmes which could not be implemented because the ministry refused to make the necessary budgetary allocation (Sehgal 1999: 18). The then Information and Broadcasting Minister Arun Jaitley reacted to the furore caused by the retirement issue by dismissing the charge that his party had a hidden agenda. At a debate sponsored by Jaipal Reddy on this issue, he said, 'there is no question of appointing persons of one ideology or another'. He asserted that his government had not made a single appointment, so how could it be accused of 'saffronizing' (the colour now associated with the Hindu right wing) DD and AIR (quoted in *The Economic Times* 2000g: 2).

However, the government's 'saffronizing' agenda has apparently not been limited to the broadcast media, and appears to be part of a wider movement. It is a fact that in the year 2000 many liberals and Marxists complained of the growing saffronization of educational institutions including the Indian Council of Historical Research and Indian Council of Social Science Research. Narayani Gupta, an eminent historian, felt that saffronization had affected educational institutions such as the National Council of Educational Research and Training (NCERT). In fact, she expressed the opinion that the prevailing political ideology, with its emphasis on Hinduism, had affected educational institutions; the effect was that mediocrity was rewarded and no real scholarship was emerging under the saffron banner. There has also been a concerted effort to rewrite history along 'Hindu' lines (Gupta 2001).

According to a press report in the English language daily *The Hindu*, senior civil servants had eyed slots in the proposed Communications Commission of India (CCI). This had apparently displeased the industry heavy-weights as well legal experts. The cellular companies had also expressed their apprehensions about officers on deputation from the Government being prejudiced and compromising the independence of the proposed CCI (Dikshit 23 October 2000: 11). The legal experts objected on the grounds that, 'appointees from the civil service will be found wanting in making the CCI a benevolent and understanding 'super-regulator' and 'super-facilitator' '(Dikshit 23 October 2000).

The large number of committees appointed to examine various aspects of broadcasting may indicate the importance of this sector from a political viewpoint. Khanna (2000) is instructive on this point:

> Like most government actions, the only thing which is apparent is a plethora of committees. There is a Group of Ministers (GOM), headed by finance minister Yashwant Sinha, which is looking at the new converged environment. There is another GOM, headed by home minister LK Advani, which is looking at direct-to-home (DTH) television. There is a committee, headed by legal-eagle and MP Fali Nariman, which is drafting the new information, communication and entertainment Bill. A Prasar Bharati review committee comprising Kiran Karnik, Shunu Sen and NR Narayana Murthy has just submitted a report on the recast of Prasar Bharati (Khanna 2000: 3).

While the multitude of committees at least suggests the importance of broadcasting on the political agenda, the lack of progress in amending the Prasar Bharati, and in making appointments to the board in this decade, speaks for itself. Masterly inaction may itself be a government policy, stymieing any attempts at real autonomy for the Prasar Bharati.

STATE'S RESPONSE

In an examination of statehood in South Asia, Ainslie Embree expresses the opinion that the state should have a local, federal structure, rather than nationalism imposed from above.[4] In the five decades that India has been independent, concern for national unity has had two broad aspects, namely, preservation of territorial integrity, and the creation of a unifying national consciousness (Embree 1997). The broadcast media's role in the creation of a 'national consciousness' in India has been well documented. In fact, DD and AIR have been accused of attempting to promote 'nationalism from above', since there has been a dearth of more local, participatory programming (Melkote 1991).

Historically, in the post-Independence era, India had pursued a state-led model of economic development, which rested on the foundations of a mixed economy. The emphasis was on import-substitution and self-reliance. Politically, India, along with some other post-colonial nations, was a vigorous supporter of the Non-Aligned group of nations during the Cold War. India was also vociferous in her support of the New World Information Order, which favoured greater equality of information flows between the developed and the developing countries (McDowell 1997). Unlike some East Asian countries which achieved high rates of economic growth, for many years India was dogged by a low rate of economic growth, which was labelled the 'Hindu rate of growth' by the economist Raj Krishna.

The Political Economy of the Indian State

In a classic work on the political economy of the Indian state, Rudolph and Rudolph (1987), two eminent political scientists, have examined the unique character of this sub continental state.[5] In their words, 'India is a political and economic paradox: a rich-poor nation with a weak-strong state' (McDowell 1997: 1). The characterization of India's state as weak-strong conveys the paradoxical nature of the state, where it has oscillated between autonomous and reflexive relations with society (Skocpol 1985; Evans and Rueschmeyer 1985).

In arriving at an understanding of the Indian state and its complex nature, a word about India's political culture may be informative. As Nandy (1980) informs us:

> At different times in their political history, a people choose to remember different features of their past, and to emphasise different elements of their culture. One characteristic of a protean civilization such as India's is that it has many pasts; depending on the needs of each age, the nation brings a particular past into its consciousness.... In this respect, cultural history is a projection: one reads into it or takes out of it according to present-day needs (Nandy 1980: 47–8).

Thus, politicians and the ideology put forward by institutions of the state have drawn on different traditions at different points of time in order to legitimize their existence.

The importance of the state in India has historical roots in the institutions created by over 350 years of Mughal and British rule. The level of 'state-ness' and administration in India surpassed many other developing countries at the time when she became independent.

The authors identify the centrist pattern of partisan politics with the ideology of secularism, socialism, democracy, the mixed economy, and non-alignment as a major source of strength for the Indian state. Another source of strength is its professional and well-institutionalized bureaucracy. Thus, the Indian state could create a basic industries sector and occupy the 'commanding heights' of the economy in the 1960s. However, Rudolph and Rudolph argue that, 'to varying degrees and in different times and arenas, the third actor has served public interest or socialist objectives, the interests of private capital, and its own partisan, patronage, and resource interests. In the early 1970s, the third actor came increasingly to serve itself' (1987: 2). The 'third actor' refers to the state, the other two actors being labour and capital.

Rudolph and Rudolph (1987) argue that class politics has been marginal in India, as 'in the context of regulated conflict, India's parties do not derive their electoral support or policy agendas from distinct class constituencies, or from organized representatives of workers and capital' (1987: 20). The 'two historical adversaries' of class politics, capital and labour, are marginal in the Indian context because of the presence at centrestage of a 'third actor', namely the state. The dominance of the state in the period since Independence lies in its control of capital, market power, and employment. The classic antagonism between labour and capital are diluted because of the larger than life presence of the state. The state has presented itself as the representative and protector of organized labour, rather than its class enemy. Organized capital also faces 'formidable ideological, sectoral, and structural constraints that inhibit its capacity and will to engage in class politics' (Rudolph and Rudolph 1987: 25). Private capitalism in India has grown up under the aegis of the state; it is dependent on it for patronage and protection.

External factors are less important for explaining India's economic and political development up till the 1990s because it had a fairly autarkic economy till then. When one examines internal factors at work in changing the nature of the Indian state, Rudolph and Rudolph argue that:

> Four developments have given concrete shape to state weakness: (1) governments led by Indira Gandhi deinstitutionalized the Congress

party and state structures; (2) increasing levels of political mobilization, embodied in demand groups that press for immediate and hard-to-fulfil demands, have created an overload on the state; (3) unofficial civil wars among castes and classes have beset the countryside, particularly in North India; and (4) a new religious fundamentalism is exacerbating hitherto latent or low level social cleavages, making it difficult for the state to accommodate them (Rudolph and Rudolph 1987: 6–7)

In their opinion, the Indian State is located between constrained and autonomous, in the continuum of reflexive, constrained, autonomous, and totalistic reflecting the relationship of the state to society. Autonomy has two aspects. First, it could imply that the state is above social forces that could appropriate it to vested ends. Second, autonomy could also mean the 'state for itself', an entity that appropriates public powers and resources to partisan interest (Rudolph and Rudolph 1987: 14). While the former description of autonomy can be applied to the Nehruvian state of the 1950s, the latter description of autonomy can be applied to the state under Indira Gandhi's government in 1975–7 when the Emergency was imposed and the opposition was intimidated.

Rudolph and Rudolph further conceptualize the state with respect to policy formulation in terms of the command polity and demand polity heuristic, while society is examined in its political manifestation in terms of demand groups. The demand polity and command polity models help us to understand 'the tension between conflicting requirements of state sovereignty and popular sovereignty, which determines the degree of state autonomy on the one hand and state responsiveness on the other' (Rudolph and Rudolph 1987: 211). In the command polity model, the state is sovereign; it is autonomous, and has domination or control over policy and politics. The demand polity model, on the other hand, is characterized by voter sovereignty; the state is connected to societal values and interests by 'processes of representation and accountability' (Rudolph and Rudolph 1987: 14). While periods of command politics can gear policy towards future societal benefits and public goods, they can also be associated with appropriation by state elites, officials, and employees. Demand politics conversely direct policy in the direction of fulfilling the short-run consumption needs of mobilized constituencies.

In India, political mobilization has revolved around the actions of demand groups. Demand groups, unlike organized groups which have permanent organizations and pursue long-term goals, are more akin to social movements. They are more visible in the unorganized economy, and they use ad hoc organizational means to pursue their objectives. Rudolph and Rudolph emphasize the importance of demand groups in understanding the behaviour of the state:

> If interests, more than classes, provide the main link between state and society in India, mobilized interests have proved as decisive as organized interests for policy determination and state formation. In the multifaceted political economy of the Indian state, the demand group stands out as both a distinctive and a powerful determinant of the state in its policy mode (Rudolph and Rudolph 1987: 15)

Thus, the Indian state in its policy mode has its own peculiarities, and unravelling the strands of influence in a particular policy—for example, as pertains to the broadcasting sector—is a complex task.

In analysing the nature and behaviour of the Indian state, Rudolph and Rudolph have characterized the Nehruvian period up to about 1964 as one having a democratic regime and command politics. The following period, first under Lal Bahadur Shastri, then Indira Gandhi, up to 1975, has been defined as having a democratic regime and demand politics. The period 1975–7, when Indira Gandhi imposed the Emergency, has been categorized as one of authoritarian regime combined with command politics. The successive governments under Morarji Desai, Indira Gandhi and, Rajiv Gandhi have been characterized by a democratic regime and demand politics.

The Indian state, like others in South Asia, has changed in political climate from the point of time when it won its independence, to the current period. Candland comments on the nature of political leadership in South Asia:

> In India, as in Bangladesh, Pakistan, and Sri Lanka, the generation of leaders who held power after Independence has been replaced by a generation of leaders whose constituents and issues are more representative of society as a whole. The national parties that led in important phases of the independence struggle including the Communist Party of India

and the Congress have been in long term decline. Throughout South Asia, the national political parties that led independence movements tended to dominate government in the formative years of independence, only to give way to increasingly agrarian, confessional, regional, and vernacular political parties (Candland 1997: 31)

Thus the rise of demand politics and a constrained state is not surprising.

In examining developments in broadcasting in India in the last two decades, it is useful to apply the theoretical constructs adopted by Rudolph and Rudolph in their examination of the political economy of the Indian State.

Liberalization in India

By the 1980s, India's economic policies and model of development were coming under scrutiny from many groups, both in India and abroad. Matters came to a head when India suffered a massive foreign exchange crisis as the result of the Gulf War. By the early 1990s, India underwent massive trade, investment, and regulatory liberalization across the board. The end of the 'license raj' was at hand.[6] The then Prime Minister Narasimha Rao invited Manmohan Singh to take the office of Finance Minister in June 1991. Manmohan Singh was the architect of reforms which attacked the problems of fiscal and balance of payments crisis, as well as poor productivity plaguing the Indian economy (Ahluwalia and Little 1998).

In the opinion of two economists, Ahluwalia and Little, 'Manmohan Singh's historic contribution to Indian economic policymaking in 1991 was to initiate a decisive break away from the strongly inward-oriented trade policy regime in India, thereby providing an environment for efficient industrialization and better export performance' (Ahluwalia and Little 1998: 4). Since the reforms were put into motion in response to a crisis, in the initial phase, they had to focus on macroeconomic stabilization. The reforms initiated spanned the breadth of the Indian economy. Sachs, Varshney and Bajpai (1999) sum up the situation:

> Put simply, India's reform strategy has been to dismantle four decades of central economic control. Among other things, this included controlling

fiscal deficit, cutting and rationalizing corporate and personal income taxes, abolishing industrial licensing, encouraging foreign investment, liberalizing import rules and cutting import duties, encouraging exports, and deregulating India's archaic capital markets (Sachs, Varshney, and Bajpai 1999: 4).

These reforms were instituted more or less simultaneously.

It is interesting that the government of the time chose to undertake liberalization measures rather than an outright privatization of many sectors in the economy. Sinha (1995) is of the opinion that:

> During the economic reform process as a whole (popularly known in India by the catch-all phrase 'liberalization'), and for the telecommunications reforms in particular, the government has constantly had to trade off among four often opposing objectives: to push through the economic reforms; to do so within the limits of a parliamentary and federal democracy governed by the rule of law; to ensure that the political fallout of the reforms does not hurt the ruling party's electoral prospects; and to counter opposition from political, industrial and labor groups.

Accommodation of different interest groups may be the reason why India did not adopt a policy of complete privatization in both the broadcasting as well as the telecommunications sectors. For example, the potential political protest from the unions and workers employed in the state owned Post Telephone and Telegraph (PTT) makes the policy choice of outright privatization a difficult, if not an impossible one.

In examining the results of India's reform strategy initiated two decades ago, it would appear that there are some satisfactory results in the area of macroeconomic stabilization and growth. The annual rate of inflation has more or less been contained. Foreign currency reserves which stood at $1 billion in mid-1991 rose to $27.4 billion in January 1999. Foreign Direct Investment (FDI) inflows also increased from $135 million in 1991–2 to $3 billion in 1997–8 (Sachs, Varshney, and Bajpai 1999: 2–3). Notwithstanding these success stories, problems such as poverty remain.

State's Actions with respect to Broadcasting 1990–2001

In examining the actions of the state in the period 1990 onwards, one may characterize Narasimha Rao's government as one of command politics in a democratic regime. Such a radical change in policy as represented by the Indian state in this period can only point to a certain amount of autonomy on the part of the state. Subsequent governments seem to point towards democratic regimes, but demand politics. During 1990–2000 alone, there have been six different union ministries taking the reins of government at the Centre. In the absence of a clear majority, 'hung parliaments' have made an appearance. The 9th General Election in 1989, 10th in 1991, 11th in 1996 all resulted in hung parliaments. The regional parties, especially in the South, have increased in importance. The changing nature of political parties has impacted the policy-making functions of the state.

Regarding the broadcasting sector, this period has seen the state in policy mode as witnessed by the Prasar Bharati Bill, the Broadcasting Bill, and various drafts of the latest Communications Bill. The National Front government, following its commitment in its election manifesto, introduced the Prasar Bharati Bill in its first session of Parliament, when it came into power at the end of 1989 (Gill 1991). This was a significant development. This government, with Vishwanath Pratap Singh as the Prime Minister, was a minority government, supported by political parties from outside. Vishwanath Pratap Singh came to power, as forces coalesced to support him as an alternative to the Congress (I). It is interesting that the autonomy of DD and AIR should have been an election issue for the National Front government. However, this government was not destined to last long. V. P. Singh's populist policies of job reservations for the lower castes created contradictions which could not be resolved. The upper castes and middle classes became hostile. The BJP, which relied on this constituency, felt threatened and withdrew its support.

In November 1990, Chandra Shekhar was sworn in as the new Prime Minister with the support of the Congress (I). The weak coalition supporting Chandra Shekhar also broke down and a mid-term poll for the 10th General Election was held. This again resulted in a 'hung parliament' leading to a minority government with Narasimha Rao of the Congress (I) assuming Prime Ministership. While the

Rao government has gone down in history for ushering in powerful reforms across the board, the Congress government did not proceed with the issue of autonomy for DD and AIR.

A content analysis of the *Lok Sabha Debates* (the record of the proceedings of the Lower House of Parliament) for the period March–April 1990 reveals that most of the Parliament questions relating to broadcasting tackled by the Minister of Information and Broadcasting, Mr. P. Upendra pertained to issues such as content on DD, and expansion of transmitters in various states. During this period, it would appear that the question of competition for DD was not on the agenda in the Parliament. The questions asked by Lok Sabha members pertained mostly to specifics such as programming in regional languages, or the expansion of the reach of DD in their constituencies.

The minister, however, did refer to the question of the autonomy of DD and AIR on one occasion. In reply to a question on the establishment of an Indian Broadcasting Programme Service (IBPS), with a view to bring in greater professionalism in the media, Mr. P. Upendra stated, 'while the government is in favor of constituting the proposed IBPS, the question now has to be examined in the context of the decision to convert All India Radio and DD into an autonomous corporation' (*Lok Sabha Debates*, 9th series, 1990, V. 2, No. 5, 16 March 1990: 57). The *Lok Sabha Debates* for this period also reveal that some state governments had demanded that the second channel of DD be handed over to them for programming in regional languages. The minister said this was not necessary as the Prasar Bharati Bill dealt with such issues. This shows some of the tension that existed around the monolithic structure imposing programming in a centralized fashion.

The new Congress government assumed office in mid-1991. A content analysis of the *Lok Sabha Debates* during July-September 1991 reveals that the parliamentary questions posed to the then deputy minister of Information and Broadcasting, Girija Vyas also touched upon issues such as the advertising revenues of DD, the expansion of DD, the desire for more regional and local programming in different regions, infrastructure, and the content of specific programmes. The issue of the provision of the second channel of DD to the state governments surfaced again. There were a few queries about the telecast of election results and time given to political parties in news coverage.

What emerges from an analysis of these parliamentary debates for this period is that broadcasting issues appeared to have been low on the agenda. Issues such as the economic crisis facing the nation, and even political issues such as Kashmir and the contentious Babri masjid/Ram temple at Ayodhya appeared to be salient. In fact, the Lok Sabha Debates for July included the historic budget speech of the finance minister Manmohan Singh, where he charted the course of sweeping economic reforms.

Why was the Prasar Bharati Bill introduced by the National Front government captained by V. P. Singh swept under the carpet for the next seven years? The answer is not simple. One may argue that the V. P. Singh and Chandra Shekhar governments were in office for extremely short periods of time. Chandra Shekhar's priority being survival, the broadcast sector took a back seat, since he was negotiating politically between various parties and factions for much of the time he was in office. Autonomy for the broadcasting sector may not have been high on the public agenda. However, the Narasimha Rao government was in office for a full term. While the introduction of sweeping economic reforms and liberalization may be an instance of command politics on the part of the state in 1990–91, this did not spill over into the broadcast sector.

It may be argued that the state as represented by the Congress (I) government at this period of time was similar to other earlier Congress governments, in that it discouraged autonomy for the electronic media. DD and AIR may have been too valuable for internal propaganda. After all, the Rao government was also a minority government, which needed to present the economic reforms to the nation in a positive light, so as to generate favorable public opinion. Private broadcasters had not really impacted DD in the first few years that Rao was in office. Hence, DD and AIR were still in a monopolistic position as far as the populace's minds and hearts were concerned.

During the period 1991–6, when the Rao government of the Congress (I) was in power at the Center, DD was expanding its terrestrial infrastructure. In fact, over this period, approximately 240 additional transmitters were installed. It is also significant that during 1994–6, the period leading up to the 11th General Election in

April-May 1996, approximately 200 transmitters were installed by DD (Figure 5.7a). As described earlier, DD also expanded the programming available by increasing the hours of transmission, and introducing new channels. Thus, the sidelining of the Prasar Bharati Bill may actually be a strong policy statement on the part of the Congress (I) government. The adherence to the status quo may have actually suited the government very well, where DD and AIR were directly controlled by the MIB.

Another reason that the Rao government did not take action on the Prasar Bharati Bill, or formulate a comprehensive broadcasting bill dealing with the issues posed by the entry of satellite television, may be because they did not figure prominently in the popular agenda at that time. An analysis of the *Lok Sabha Debates* during July 1991 reveals the low salience awarded to broadcast related issues in Parliament. When this government assumed office, India's mass politics and electoral agenda were driven by issues such as job reservations for the 'lower castes', and Hindu-Muslim tensions following the BJP-led Rath Yatra[7] in 1990 and the mosque-temple controversy at Ayodhya (Sachs, Varshney, and Bajpai 1999: 15). Thus, the Union government at that time appeared to be confronted with caste and religious issues, as well as being faced with a severe fiscal and balance-of-payments crisis on the economic front.

While the issue of autonomy for Prasar Bharati was shelved, the Rao government did push through the Cable Act of 1995 while it was in office. This may have been because the cable industry with its large-scale relaying of satellite TV channels had mushroomed in an unregulated manner, and the state was belatedly trying to bring it under its control. However, even in this there was delay, so there did not seem to be any great urgency in tackling the cable industry's problems.

In the period following 1991, economic reforms have not figured prominently in electoral politics. Unlike V. P. Singh's government, broadcast-related issues did not appear on the electoral agenda at all. On the contrary, 'the electoral agenda has been dominated by secular versus religious politics, affirmative action, corruption, and personalities' (Sachs, Varshney, and Bajpai 1999: 14). The Eleventh General Election in 1996 again resulted in a 'hung parliament', with the pro-Hindu BJP garnering the largest number of seats. Although the BJP was invited to form the government, it did not have a majority and resigned within two weeks. Finally the United Front, which was a combination of the National Front and Left Front, came to power as a 13-party coalition. Four of the prominent regional parties in this coalition were the Telegu Desam Party, the Dravida Munnettra Kazhagam, the Tamil Manila Congress, and the Samajwadi Party. The ascendance of confessional and caste based politics is reflected in the growth of parties such as the Akali Dal representing the Sikhs, the Bahujan Samaj Party (BSP) for the dalits, and the Samata Party in Bihar. While parties such as the Samajwadi Party and the BSP are caste-based, the Shiv Sena is a language and local identity based party in Maharashtra (Thomas 2010: 72).

The coalition government following the 1996 General Election, can also be considered to be a case of demand politics, since representation of so many entities was achieved. The state's policies in this period with respect to the broadcasting sector reflect a desire to grapple with the issues of autonomy for Prasar Bharati and regulation for the industry through the passage of the Broadcast Bill. An analysis of the Lok Sabha Debates for the period February–August 1997 does reflect the rising salience of issues such as the restriction on foreign satellite channels, broadcast regulation, and autonomy for Prasar Bharati.

It would appear that the unregulated proliferation of private television was a matter of concern to this government, as the government wished to bring these broadcasters under its control. Speaking in reply to a question pertaining to private broadcasters in Parliament, the then Minister for Information and Broadcasting, C. M. Ibrahim stated:

> Private TV channels beam their programs from outside the country. Some of these channels, at times, do not exhibit the requisite degree of sensitivity to Indian values and culture. Government intends to introduce a bill in the Parliament which would seek to facilitate the broadcasting of such channels within the ambit of the proposed law and, inter-alia, provide for application of a broadcasting and advertising code on such satellite channels.... As regards presentation of the Bill, the matter is already pending before the cabinet. We'll try to present and pass both the Broadcasting Act and the Prasar Bharati Bill in this session itself. After getting the approval of the Cabinet, I would like it to be

discussed on various fora throughout the country because such a law is being enacted for the very first time in this country (*Lok Sabha Debates*, 11th Series, 27 February 1997: 14–17).

The intentions of the Union government in the introduction of the proposed legislation on broadcasting were fairly clear. Amongst other things, the government wished to exert authority over the private broadcasters by seeking adherence to a broadcasting code. The issue of cultural imperialism or cultural degradation was also coming up in Parliament repeatedly. The following extract from the *Lok Sabha Debates* is illustrative. The following question was addressed to the Minister of Information and Broadcasting, C. M. Ibrahim, in the Lok Sabha by a member, P. J. Kurien:

> It has been accepted by all that most of the programmes being telecast by private T.V. channels, and some of the programmes of the Doordarshan also, are more Westernised, alien to our culture, and are capable of misleading our youth. This has been brought to your notice earlier also. I would like to know as to what action you are going to take in this regard...
>
> C. M. IBRAHIM: The answer to your first question is: 'Yes'. I have made up my mind. Some of the programmes are not only Westernised, but they are also destroying our culture. As on today, I have no powers to control them. That is why, in the Broadcasting Bill, we are bringing them under the purview of licensing. Once they are brought under the purview of licensing, then I can have all these conditions (*Lok Sabha Debates*, 11th series, vol. 10, no. 11, 6 March, 1997: 15–6).

Some other examples of the preoccupation with foreign channels and their impact on Indian culture are given below. The following questions were addressed to Mr. C. M. Ibrahim by members of the Lok Sabha:

> SHRIMATI RATNMALA D. SAVANOOR: Mr. Deputy Speaker, Sir, through you, I would like to know from the Hon'ble Minister whether the programs being beamed in India through foreign satellite channels are in conformity with the Indian culture and whether these programs are not affecting our social milieu. Now-a-days, no one likes to watch TV along with his family members. I would like to know from the Hon'ble Minister as to what measures are being taken to protect the Indian culture and social values, because such programs are giving

rise to immorality in our society and casting adverse impact on women and children.

SHRI C. M. IBRAHIM: Mr. Deputy Speaker, Sir, I agree with the Hon'ble member. As no law pertaining to broadcasting has been formulated in the country so far, the department has decided to enact a law in this regard and after enactment of law, all the foreign channels would be able to beam their programs only after procuring a licence and at the time of issuing such licences, a restriction would be imposed on them that the programs not in conformity with the Indian culture would be banned effectively (*Lok Sabha Debates*, 11th series, vol. 10, no. 11, 6 March, 1997: 15).

Yet another question about the role of television and an attack on Indian culture was addressed to C.M. Ibrahim.

SHRIMATI BHAVNABEN DEVRAJ BHAI CHIKALIA: Our culture is under attack and our TV channels are under attack from the foreign channels, but the government is unable to do anything about it. Whether the government would deliberate upon this matter in order to improve the situation?

SHRI C. M. IBRAHIM: I have made it amply clear in the beginning that this is a very serious issue. India is a vast country. Here, permission of house owners is required to gain entry into even an ordinary household but on the contrary no permission is required for entering this country of 95 crore people. Anyone who is willing is beaming programmes without seeking any permission. Hence, we are trying to enact legislation as soon as possible so that after its enactment, strict action could be taken against those trying to beam such programs which go against the culture of our country and our national unity (Lok Sabha Debates, 11th series, V. 10, No. 11, 6 March, 1997: 16).

The statements of C. M. Ibrahim indicate that the issue of private broadcasters and satellite television was slowly gaining salience in the ministry's agenda. The paternalistic nature of the Indian state was also revealed by the emphasis on protecting national culture, as if the individual consumers of media products were helpless against the onslaught of foreign satellite channels. Here indeed is an expression of the fear of the nation-state, evoked by the spectre of global television. All these factors came into play in the drafting and introduction of the Broadcasting Bill in 1997.

While much has been said about the Union government in the interpretation of the state's role, the analysis is not complete unless one touches upon the seat of 'permanent government', or the role of the bureaucracy. The Indian Administrative Service (IAS) is a post-Independence version of the colonial Indian Civil Service (ICS), or the 'steel frame' of India. As interpreted by Rudolph and Rudolph (1987), post-Independence India inherited a high degree of 'stateness' from several centuries of Mughal and British rule. The bureaucracy was an integral part of the state's machinery. With respect to the broadcasting sector, the post of Director General of DD was generally held by a civil servant from the IAS, rather than a professional broadcaster. Even after the Prasar Bharati has been granted autonomy, the post of CEO has been held by an IAS officer on deputation.

The implication is that a professional ethos cannot prevail. As indicated earlier, interference from the PMO and the MIB has been tolerated by DD in its day-to-day working. It stands to reason that a serving civil servant cannot be wholly insulated from political pressures.

Recent Developments

While the contents of the Communications Bill (2000) draft have been debated, some of the provisions of the erstwhile Broadcast Bill have been de-linked as separate policies, such as, uplinking for private Indian networks and DTH, and notification for must-carry provisions for two DD channels—DD National and DD Metro—on the cable operators prime band (Editorial, *Business India*, 4–17 October 1999: 9).

In the initial phase of satellite television, foreign broadcasters were not allowed to broadcast from India. There was a change in 1998, when Indian companies with Indian equity of at least 80 per cent and management control in Indian hands were permitted to uplink from India through Videsh Sanchar Nigam Limited (VSNL). Clearance from the MIB was also required for this. This policy was liberalized in 1999 to permit Indian companies to uplink on any platform they chose. In 2000, further liberalization occurred and all broadcasters were allowed to uplink from India. The government announced more changes in 2003. News and current affairs channels uplinking from

India were limited to not more than 26 per cent foreign equity or foreign holding of any kind. The MIB in 2005 also issued guidelines for downlinking of channels that were uplinked from outside India. According to these guidelines, it was mandatory for such broadcasters to have companies registered in India, so that they were tax-paying entities and did not repatriate money earned in India (Kohli–Khandekar 2010: 104).

Regarding the period 2000 onwards, the Union cabinet approved the new domestic satellite uplinking policy in July 2000. While this policy relaxed various constraints, it gave the government a tool with which to control the content of all the telecast channels. Firstly, this policy allowed any Indian firm (even if not a broadcaster/telecaster) to establish uplinking hubs or teleport facilities for hiring these out. Limitations on foreign equity were set at 49 per cent, the same as in the telecommunications sector. Secondly, these firms were permitted to uplink only those TV channels allowed by the government. In other words, all TV channels could uplink from India if they complied with the official code on content. Thirdly, all news agencies incorporated in India and accredited by the Union's Press Information Bureau, and fully owned by Indians were allowed to establish/use up linking. Thus, the government retained its control over the satellite television industry by mandating adherence to the programme code.

Speaking to the Parliament on this issue, the then Information and Broadcasting Minister Arun Jaitely remarked, 'this new policy will not only bring a large number of TV channels within the discipline of our broadcasting codes, but also generate substantial employment opportunities as India becomes an important hub, offering state-of-the-art facilities for up linking' (*Times of India* 2000d: 10). Therefore, even though this change in policy to allow private parties to uplink from India seemed like a liberal move, the interest of the state is fairly clear; to bring the satellite TV channels within the ambit of Indian jurisdiction, especially on matters pertaining to content.

Another major policy initiative was that the decision allowing DTH television had finally been taken by the government in November 2000. The opening up of this sector compounded the liberalization in the broadcasting sector resulting from a change in policy allowing up linking. The DTH story had been unfolding over the last decade, when STAR TV indicated its desire to enter this platform.

The government used delaying tactics and did not take a decision on DTH till 2000. According to an editorial in *The Economic Times*, 'DTH is an example of a technology which has been delayed by political manoeuvring. It should have been introduced three years ago in 1997, but the United Front government came out with a notification banning DTH broadcasts using the Ku band' (*The Economic Times* 2000f: 12).

The group of ministers examining DTH was headed by Home Minister L. K. Advani, a stalwart of the BJP. The DTH policy announced by the government had capped FDI at 20 per cent. The limit of the total foreign investment, including that of NRIs, OCBs and, FIIs, had been delineated as 49 per cent. The government further indicated that no individual company would own more than 20 per cent of the paid up capital of a DTH company, with a view to prevent monopoly (Sinha 21 November 2000: 13). Some media analysts felt that though long delayed, the DTH policy finally announced had some inconsistencies. For example, the condition that the licence was valid only for DTH broadcasting, and voice, data, fax, and internet would require specific and additional licences. Since 'convergence' was supposedly being encouraged by the state, this separation of licences struck an odd note. Another condition was that the DTH licensee would be bound to carry channels of Prasar Bharati on the 'most favourable financial terms offered to any other channel' (Nagaraj 3 November 2000: 5). N. Bhaskar Rao, chairman of the New Delhi based Centre for Media Studies, believed that while there might be technological convergence taking place, the DTH policy was in fact divergent (Rao 2001).

The Information Minister Sushma Swaraj finally announced the DTH guidelines in March 2001. The ban on the reception and distribution of television signals on Ku band was withdrawn. As mentioned earlier, the foreign equity holding had been capped at 49 per cent, while the FDI component had been capped at 20 per cent. An additional requirement was that the applicant company should have Indian management control, with majority representatives on the board, as well as the chief executive of the company being a resident Indian. The government has attempted to prevent media monopolies by stipulating that broadcasting companies and/or cable network companies shall not be eligible to collectively own more than 20 per cent of the total equity of the applicant company at any time during the licensed period. In parallel fashion, the applicant company should not have more than 20 per cent equity in a broadcasting and/or cable network company. There would be no restriction on the total number of DTH licences, as long as certain minimum requirements were met (*Times of India* 2001b: 1).

The MIB came down once more with a heavy hand against 'improper content' in 2001. The Ministry objected to semi-nudity on FTV, the French fashion channel being aired in India. Short of an outright ban, the FTV head had to himself assure the MIB that Indian sensibilities would be respected (Anand 2001c). However, in spite of these assurances, it would appear that the content on FTV currently was not significantly different from earlier.

The furore over FTV was followed by the controversy about surrogate advertising of alcoholic products. In fact, the MIB issued a note to the private channels in May 2001, stating that the advertisements shown on these channels were not in strict adherence to the programming and advertisement codes of the Cable Television Networks Act, 1995. Officials of some of the major private television channels felt that most channels were attempting to abide by the official codes, and that the government was out to curb their freedom (Anand 2001c).

The MIB attempted to draft the Broadcasting Services Regulation Bill in 2006. The media industry was also invited to give its comments on the draft bill. This draft proposed the Broadcast Regulatory Authority of India as an independent authority to oversee the development of broadcasting. It included carriage, content, spans broadcasting, cable, DTH, radio, satellite radio, and others. The draft versions of the bill suggested restrictions on cross media ownership, with a view to preventing monopolies. Other provisions included restriction of shareholding of a content provider in a broadcaster and vice versa, caps on the number of channels owned by a company, and public service obligations for all broadcasters. More importantly, it also proposed to repeal the Cable Networks Regulation Act of 1995 (Kohli–Khandekar 2010: 107). As of mid-2011, this Act was still in limbo, and was yet to be tabled in Parliament.

In 2007, the government floated a draft content code, partially in response to public interest litigations against obscene content, and debate about the low standards of news channels. In turn, the broadcast industry responded to this move by attempting to create its own guidelines under the Indian Broadcasting Federation. Thus, things moved in the direction of self-regulation (Kohli–Khandekar 2010: 108). The News Broadcasters Association (NBA) was formed in August 2008 with the aim of setting up and enforcing its broadcasting standards and ethics.

In 2008, the MIB issued guidelines for state and district monitoring committees for private television channels, regarding adherence to the norms outlined in the Programme and Advertising Codes outlined in the Cable Television Network Regulation Act of 1995. The televised coverage of the landmark Arushi case also demonstrated a new low in sensationalism of what was essentially a tragic murder, the victim being a minor. The ministry took exception to some of this coverage and had to caution certain offending channels such as India Live (Kumar 2010: 341). In early 2010, the Associated Chambers of Commerce and Industry in India made a demand for an independent regulator which would set out guidelines whereby the broadcaster was restrained from unprofessional or unethical broadcasts such as the media coverage of the 26/11 terrorist attacks in Mumbai, wherein the TV channels showed little self-restraint in the race for ratings. This was expressed in a note submitted to the MIB.

*　　*　　*

From the preceding sections it is apparent that there are intricate and myriad links between the state and the broadcast sector. While the state has radically changed its economic strategies in the last two decades, the case of the broadcasting sector is peculiarly complex. Various governments seemed to cherish DD and AIR for their propaganda value. Thus, the state appeared to be reluctant to grant these institutions autonomy, although some half-hearted attempts were made in this direction. Incidentally, these pro-active measures have been taken by non-Congress governments, most of which did not even enjoy an electoral majority. According to Karnik (2001) this may be because these governments felt it would be in their benefit to push through autonomy for the state broadcaster, as their governments, in all probability, would not last long. The changing nature of politics has also impinged upon the broadcasting sector, with the increased representation of other demand groups.

For most of the decade 1990–2000, the state managed to hold the reins of the national broadcaster. It is interesting that even when broadcast-related issues surfaced on the public agenda, they revolved around autonomy for Prasar Bharati, and not domestic competition in a terrestrial form. The argument was moot when fierce competition emerged in the form of satellite competition. Initially, the state appeared to be caught unprepared for this onslaught. However, it did not react by banning satellite TV as in other Asian nations. This may have been because this measure might have been unpopular in a democracy, which prides itself on its freedom of press. Alternatively Sinha (1998) suggests that this may have been a strategy pursued by the state as a plank in its economic liberalization measures which relied on opening up an autarkic economy and encouraging consumerism. Mishra (2001) is of the opinion that true to form, the state reacted in a paternalistic fashion. One may also argue that the safest option for the state was to do nothing initially, as satellite TV was only available to the high-income populace, in mostly urban locations. With the increasing popularity of satellite and cable TV, however, the picture changed.

The issue of foreign satellite channels was making an appearance and gathering momentum in the print media and even Parliament by the second half of the 1990s. While the old chestnuts about cultural imperialism and the threat to Indian values were re-examined, there was increased pressure on the state to react to the developments. It may be cynical to observe that the notification allowing the Prasar Bharati Act was made in 1997, resulting in formal autonomy for DD and AIR at this time, when de facto liberalization had already occurred in the industry. Since the government no longer monopolized the airwaves, it may as well make the Prasar Bharati autonomous, at least on paper.

There was a fresh impetus by the state to redraw the contours of its control by seeking to regulate the new entrants. The MIB tried to bring the satellite channels within the ambit of the government's regulations by seeking their adherence to a programming and advertising code. The draft Broadcasting Bill of 1997 also tried to make it mandatory for all satellite broadcasters to uplink from India so that they could be subject to stringent regulation. These terms proved unworkable and ultimately fell through. The various drafts of the Communications Bill of 2000 also reflected the state's concern with establishing control over an industry that was still regulated on the basis of an archaic piece of legislation.

It is a truism that liberalization is often accompanied by or followed by increased regulation. After all, deregulation often requires re-regulation. It is a mistake to perceive liberalization as a simplistic withdrawing on the part of the state. While the state may withdraw from some areas, it may actually advance in others. While the broadcasting sector has undergone a de facto liberalization in India in the last two decades, the state had initially responded by attempting a comprehensive regulation of both broadcasting and telecommunications under one bill. In the area of Information Technology, the Indian state has actually been proactive, encouraging foreign investment in this sector.

While Prasar Bharati was finally granted its autonomy in 1997, the dilution of the state's development agenda started much earlier. As indicated earlier, DD had begun to show increasing amounts of entertainment as compared to educational programming over its national and regional networks. However, this may also be viewed as a survival tactic on the part of the state. Increased competition meant that DD had to be concerned about audiences, revenues, and ratings. The dilution of its public broadcasting mandate, especially the commercialization of DD2 (DD Metro), are a direct result of DD's battle to keep its market share.

The overall picture that emerges is that the Indian state, for the first part of the decade 1990–2000, responded to developments in the broadcasting sector by permitting global competition more by default than by design. Local enterprise in the shape of the cable industry was the subject of regulation by 1994–5. The second half of the 1990s witnessed much stronger competition for the national broadcaster, which had 'glocal' dimensions. The state's reaction to its dilution in control has been apparent in the area of regulation.

In studying the state's response to changes in the broadcasting sector in India in the last two decades, several factors have been taken into account. These include (but are not limited to) the actions of various broadcasters—transnational, national, and local—and the policy statements and replies to parliamentary questions emanating from the Ministry of Information and Broadcasting. Prasar Bharati and the role of DD have been explored in depth.

To sum up, while the Congress government for the period 1991–6 introduced widespread economic liberalizing measures, this did not spill over into the broadcasting sector. Even though the state in this period is characterized as one of command polity in a democratic regime, or one of relative autonomy, no direct measures encouraging domestic competition or autonomy for DD were undertaken. However, it has been argued elsewhere that inaction can also be interpreted as a policy statement on the part of the state. Thus, one may argue that a strong state could afford to disregard the whole issue of autonomy for DD. Secondly, even though the state did not actively encourage liberalization in broadcasting, it did not discourage it by imposing an outright ban on satellite television either.

Given the democratic ethos of the country, the option of banning satellite television would have been an unpopular one. The paternalistic nature of the state is also indicated by the fact that the argument for allowing transnational and local television was couched in language that stressed that a variety of information sources were in the citizen's interest. It is interesting that the state chose to ignore the issue of satellite television while it had a small viewership. As the viewership increased and concerns about national sovereignty and cultural imperialism began surfacing, the state tried to bring satellite television under its sphere of control. This control was exercised through the distribution mechanism for satellite television under the rubric of the Cable Television Regulation Act. Specifically, satellite television was to be brought under the state's control with the requirement that it adhere to the programming and advertising code as stipulated in the Act.

The subsequent governments that came to power at the Centre during 1996–2001 were all non-Congress coalitions, representing diverse groups. They may be characterized as those of demand polity in a democratic regime. In addition, the state during this period may be considered to be constrained, rather than autonomous. Given its constraints, including the rise of religion-related and coalition politics, the state's actions in the broadcasting sphere are harder to interpret for this period. The increasing salience of broadcasting related issues in various forums such as the print media and Parliament may have necessitated some accommodation on the part of a state exhibiting the characteristics of a demand polity. Thus, the Prasar Bharati Bill was finally notified, and the Broadcasting Bill was introduced in Parliament in 1997.

While these may seem to be far reaching changes, in reality, the state continued to exercise its authority in various ways. The 'autonomy' of Prasar Bharati has been considered to be a sham as it still has links at many levels to the MIB. Thus, the Central Government has been fairly successful at stifling any real independence on the part of DD. The Broadcasting Bill of 1997 also has provisions where the Central Government can step in and override the proposed broadcasting regulatory authority in the interest of the security of the state, or other specified conditions. Thus, the presence of the state looms large, even in this proposed piece of legislation.

While the provisions of the Broadcasting Bill (1997) had already been rendered obsolete by the fast pace of technological change, the Communications Draft Bill of 2000 had been under consideration. What is evident is that an independent regulatory authority for broadcasting has still not come into existence in the year 2011. The state continues to perform this important function. Interestingly, the state has also not permitted domestic terrestrial competition. Thus, the state in the shape of the national broadcaster continues to monopolize audiences in rural areas, which have yet to be substantially penetrated by cable. Since approximately 60 per cent of the population still resides in villages, the government still has clout in the countryside, which adds up to access to substantial vote-banks.

In examining the broadcasting policies with respect to various Congress lead governments during 2000–10, one has to first examine the changing pattern of the Congress party vis-à-vis elections. While the Congress garnered 70 per cent of the seats in the first Lok Sabha in 1952–7, it only managed to muster 27.7 per cent of the seats in the 14th Lok Sabha in 2004–9. This implies that the government was constrained by coalition politics, rather than being autonomous. The trend in this decade has reflected the decline of power of the Central Government and the emergence of a more federal power structure (Thomas 2010: 72). Regional and caste-based politics have continued to be important.

In studying the link between politics and broadcasting, it is necessary to also examine the role of private broadcasters such as Sun TV. This is especially important in the light of the rise of regional political parties and their links to media houses. The regional Tamil political party, the Dravida Munnettra Kazhagam (DMK), is closely linked to the Sun TV network. While this party had historical links with the film industry, the DMK continues to enjoy the support of the Sun TV network. The erstwhile Chief Minister of the state, M. Karunanidhi, is closely related to the Maran family, who established this network in 1993.

In fact, Dayanidhi Maran was the former Union Communications Minister in the United Progressive Alliance (UPA). During his tenure, the Sun network expanded its operations substantially and he has been accused of giving preferential treatment to the Sun network. For example, it has been suggested that he used his position to coerce the Tatas into giving Sun TV a stake in their Tata-Sky DTH operations. Today, the Sun network is the dominant player in South India, integrated across the segments of cable and satellite television, it is a major multi system operator (MSO), a player in FM radio, as well as having interests in the press including the Tamil daily *Dinakaran* (Thomas 2010: 74). It is apparent that the Sun network's support is required for the DMK's electoral success. In terms of policy formulation, the rise of regional parties and their links to media groups implies that policies are being affected in a diverse manner, as compared to the earlier period when the Congress party in power had a large electoral majority.

The conclusions arrived at and the implications of this study are the subject matter of the next chapter.

NOTES

1. The control measures employed by the state are discussed at length later in the chapter.
2. The imposition of the Emergency during 1975–7, imposed by the Indira Gandhi Congress government implied a period of widespread suspension of civil liberties and unparalleled restrictions on the freedom of the press.
3. Red Lion Broadcasting Co. versus FCC, 395 U.S. 367 (1969).

4. The historical reasons for nationalism imposed from above include the colonial top-heavy structures of governance, the centralization of authority during this period, and the attempt to unite peoples who were diverse ethnically, culturally, linguistically, and in terms of religion.

5. The complexity of the Indian state is evident from the following extract from Rudolph and Rudolph (1987): 'like Hindu conceptions of the divine, the state in India is polymorphous, a creature of manifold forms and orientations. One is the third actor whose scale and power contribute to the marginality of class politics. Another is a liberal or citizens' state, a juridical body whose legislative reach is limited by a written constitution, judicial review, and fundamental rights. Still another is a capitalist state that guards the boundaries of the mixed economy by protecting the rights and promoting the interests of property in agriculture, commerce, and industry. Finally, a socialist state is concerned to use public power to eradicate poverty and privilege, and tame private power. Which combination prevails in a particular historical setting is a matter for inquiry' (1987: 400–401).

6. The 'licence raj' implies the pre-liberalization period when the industrial licensing regime existed.

7. The BJP led RathYatras were attempts at political rallying by politicians seated on chariots. These chariot led journeys tried to invoke the imagery of the triumphal marches of the Hindu gods Ram and Krishna from the epics Ramayana and Mahabharata. These epics were very popular on DD when they were aired in the late eighties.

CONCLUSION

This study concludes by considering the contribution made to the larger debate about global/local dimensions of television, and the role of the state in this regard. More specifically, the study has focused on India. The major findings are highlighted and the interpretations summarized. The processes of globalization, which are multi-dimensional and exist in social, political, economic, and cultural spheres, have been linked to privatization, liberalization, and deregulation issues. The role of the state has been examined at length.

Worldwide, there has been a move towards privatization and liberalization in telecommunications, as well as in broadcasting. It has been an interesting exercise to examine whether the effects of these reform processes would lead to global integration and local resurgence, with a concomitant loss of authority for the nation-state. In India, the state appears to be accommodating the needs of international and local players in a fashion so that its own interests are met in the short-run.

Regarding case studies, Stake (1994) is of the opinion that the epistemological question that needs to be answered is: what can be learned from a single case? In answering this question, some lessons may be learned which are specific to the Indian context, while other generalizations can be made which have applications elsewhere. It is hoped that this particular study has shed some light on the general questions posed here.

It would appear that adopting Rosenau's global/local theoretical framework to study developments in the Indian television industry in the last decade has borne fruit. Since this hitherto closed industry has been blasted open to transnational forces, there has also been a germination of private domestic broadcasting. While the state's monopoly over electronic means of communication has broken down in the last two decades, a cacophony of new voices has emerged in television. The state's direct control over its mouthpiece Doordarshan (DD) has also been impacted with the Prasar Bharati being granted autonomy in 1997. Thus, the hypothesis that control/authority of the state has in some sense been relocated with loci emerging at the global and local levels, does appear to bear support.

The devolution of authority and control of the state has been examined quantitatively in terms of advertising revenues, ownership, and content, and also qualitatively in terms of content. There are clear indications that DD has been fighting a losing battle in terms of revenues and audience share. The development agenda of educational programming has also been watered down. However, DD is still a force to reckon with, especially for audiences who do not subscribe to cable or DTH. The satellite and cable industry has burgeoned from zero in 1990 to the lion's share of revenues in the last decade. It would definitely seem that DD's hold over the audiences has waned. Ultimately, content is of supreme importance, and DD seems to be losing its grip by failing to air programs that have a magnetic appeal, as compared to the private broadcasters.

The role of the state has also been examined in its wider context as a policy making body and an entity in its own right. The examination of the state has been theoretically informed with literature that concentrates on the political economy of the state. The policy statements emanating from the Ministry of Information and Broadcasting (MIB) have been examined with a view to understand the behaviour of the state with respect to broadcasting. While the indexes used as indicators of control and authority, such as advertising revenues, have indicated a decrease for the national broadcaster, the role of the state with respect to regulation tells a different story. At every turn, successive governments have opposed the liberalization of the broadcasting sector. Domestic private terrestrial competition was never allowed as an alternative to DD. The state, thus, monopolized the airwaves right up to the 1990s. Even when competition emerged in the form of satellite competition, the state did nothing to encourage this de facto competition. In fact, various drafts of the Broadcasting Bill (1997) and the Convergence Bill (2001), as well as the Draft Broadcasting Regulation Bill (2007) have indications that the government wished to control private broadcasters via adherence to a government-stipulated code for content, as well as seeking to control the satellite broadcasters by restrictions on uplinking, downlinking, private FM Radio, and so on.

Any analysis of the role of the state in India in the last two decades, particularly with respect to policies in a particular sector, is fraught with difficulties. As indicated in the earlier chapter, the Indian state is polymorphic in character. The last two decades have also seen the rapid turnover of governments, and the rise in the salience of regional and caste factors in the political economy of the state. These factors add fresh layers of complexity to the analysis of the role of the state with respect to broadcasting.

With this caveat in mind, however, it would appear that an analysis of the role of the state in India with respect to broadcasting does not indicate a straightforward withering away of the state under the attack of global/local forces. While it is certainly true that the state's formal control over DD has been reduced with the granting of autonomy to Prasar Bharati, as indicated in the previous chapter, informal and subterranean methods of control linger on. The de facto liberalization of television witnessed in the last two decades may have been allowed by the state as part of the general liberalization allowed in the economy in the early 1990s. While the liberalization of the economy might have been a contributory reason to the liberalization of television in the last two decades, the reasons for permitting satellite television were couched in the language of 'public interest', indicating a paternalistic state. Although the state did not encourage satellite television, it did not actively discourage it either, by issuing an outright ban. In other words, it may have been in the best interests of the state not to oppose competition to the national broadcaster, in order to send the right signals to an economy opening up and encouraging foreign investment and consumerism. Firstly, this may be because viable competition first emerged in the form of transnational players, and not as domestic enterprise. Secondly, satellite television had a very small viewership when it came into India, and thus, it was easy for the state to ignore its existence in the early phase.

The state does not appear to have been impotent in the face of transnational and local broadcasting. Its actions in the area of regulation have already been analysed. It would appear that the behaviour of the Indian state in this period with respect to broadcasting broadly follows the 'state as a third actor' line of reasoning. In other words, the state has attempted to safeguard its own interests in the face of some reduction in its sphere of control. This has been perceived via the ministry's informal methods of control of DD in a post-autonomy Prasar Bharati scenario, as well as through the regulatory process.

During the period 1991–6, when a Congress government was in power at the Centre, the state appeared to have been relatively autonomous, as is indicated by the fact that it could push through sweeping liberalization measures on the economic front. This period can be characterized as one of command polity, judging by the state's actions. During the same period, the government did not usher in any reforms in the realm of broadcasting. Thus it seems to be in the state's short term interest to continue to hold the reins of DD and not grant it any autonomy, thereby safeguarding its interests.

In the period 1997 onwards, the governments that came to power at the Center were non-Congress governments. The period that followed was one of hung parliaments and coalition governments, till about 2004. The state during this period can be characterized as one of demand polity, and it was constrained. Since the state was one of demand polity, some amount of liberalization in the broadcasting sphere may have been permitted as an accommodation of interests within the state. The whole political structure has become less centralized in the last two decades, with the rise of regional, confessional, and caste based politics. While the Prasar Bharati Act was finally passed in this period, and the Broadcasting Bill was introduced, it is debatable how far reaching these changes are. Notwithstanding these measures, the state still exerts control over an 'autonomous' DD via the MIB. The state also exercises control over the whole broadcasting and cable sector, as it is still the regulator in the absence of an independent regulatory authority. Although a Congress-led government has been in power from 2004 onwards, it has still been constrained by coalition politics, and small electoral margins.

In a nutshell:

(1) Regarding the framework adapted from Rosenau in this study, authority or control appears to have been relocated away from the national, toward the local and global levels. The indicators of ownership, advertising revenue, and content suggest this. However, the indicator of regulation tells a different story.

(2) This relocation has occurred in a manner in which there are complex interactions and accommodations between global and local levels.

(3) The state has suffered a loss of control as measured by changes in ownership, advertising revenues, and content. However, in the area of regulation and policy-making, it is evident that the state has not 'withered away'.

(4) Throughout the last two decades, the Indian state has acted in a defensive manner, trying to minimize its losses. This behaviour leads one to categorize the state in this period as the 'third actor' with consolidation interests of its own. However, the Indian state has also continued to display elements of paternalism in the last decade.

(5) This leads to the next question—what is the self-interest of the state? One obvious answer would be survival. Even though self-interest motivates the state, it is constrained by the democratic process and the exigencies of electoral politics. These constraints, and the nature of the demand polity in the last decade, have implied that the state has not undertaken any repressive measures in this period (or could not undertake such measures even if it wanted to). Thus, the state appears to be neither malevolent, nor wholly benevolent, as it has tried to ensure its own survival.

(6) Another response by the state to the devolution of control to global and local levels, in terms of the emergence of satellite

and cable television, has been that DD itself introduced regional and international channels. This may tie in with a period which witnessed the growing regionalization of politics, and the decentralization of governance.

In conclusion, in answer to the questions posed here, there has been a loss of control suffered by the state, as this control has been relocated to the global and local levels in the realm of broadcasting. However, the state has not witnessed a straightforward 'withering away'. It has been active in the sphere of regulation and policy-making, and has done so in a manner such that its own needs are accommodated, at least in the short run. As such, the straightforward dichotomy between the state and the market, often assumed, does not apply to the case under consideration here. The state is still setting the parameters of the discussion in the broadcasting industry, as the authority for regulation still resides with the state. Even though one cannot say that the liberalization that has occurred in broadcasting has occurred at the behest of the state, the state has responded to exogenous changes by redrawing the contours of its control. In all, one can say that the state in India has been a resilient one.

IMPLICATIONS

This study sheds light on the manner in which globalization in communications is occurring in the context of a particular country. It also examines the emergence of cultural hybrids, at the junction of the global and local planes, in the field of television. Since the electronic media are intimately associated with the phenomena of globalization, in the sense that they have been considered to be both a cause as well as a consequence of globalization, a better understanding of the global processes at work with regard to broadcast media in a particular context and country may shed some light on the nature of globalization itself.

At a lower level of generality, this study has the implications of understanding communications processes at global, national, and local levels, from the viewpoint of a developing country. The issues that emerge from this study could be used to understand similar occurrences in developing countries elsewhere in the globe. For example, this study contributes to debates currently taking place within many developing countries regarding the globalization of media, cultural imperialism, and cultural resurgence. One of the findings to emerge from this study is that a one-way inflow of globalization from developed countries to developing countries is not taking place, at least not in the context of India. What is occurring is 'glocalization', in the sense that complex accommodations are taking place between global and local entities, so that they are merging and blending in the realms of economics, culture, politics, and others.

More specifically, it is hoped that this research project has shed some light on television in South Asia. Since India is a regional leader in this area, and has many similarities with other countries in South Asia in terms of its societal as well as broadcasting structure, understanding the Indian experience has ripple effects in the rest of the region. Indian television channels are also popular across South Asia. The Indian broadcasting sector today, is one of the most liberalized in South Asia, and developments in this country may outline the shape of things to come in other South Asian countries with less liberalized media environments.

One of the implications of the manner in which liberalization has occurred in the Indian television industry is that it has helped usher in a consumerist era. Again, advertising has utilized 'glocal' strategies, uniting consumer products marketed by multi-national corporations, with culturally appropriate adaptations and selling strategies. The 'glocal' mantra has paid dividends for MNCs in the Indian context.

Along with the increased inflow, India has also seen an outflow of television programming in this period. This outflow has stepped up in tempo in the last decade. In fact, India seems to be developing as a regional media hub. This is true across the spectrum of Indian films, the availability of television programming produced in India, and computer software. This seems contrary to any simplistic notions of one-way flow and cultural imperialism.

Television content has also been impacted by competition with entities that are run on purely commercial lines. A host of new genres such as game-shows, talk shows, and other reality formats have made their presence felt. Qualitatively speaking, even the roles played by female protagonists have undergone revision in this period. Unfortunately, women have not been portrayed in a more emancipated fashion on many satellite television programs in the last decade. Notions of public service broadcasting have also been re-examined with the emergence of commercial imperatives in the last decade.

The quantum jump in broadcasting and in telecommunications in India in the last two decades has been one of the most visible effects of liberalization in these two areas. This has been labeled a 'communication revolution' by Singhal and Rogers (2001). In the broadcasting sector, this increase in sheer volume of television programming has been portrayed as an 'entertainment explosion', as well as an 'information explosion'. Again, the implications are that the audience has a wider range of voices on the basis of which it can form its opinions. The formation of public opinion is of vital importance in a democracy.

The Indian case also provides a good opportunity to understand the functioning of the state, in the light of global/local processes. In addition, this study sheds light on the state's role with respect to communications policy formulation and implementation, in the context of a developing country. In India, the study of the role of the state in the last two decades has highlighted the polymorphic and complex nature of this entity. It is possible that the Indian state which has become (by some accounts) less monolithic and more diverse in the last decade, may have found it inevitable that a plurality of voices has emerged in the sphere of broadcasting.

The state in India has played a central role in the development of the broadcasting and the telecommunications sector. Critical scholars working in the field of communications have argued that the state and corporate uses of communications have, in general, reduced the array of social uses of communications (Nordenstreng and Schiller 1993). It has also been suggested that broadcasting policy in India has emphasized state control and the commercialization of the audiences, through advertising supported programming (Melkote 1991). This accusation had been made even prior to the appearance of satellite television and the mad scramble for ratings and audiences thereafter. Although the state adopted a paternalistic role with respect to broadcasting policy (as is evident in the emphasis on development programmes), this model of broadcast regulation and these policy choices made by the state actually inhibited a more decentralized, participatory, and grass-roots growth of broadcasting in India. An example of this is the constraint on community radio.

With regard to communications policy formation, the sub-theme of development is another factor, which is of concern to many developing countries. The level of interpersonal communication and the extent of mass communication within a society are important factors in a democratic society's developmental processes. India has witnessed wide-ranging changes in both these areas in the last decade. This process of reform in communications could have important consequences for development. The Indian case is particularly fascinating, as it is the world's most populous democracy, and developmental programming was the basis of growth of broadcasting in post-Independence India. What most policy makers in India have generally assumed, especially with respect to regulation, is that media have strong effects. Indeed, this may not be overtly expressed; rather, it is endogenous to many of the policies formulated for the broadcasting sector. This is hardly surprising, as the government was preoccupied with developmental strategies at the time India gained independence. Much of the early literature on communications and development has been centred on notions of strong media effects, or media as the 'magic bullet' which would act as a catalyst to development.

The road to reform of electronic communications in India has had to negotiate the difficult terrain between reaping the developmental benefits of liberalization of communications on the one hand, and coping with the problems of commercialism on the other. As the linkages between globalization, mass media, telecommunications, and the role of the state become better understood, it is important to craft policies that help in bringing about development (Samarajiva and Shields 1990; Melkote 1991; Saunders, Warford, and Wellenius 1994; Hettne 1995; Servaes 1997). Thus, by demonstrating the political and economic factors that underlie the policy-making process, this study highlights some of the conditions under which a change in policy can come about, and be successfully implemented.

Another implication of this study concerns the issue of regulation. By comprehensively studying the processes of policy formulation in television, the attempt is made to throw light on the regulation of this area. As touched upon earlier, an incredibly diverse country like

India requires a special recipe for regulation of broadcasting and cable. Regulators have to make allowances for different religions, castes, languages, and other aspects of diversity. Concerns with development and the trade-off between education and entertainment also have to be factored into the regulatory structure. Regulatory policies for the communications sector have to be viewed against the backdrop of liberalization and de-regulation in the Indian economy. The rapid rate of technological change and convergence in the electronic industries has added another dimension that regulators have to take into account.

The policy which has evolved in India in recent years with respect to broadcasting, has been a kind of ad-hoc response to the exogenous push of factors such as satellite-delivered programming from STAR TV and Zee TV. Interestingly, while the frontiers of the state are being rolled back in Europe and elsewhere, and the rash of privatization seems to be spreading, the media mandarins in India had opted for regulation of broadcasting in India along the lines of a public service broadcaster, rather than outright privatization. The Prasar Bharati Bill, which established an autonomous body for broadcasting, aimed to free this sector from the direct control of the state. However, as established in preceding sections, it may take some time before this new organizational structure becomes truly independent, since the culture of sycophancy and of acting as a mouthpiece for the central government is still well entrenched in the offices of DD.

Changes in the regulation of telecommunications, and policies pertaining to new technologies in India have also occurred, echoing changes in broadcasting in the nineties. It seems as if the whole communications environment has undergone an upheaval in recent years. The exogenous pressures for liberalizing India's economy have come from agencies like the World Bank and the International Monetary Fund (Kumar 1995). The telecommunications sector has been liberalized, and basic as well as value added phone services have been thrown open to international competition. Metropolises in India today are linked up via the latest wireless technology. Foreign investors with interests in Indian telecommunications services have included global players such as AT&T, US West, Bellsouth, Motorola, Singapore Telecommunications International, France Telecom International, and others (Mody 1995). Notwithstanding these changes in India's telecommunications structure, Mody (1995) has argued that the state in India has actually consolidated its position through the liberalization of this sector in India. According to Mody (1995), decisions about ownership of telecommunications flow from national and international accommodations between members of the ruling triple alliance of state, national capital, and foreign capital. In her opinion, the state is a central actor with consolidation interests of its own.

Thus, the implications of a dominant state combined with some amount of liberalization in broadcasting and telecommunications have been that the public sphere[1] has been slowly emerging in the last two decades. Is the concept of a public sphere in India valid and viable today? Robbins (1993), in his examination of the public sphere, asserts that the concept is so 'hazy, idealized, and distant from the actual people, places and institutions around us, that it can easily serve purposes that are anything but democratic' (Robbins 1993: xii). The concept of the public sphere holds special importance for India, as it is the world's most populous democracy. Apart from the 'tea shops' which are the equivalent of Habermas' cafes, the public sphere in India would mainly include the print and broadcast media, since large numbers of people have access to them, although the new media are gaining in popularity. With convergence and exponential growth in mobiles, this may change in the near future.

DD still occupies a salient position, since it has a vast geographical coverage and is available to the majority of the population, especially in the rural areas. The implications of a public sphere circumscribed by a dominant state for the formation of public opinion are obvious. However, the diminishing popularity of DD vis-à-vis the satellite channels means the public sphere has seen some re-vitalization in the last decade. Again, this is a debatable point, given the profit motive of the private players. However, the sheer number of news channels available over cable and satellite suggest that there is scope for various viewpoints.

In the sphere of regulation, a single regulatory body to regulate broadcasting and telecommunications could take advantage of synergies between the two sectors. In this era of technological convergence, where cable operators are providing access to the Internet and Internet telephony has become a reality in urban India, it stands to reason that regulation should also exhibit convergence. If the

American model inspires one, then it is worthwhile to note that the Federal Communications Commission (FCC) is an independent regulatory commission, which combines two bureaucracies. These broadly relate to broadcasting and telephony. In fact, this Commission has bureaus which cover radio, television, cable, cellular telephony, satellites, conventional telephony, and amateur radio operators. Interestingly, the FCC does not regulate the Internet (Krattenmake 1998). India could study this model of regulation, and make suitable adaptations to take into account its own experience and problems. Instead of a situation where the 'left hand does not know what the right hand is doing', the regulatory body could actually anticipate developments in electronic communications across the spectrum.

While this study has concentrated on political and economic aspects of television liberalization and globalization in the Indian context, many interesting questions have emerged which are deserving of study. One major area of future research could be into media effects in the context of satellite television as compared to the national broadcaster, in the subcontinent. Thus, a better understanding of the reception of television, combined with fresh insights into the political economy of the state in the arena of broadcasting, could provide a more complete picture of the liberalization that has occurred in the electronic media.

As development related issues are still on the government's agenda, studies of media-effects of particular programmes could indicate which messages are being effectively communicated. The whole area of entertainment-education would have to be explored in the context of satellite channels. This may prove to be an effective communication strategy for incorporating developmental objectives. In the light of films such as the Bollywood film *Taare Zameen Par* (released in 2007), which was both a critical and commercial success and delivered a socially relevant message, this does not seem so far-fetched.

Another area of interest is the links between the private satellite channels and the state. Is the state extending/continuing its control of the broadcasting sector through establishing links with the private broadcasters? In other words, is liberalization only one face of the coin, while the reverse side is the state exerting its authority in less visible means through the patronage of particular private broadcasters? The example of Sun TV and the Maran family, and Jaya TV and

Jayalalitha in the state of Tamil Nadu, are good examples of the nexus between politics and private broadcasters. This is an interesting issue, when state controlled broadcasters have given ground to private broadcasters to run along commercial lines. These are all directions for future research in the vibrant broadcasting sector of the most populous democracy in the world.

NOTE

1. For a detailed discussion on the concept of public sphere see Jurgen Habermas (1989).

BIBLIOGRAPHY

Abu Shair, O. 1997. *Privatization and Development*, St. Martin's Press: New York.

Aggarwal, A. 1995. 'Choking on its Own Growth', *India Today*, August.

Ahluwalia, K. 2001. Chief of Operations, *TARA Punjabi*, Interviewed by author, NOIDA.

Aiyer, S. 2000. 'Na is par na us par, phocus rahega sirf jaat-paat par', *The Economic Times*, 14 July, p. 1.

Ali, O. and Gunaratne, S. 2000. 'Pakistan', in S. Gunaratne (ed.) *Handbook of the Media in Asia*, Sage: New Delhi.

Altheide, D. 1996. *Qualitative Media Analysis*, Sage: Thousand Oaks.

Altschull, J. 1995. *Agents of Power: The Media and Public Policy*, Longman: White Plains, New York.

Anand, S. 2000. 'Now Admen Chase Cablewallah'. *The Economic Times*, 13 October, p. 5.

———. 2001a. 'Hindujas Launching 24-hour Digital Free-to-air Channel', *The Economic Times*, 4 April, p. 9.

———. 2001b. 'ZEE Decides to Launch Digital Pay Channels from June 1', *The Economic Times*, 3 May, p.15.

———. 2001c. 'Come off Naughty and Surrogate Ads, Ministry Warns Channels', *The Economic Times*, 7 May, p. 6.

Anderson, B. 1983. *Imagined Communities*, Verso: London.

Appadurai, A. 1990. 'Disjuncture and Difference in the Global Cultural Economy', in M. Featherstone (ed.) *Global Culture: Nationalism, Globalization and Modernity*, Sage: London.

Applebaum, R. and Henderson, J. 1992. *States and Development in the Asian Pacific Rim*, Sage: Newbury Park.

Arathoon, M. 2000. 'Golden M to Storm TV to Catch a Few Eyeballs', *The Economic Times*, 3 April, p. 20.

Bagdikian, B. 1992. *The Media Monopoly*, Beacon Press: Boston.

Bakshi, R. 2001. Manager Corporate Communications, Zee television. Interviewed by author, Delhi.

Bamzai, K. 2000a. 'Sangh Divided on DD', *The Indian Express*, The Express Magazine, 16 April, p. 4.

———. 2000b. 'Enabled for Cable', *The Times of India*, 3 June, p. 12.

———. 2000c. 'Not Ready to Fade out', *The Times of India*, Sunday Review, 22 October, p. 3.

———. 2001. 'Keeping Watch on the Graveyard Shift', *The Times of India*, 27 May, p. 15.

Bannerjee, P. 2001. 'There's No Room for Rajani Today', *The Times of India*, 6 May, p. 13.

Barber, B. 1992. 'Jihad vs. McWorld', *The Atlantic*. vol. 269, no. 3.

Bardhan, P. 1984. *The Political Economy of Development in India*, Basil Blackwell: Oxford.

Barker, C. 1997. *Global Television: An Introduction*, Blackwell: Oxford, UK.

Beck, U. 1994. 'The Reinvention of Politics: Towards a Theory of Reflexive Modernization', in U. Beck, A. Giddens, and S. Lash, *Reflexive Modernization: Politics, Tradition and Aesthetics in the Modern Social Order*, Stanford University Press: Stanford, California.

Besancon, L. and Kelly, T. 1997. 'Telecom Privatizations: The New Realism'. Available at http://www.itu.int/ti/papers/privatisation/gtbart.htm.

Bettig, R. 1996. *Copywriting Culture*, Random House: New York.

Beynon, J. and Dunkerley, D. (eds) 2000. *Globalization: The Reader*, The Athlone Press: Random House.

Bhabha, H. (ed.) 1990. *Nation and Narration*, Routledge: London.

Bhagwati, J. 1993. *India in Transition: Freeing the Economy*, Clarendon Press: Oxford.

Bhandari, M. 2000. 'The Media Magic, 2000', *The Economic Times*, Investors Guide, 5 June, p. 5.

Bhardwaj, N. 2000. 'Asia, Food Retailing Grows with a Local Touch', *The Times of India*, 15 November, p. 17.

Bhaskar Rao, N. 2001. Director, Center for Media Studies. Interviewed by the author, Delhi.

Bhatia, S. 2000. 'From KFC to KBC, Wooing and Winning of Middle India', *The Times of India*, 5 September, p. 14.

Bhuiyan, S. and Gunaratne, S. 2000. 'Bangladesh', in S. Gunaratne (ed.) *Handbook of the Media in Asia*, Sage: New Delhi.

Biersteker, T. 1992. 'The "Triumph" of Neoclassical Economics in the Developing World: Policy Convergence and the Bases of Governance in the International Economic Order', in J. Rosenau and E. Czempiel (eds) *Governance without Government: Order and Change in World Politics*, Cambridge University Press: New York.

Bird, J., Barry Curtis, Tim Putnam, George Robertson, and Lisa Tickner (eds) 1993. *Mapping the Futures: Local Cultures, Global Change*, Routeledge: London.

Boyer, R. and Daniel, D. (eds) 1996. *States against Markets: The Limits of Globalization*, Routledge: London.

Brahmankar, S. and Gupta, T. 2000. 'Rural India: Market on Fast Track?', in *The Economic Times*, 13 July, p. 14.

Business India. 1999. Editorial. 'Watching the Waves', 4–17 October, p. 9.

Buzan, B. and Segal, G. 1996. 'The Rise of 'lite' Power: A Strategy for the Postmodern States', *World Policy Journal*, vol. 13, no. 3, Fall, pp. 1–10.

Candland, C. 1997. 'Congress Decline and Party Pluralism in India', in *Journal of International Affairs*, vol. 51, no. 1, Summer, pp. 19–35.

Cerny, P. 1990. *The Changing Architecture of Politics: Structure, Agency and the Future of the State*, Sage: London.

———. 1995. 'Globalization and the Changing Logic of Collective Action', *International Organizations*, vol. 34, no. 2.

Chakravarti, P. 2001. Manager, New Delhi Television. Interviewed by author, Delhi.

Chandrasekhar, S. 2001. Previous Director, Audience Research Unit, Prasar Bharati. Interviewed by author, Delhi.

Chase-Dunn, C. 1994. 'Technology and the Logic of World Systems', in R. Palan and B. Gills (eds), *Transcending the State-Global Divide: A Neo-Structuralist Agenda in International Relations*, Lynne Reinner: Boulder.

Chasia, H. 1997. FCC's Annual Symposium, 'New Priorities and Future Directions: Liberalization and Competition in Telecommunications, the Role of the ITU'. Available at http://www.itu.int/chasia/speeches/1997/fccspe.htm.

Chatterjee, M. 2001. 'STAR Turns 10, Faces Reality', *The Times of India*, 22 April, p. 16.

Chatterjee, P. 1993. *The Nation and its Fragments: Colonial and Postcolonial Histories*, Princeton University Press.

———. 1997. *State and Politics in India*, Oxford University Press: New Delhi.

274   *Bibliography*

Chatterjee, P. 1999. *The Partha Chatterjee Omnibus*, Oxford University Press: New Delhi.

———. 2010. *Empire and Nation: Selected Essays*, Columbia University Press: New York.

Chaterjee, S. 2000. 'Spectranet's Net-on-cable from Sept 1', *The Times of India*, 26 August, p. 15.

Chatterji, P. C. 1991. *Broadcasting in India*.

Chauhan, C. 2009. '38 Per cent Indians are Poor: Report', *The Hindustan Times*, 20 August.

Chen, A. and Choudhury, A. 1991. 'Asia and the Pacific', in J. C. Merrill (ed.) *Global Journalism*, Longman: New York.

Chopra, R. 2000. 'Now media companies hit primary market', in *The Economic Times*, 19 October, p. 5.

Comor, E. (ed.) 1994. *The Global Political Economy of Communication*, Macmillan: Basingstoke.

Conlon, C. 2000. 'Bhutan', in S. Gunaratne (ed.) *Handbook of the Media in Asia*, Sage: New Delhi.

Cooper, T. 1989. 'Introduction', in T. Cooper, C. Christians, F. Plude, and R. White (eds) *Communication Ethics and Global Change*, Longman: New York.

Cox, R. 1992. 'Towards a Post-hegemonic Conceptualization of World Order: Reflections on the Relevancy of Ibn Khaldun', in J. Rosenau and E. Czempiel (eds) *Governance without Government: Order and Change in World Politics*. Cambridge University Press: New York.

Crook, C. 1997. 'India's Economy, Work in Progress', *The Economist*, 22 February.

Czarniawska, B. 1998. *A Narrative Approach to Organization Studies*, Sage: Thousand Oaks.

Das, A. 1999. 'Now You See Them, Now You Don't', *The Indian Express*, The Express Magazine, 5 December, p. 1.

Dasgupta, K. 2000. 'The New Gold Rush; Q&A with Kunal Dasgupta', *The Times of India*, 5 September, p. 14.

Dasgupta, R. 2000. 'McConverti: Big Mac Bows to Indian Taste Yet Again', *The Economic Times*, 8 September, p. 1.

Davies, S. 1995. 'The 53 Country Question'. *Multichannel News International*, May.

Denzin, N. and Lincoln, Y. 1994. 'Introduction: Entering the Field of Qualitative Research', in N. Denzin and Y. Lincoln (eds) *Handbook of Qualitative Research*. Sage: Thousand Oaks.

Denzin, N. and Lincoln, Y. 1998. *Strategies of Qualitative Inquiry*, Sage: Thousand Oaks.

Desai, M. 1977. *Communication Policies in India*, Unesco Publications: Belgium.

Desai, S. 2000. 'Filmi Chakkar', *The Economic Times*, Brand Equity, 21–7 June, p. 2.

Deutsch, K. 1966. *The Nerves of Government: Models of Political Communication and Control*, Free Press: New York.

Dewey, J. 1934. *Art as Experience*. Penguin: New York.

Dey, S. 2000a. 'Zee to Launch Chakra Channel in US, Europe', *The Economic Times*, 30 October, p. 18.

———. 2000b. 'Channels Scramble to Line up KBC Look Alikes', *The Economic Times*, 26 December, p. 11.

Dikshit, S. 2000. 'Civil Servants Eyeing Slots in Communications Panel', *The Hindu*, 23 October, p. 11.

Dilipkumar, R. 2010. 'Innovations Set to Power DTH', *The Asian Age*, 17 May, p. 11.

Dirlik, A. 1996. 'The Global in the Local', in R. Wilson and W. Dissanayake (eds) *Global, Local: Cultural Production and the Transnational Imaginary*, Duke University Press: Durham.

Doordarshan. 1994. *Reports of the Audience Research Unit*, Doordarshan Directorate General: New Delhi.

———. 1995. *Reports of the Audience Research Unit*, Doordarshan Directorate General: New Delhi.

———. 1997. *Reports of the Audience Research Unit*, Doordarshan Directorate General: New Delhi.

———. 1998. *Reports of the Audience Research Unit*, Doordarshan Directorate General: New Delhi.

———. 1999. *Reports of the Audience Research Unit*, Doordarshan Directorate General: New Delhi.

———. 2000. *Reports of the Audience Research Unit*, Doordarshan Directorate General: New Delhi.

Duch, R. 1991. *Privatizing the Economy: Telecommunications Policy in Comparative Perspective*, The University of Michigan Press: Ann Arbor.

Dunn, H. (ed.) 1995. *Globalization, Communications and Caribbean Identity*, St. Martin's Press: New York.

Durham, M. and Kellner, D. (eds) 2006. *Media and Cultural Studies*, Key Works, Revised edition, Blackwell Publishing: Oxford.

Dyson, K. and Humphreys, P. (eds) 1990. *The Political Economy of Communications: International and European Dimensions*, Routledge: London.

Eade, J. 1997. 'Introduction', in J. Eade (ed.) *Living the Global City: Globali-zation as a Local Process*, Routledge: London.

Election Commission of India. 2000. *Elections in India: Major Events and New Initiatives*, Publications Division, Election Commission of India: New Delhi.

Embree, A. 1997. 'Statehood in South Asia', *Journal of International Affairs*, vol. 51, no. 1, pp. 1–18.

Evans, P., Rueschmeyer, D. and Skocpol, T. (eds) 1985. *Bringing the State Back In*, Cambridge University Press: New York.

Evans, P. 1985. 'Transnational Linkages and the Economic Role of the State: An Analysis of Developing and Industrialized Nations in the Post-World War II World', in P. Evans, D. Rueschmeyer and T. Skocpol (eds) *Bringing the State Back in*, Cambridge University Press: New York.

Featherstone, M. 1990. 'Global Culture: An Introduction', in M. Featherstone (ed.) *Global Culture: Nationalism, Globalization and Modernity*, Sage: London.

Featherstone, M. 1993. 'Global and Local Cultures', in J. Bird, Barry Curtis, Tim Putnam, George Robertson, and Lisa Tickner (eds) *Mapping the Futures: Local Cultures, Global Change*, Routeledge: London.

Featherstone, M. and Lash, S. 1995. 'Globalization, Modernity and the Spa-tialization of Social Theory: An Introduction', in M. Featherstone, S. Lash, and R. Robertson (eds) *Global Modernities*, Sage: London.

FICCI and PricewaterhouseCoopers. 2008. 'The Indian Entertainment and Media Industry. Sustaining Growth', Report.

French, D. and Richards, M. (eds) 1996. *Contemporary Television: Eastern Perspectives*, Sage: New Delhi.

Freston, T. 2000. 'Young, Cool and Connected', *The Economic Times*, The Millennium Series, May, p. 2.

Frieden, R. 1996. *International Telecommunications Handbook*, Artech: Norwood, MA.

Fukuyama, F. 1989. 'The End of History?', *The National Interest*, no. 16, Summer, pp. 3–18.

———. 1992. *The End of History and the Last Man*, The Free Press: New York.

Galal, A. and Shirley, M. 1994. 'Does Privatization Deliver? Highlights from a World Bank conference', The World Bank: Washington D.C.

Giddens, A. 1990. *'The Consequences of Modernity'*, Polity: Cambridge.

———. 1994. 'Living in a Post-Traditional Society', in U. Beck, A. Giddens, and S. Lash, *Reflexive Modernization: Politics, Tradition and Aesthetics in the Modern Social Order*, Stanford University Press: Stanford.

Giddens, A. 1995. *Politics, Sociology and Social Theory: Encounters with Classical and Contemporary Social Thought*, Stanford University Press: Stanford, CA.

Gill, S. 1991. 'Freeing Prasar Bharati', in *Manorama Year Book 1991*, pp. 422–7.

Golding, P. 1995. 'The Mass Media and the Public Sphere: The Crisis of Information in the "information society"', in *Debating the Future of the Public Sphere*, S. Edgell, S. Walklate, and, G. Williams (eds) Aldershot, Averbury: England.

Golding, P. and Harris, P. (eds) 1997. *Beyond Cultural Imperialism: Globalization, Communication and the New International Order*, Sage: London.

Government of India. 1966. 'Radio and Television: Report of the Committee on Broadcasting and Information Media', Government of India: New Delhi. Also referred to as the Chanda Committee Report.

Government of India. 1978. 'Akash Bharati: Report of the Working Group on Autonomy for Akashvani and Doordarshan', Government of India: New Delhi. Also referred to as the Verghese Committee Report.

———. 1979. *Akash Bharati Bill of 1979*, Government of India: New Delhi.

———. 1985. *An Indian Personality for Television: Report of the Working Group on Software for Doordarshan*, Government of India: New Delhi. Also referred to as the Joshi Committee Report.

———. 1990. *Prasar Bharati Act of 1990*, Government of India: New Delhi.

———. 1996. 'Broadcasting Bill: Issues and Perspectives. The Ministry of Information and Broadcasting' in M. Price and S. Verhulst (eds) *Broadcasting Reform in India, Appendix B*, Oxford University Press: Delhi, pp. 223–33.

———. 1997. Broadcasting Bill (1997), Bill No. 71 of 1997.

———. 2000. *The Constitution of India, Ministry of Law, Justice and Company Affairs*, Government of India: New Delhi.

Grugel, J. and Hout, W. (eds) 1999. *Regionalism Across the North–South Divide: State Strategies and Globalization*, Routledge: London.

Gunaratne, S. 2000. 'Overview', in S. Gunaratne (ed.) *Handbook of the Media in Asia*, Sage: New Delhi.

Gunaratne, S. and Wattegama, C. 2000. 'Sri Lanka', in S. Gunaratne (ed.) *Handbook of the Media in Asia*, Sage: New Delhi.

Gunder Frank, A. 1969. *Latin America: Underdevelopment or Revolution. Essays on the Development of Underdevelopment and the Immediate Enemy*, Monthly Review Press: New York.

Gupta, N. 1998. *Switching Channels: Ideologies of Television in India*, Oxford University Press: Delhi.

Gupta, N. 2001. Professor of History, Jamia Milia Islamia University, Interviewed by author, Delhi.

Habermas, J. 1989. *The Structural Transformation of the Public Sphere*, MIT Press: Cambridge, Massachusetts.

Hall, S. 1992. 'The Question of Cultural Identity', in S. Hall, D. Held and T. McGrew (eds) *Modernity and its Futures*, Polity: Oxford.

Hamelink, C. 1996. *World Communication*, Zed Books: London.

Hannerz, U. 1990. 'Cosmopolitans and Locals in World Culture', in M. Featherstone (ed.) *Global Culture: Nationalism, Globalization and Modernity*, Sage: London.

Harding, A. and Le Gales. 1997. 'Globalization, Urban Change and Urban Policies in Britain and France', in Scott, A. (ed.) 1997. *The Limits of Globalization: Cases and Arguments*, Routledge: London.

Harkavy, R. E. 1995. 'Competing Images of the Emerging International System', *Working Papers*, Institute for Policy Research and Evaluation, The Pennsylvania State University, IPRE-WP-95-2.

Held, D., McGrew, A., Goldblatt, D. and Perraton, J. 1999. *Global Transformations: Politics, Economics and Culture*, The Polity Press: Cambridge, UK.

Herman, S. and McChesney, R. 1997. *The Global Media: the New Missionaries of Global Capitalism,* Cassell: London.

Hettne, Bjorn. 1995. *Development Theory and the Three Worlds*, Longman: New York.

Hilliard, R. and Keith, M. 1996. *Global Broadcasting Systems*, Focal Press: Boston.

Hiremath, S. 2001. 'Radical Feminists? Only Very Rarely', *The Times of India*, 6 May, p. 13.

Holm, H. and Sorensen, G. 1995. *Whose World Order: Uneven Globalization and the End of the Cold War*, Westview Press: Boulder.

Holton, R. 1998. *Globalization and the Nation-State*, St. Martin's Press: New York.

Hudson, H. 1997. *Global Connections: International Telecommunications Infrastructure and Policy*, Van Nostrand Reinhold: New York.

Humbert, M. (ed.) 1993. *The Impact of Globalization on Europe's Firms and Industries*, Pinter Publishers: London.

Huntington, S. 1993a. 'The Clash of Civilizations?', *Foreign Affairs,* vol. 72, no. 1, pp. 22–49.

———. 1993b. 'If Not Civilizations, What? Paradigms of the post-Cold War World', *Foreign Affairs*, vol. 72, no. 5, pp. 186–94.

Huntington, S. 1996. *The Clash of Civilizations and the Remaking of World Order*, Simon and Schuster: New York.

Immerfall, S. (ed.) 1998. *Territoriality in the Globalizing Society: One Place or None?* Springer: Berlin.

Iyengar, J. 2000. 'Bollywood Cuts to Diaspora, Reels in the Megamoolah', in *The Economic Times*, 30 August, p. 1.

Jackson, R. and James, A. (eds) 1994. *States in a Changing World*, Oxford University Press: Oxford.

Jacobson, H., Reisinger, W. and Mathers, T. 1986. 'National Entaglements in International Governmental Organizations', *American Political Science Review*, vol. 80, pp. 141–59.

Jaitely, A. 2000. 'Q&A with Arun Jaitely, Converge and Connect', *The Times of India*, 5 May, p. 14.

Jameson, F. 1995. 'Postmodernism, or the Cultural Logic of Late Capitalism', *New Left Review*, no. 146.

Jensen, K. and Jankowski, N. (eds) 1991. *A Handbook of Qualitative Methodologies for Mass Communication Research*, Routledge: London.

John, S. 2001. 'Cartoon Network Moves on Brand Building Plans', *The Times of India*, 2 May, p. 17.

Jones, M. 1996. *Studying Organizational Symbolism: What, How, Why?* Sage: Thousand Oaks.

Joshi, I. 1999. 'It May End with the Closing of the Indian mind', Interview with Romila Thapar, *Outlook*, 6 December, pp. 10–12.

Joshi, M. 1999. 'Practice of Democracy; Now Let Us Have Good Governance', in *The Times of India*. 13 September, p. 14.

Joshi, N. 2000. 'The Role Reversal', in *Outlook*, 27 March, p. 30.

Kapoor, P. 2001. 'Kyonki Kekta bhi Kabhi Ekta thi!', *The Times of India*, *Delhi Times*, 27 April, p. 1.

Karnik, K. 2001. Managing Director, Discovery Communications, India. Interviewed by author, Delhi.

Karthigesu, R. 1998. 'Transborder Television in Malaysia', in A. Goonasekera and P. Lee (eds) *TV Without Borders: Asia Speaks Out*, Stamford Press: Singapore.

Kazmi, N. 2001. 'From Power Ladies to Powder Bahus', *The Times of India*, 6 May, p. 13.

Keohane, R. and Nye, J. 1989. *Power and Interdependence*, Harper Collins: Cambridge, MA.

Keyman, E. 1997. *Globalization, State, Identity/Difference: Toward a Critical Social Theory of International Relations*, Humanities Press: New Jersey.

Khanna, A. 2000. 'Broadcast Law May Beam in Free Digital World', *The Economic Times*, 31 May, p. 3.

———. 2000. 'Advertisers Need to Move in a Rapidly Changing Market', *The Economic Times*, 15 June, p. 3.

King, A. (ed.) 1997. *Culture Globalization and the World-System: Contemporary Conditions for the Representation of Identity*, University of Minnesota Press: Minneapolis.

King, G., Keohane, R. and Verba, S. 1994. *Designing Social Inquiry: Scientific Inference in Qualitative Research*, Princeton University Press: Princeton.

Kirk, J. and Miller, M. 1986. *Reliability and Validity in Qualitative Research*, Qualitative Research Methods, vol. 1, Sage: London.

Kirschten, D. 1995. 'Restive Relic', *National Journal*, April, pp. 976–80.

Kishore, K. 1994. 'The Advent of STAR TV in India: Emerging Policy Issues', *Media Asia*, vol. 21, pp. 96–103.

Kohli, A. 1987. *The State and Poverty in India: the Politics of Reform*, Cambridge University Press: Cambridge.

———. 1988. *India's Democracy: An Analysis of Changing State-Society Relations*, Princeton University Press: Princeton, New Jersey.

———. 1990. *Democracy and Discontent; India's Growing Crisis of Governability*, Cambridge University Press: Cambridge.

Kohli-Khandekar, V. 2010. *The Indian Media Business*, Response (Sage): New Delhi.

Krieger, J. 1993. 'State', in *Oxford Companion to the Politics of the World*, Oxford University Press: New York, pp. 878–82.

Kulkarni, N. 2000. 'Cable Knit', *The Economic Times*, Brand Equity. 25–31 October, p. 1.

Kumar, K. 1995. 'Telecommunications and New Information Technologies in India', *Gazette*, v. 54, pp. 267–77.

Kwang, M. 1995. 'STAR TV, Murdoch's Big Bucks Gamble', *International Cable*, September.

Lamberton, D. (ed.) 1997. *The New Research Frontiers of Communications Policy*, Elsevier: Amsterdam.

Laski, H. 1960. *The State in Theory and Practice*, George Allen and Unwin: London.

Lee, P. and Wang, G. 1995. 'STAR TV in Asia', *Telecommunication Policy*, vol. 19, 2 March.

Lindlof, T. (ed.) 1987. *Natural Audiences: Qualitative Research of Media Uses and Effects*, Ablex: Norwood, NJ.

Lok Sabha Debates. 1997. *Restriction on Foreign Satellite Channels*, 11th Series, vol. ix, no. 6, February 27, pp. 14–17.

Maddock, R. 1997. 'Telecommunications and Economic Development', in D. Lamberton (ed.), *The New Research Frontiers of Communications Policy*, Elsevier: Amsterdam.

Mahajan, A. and Luthra, N. 1993. *Family and Television*, Gyan Publishing: New Delhi.

Malakar. 2001. Deputy Director General Programming, Prasar Bharati. Interviewed by author, Delhi.

Malhotra, I. 1995. 'Satellite and Cable in India, 1995 and Beyond', *Multichannel News International*, February.

Mander, J. and Goldsmith, E. (eds) 1996. *The Case Against the Global Economy: and a Turn Towards the Local*, Sierra Club Books: San Francisco.

Maran, K. 2000. 'Sunshine Superman, Q&A with Kalanithi Maran', *The Times of India*, 15 August, p. 14.

Mattoo, A. 2001. Professor of Political Science, Jawaharlal Nehru University. Interviewed by the author, Delhi.

McDowell, S. 1997. 'Globalization and Policy Choice: Television and Audiovisual Services Policies in India', *Media, Culture & Society*, vol. 19, pp. 151–72.

McDowell, S. 1997. *Globalization, Liberalization and Policy Change. A Political Economy of India's Communications Sector*, St. Martin's Press: New York.

———. 1998. 'Telecommunications Regulation in India: Context and Institutional Change', Paper presented at the Intercultural and International Communication Section, International Communication Association Meeting, Jerusalem.

McQuail, D. 2000. *Mass Communications Theory*, Sage: New Delhi.

McVeigh, B. 1998. *The Nature of the Japanese State; Rationality and Rituality*, Routledge: London.

Mehta, D. 1979. *Mass Communication and Journalism in India*, Allied Publishers: New Delhi.

Melkote, S. 1991. *Communication for Development in the Third World: Theory and Practice*, Sage: New Delhi.

Melody, W. (ed.) 1997. *Telecom Reform: Principles, Policies and Regulatory Practices*, Den Private Ingeniorfond: Denmark.

Menon, V. 2000. 'No Marx For This One', in *Outlook*, 22 May, pp. 68–9.

Merrill, J. and Odell. 1983. *Philosophy and journalism*, Longman: New York.

Merton, R. 1957. *Social Theory and Social Structure*, Free Press: Glencoe, Il.

Miller, G. and Dingwall, R. (eds) 1997. *Context and Method in Qualitative Research*, Sage: London.

Mishra, R. 2001. Joint Secretary, Broadcasting Policy, Ministry of Information and Broadcasting. Interviewed by the author, Delhi.

Mitra, A. 1993. *Television and Popular Culture in India: A Study of the Mahabharat*, Sage: New Delhi.

Mody, B., Bauer J. and Straubhaar, J. (eds) 1995. *Telecommunications Politics: Ownership and Control of the Information Highway in Developing Countries*, Lawrence Erlbaum: Mahwah, NJ.

Mody, B. and Tsui, L. 1995. *The Changing Role of the State*, in B. Mody, J. Bauer, and J. Straubhaar (eds) *Telecommunications Politics: Ownership and Control of the Information Highway in Developing Countries*, Lawrence Erlbaum: Mahwah, New Jersey.

Mohan, R. 2001. Joint Secretary, Broadcasting Policy. Ministry of Information and Broadcasting. Interviewed by author, Delhi.

Moragas Spa, M. and Garitaonandia, C. (eds) 1995. *Decentralization in the Global Era: Television in the Regions, Nationalities and Small Countries of the European Union*, John Libbey: London.

Morgan, R., Lorentzen, J., Leander, A. and Guzzini, S. (eds) 1993. *New Diplomacy in the Post-Cold War World: Essays for Susan Strange*, St. Martin's Press: London.

Mosco, V. 1996. *The Political Economy of Communication*, Sage: London.

Mowlana, H. 1996. *Global Communications in Transition: The End of Diversity?* Sage: California.

Mozumder, S. 2000. 'US Game Show Losing Viewers', *The Economic Times*, 1 November, p. 24.

Mueller, J. 1989. *Retreat from Doomsday: The Obsolescence of Major War*, Basic Books: New York.

Mukerjea, P. 2000. *Trekking New Frontiers, Q&A with Peter Mukerjea, The Times of India*, 9 June, p. 14.

Mukherjee, R. and Gairola, M. 2000. 'Zap or Call', *The Economic Times*, Corporate Dossier, 14–20 July, p. 3.

Mukul, A. 2000. 'Convergence Bill to be Introduced', *The Times of India*, 20 October, p. 13.

Murali, N. 2000. 'No Foreign Imprint', *The Times of India*, 7 November, p. 14.

N, Bhaskar Rao. 2001. Chairman Center for Media Studies. Personal interview, New Delhi.

Nariman, F. 2000. 'Catching Up with Convergence', *The Economic Times*, 3 November, p. 12.

Nagaraj, S. 2000. 'Few Takers for Convergence of Three Ministries', *The Economic Times*, 25 October, p. 4.

Nagaraj, S. 2000. 'DTH Policy is too Divergent: Experts', *The Economic Times*, 3 November, p. 5.

———. 2001. 'Bangalore Readying to Host Global E-parliament', *The Economic Times*, 27 June, p. 12.

Nandy, A. 1980. *At the Edge of Psychology; Essays in Politics and Culture*, Oxford University Press: Delhi.

Nanjundaiah, S. 1995. 'Deregulation of Television Broadcast in India, Cultural and Informational Impacts', *Asian Journal of Communication*, vol. 5, no. 1, pp. 71–87.

Narula, N. 2001. Proprietor Rukku Cable Networks. Interviewed by author, Delhi.

Nayak, R. 2000. 'Straight Answers', *The Times of India, Delhi Times*, 23 June, p. 1.

Nayar, B. 1990. *The Political Economy of India's Public Sector: Policy and Performance*, Popular Prakashan: Bombay.

Ninan, S. 1998. 'History of Indian Broadcasting Reform', in M. Price and S. Verhulst (eds) *Broadcasting Reform in India*. Oxford: University Press: Delhi, pp. 1–21.

Ninan, S. 2000. 'Channel Wars', *The Hindu*, 13 August, p. 3.

Nordenstreng, K. and Schiller, H. (eds) 1993. *Beyond National Sovereignty: International Communication in the 1990's*, Ablex: Norwood, NJ.

Nye, J. 1990. 'Soft Power', *Foreign Policy*, vol. 80, pp. 153–71.

Ohmae, K. 1995. *The End of the Nation State: The Rise of Regional Economies*, Harper Collins: London.

Palan, R., Jason, A. and Deans, P. 1996. *State Strategies in the Global Political Economy*. Pinter: London.

Page, D. and Crawley, W. 2001. *Satellites over South Asia: Broadcasting, Culture and the Public Interest*, Sage Publications: New Delhi.

Panda, M., Darbha, G. and Parikh, K. 1999. 'Macroeconomic Development and Prospects', in K.S. Parikh (ed.) *India Development Report 1999-2000*, Oxford University Press: Delhi.

Parenti, M. 1986. *Inventing Reality, the Politics of the Mass Media*, St. Martins Press: New York.

Parikh, K. and Shah, A. 1999. 'Second Generation Reforms', in K.S. Parikh (ed.) *India Development Report 1999-2000*, Oxford University Press: Delhi.

Petrazzini, B. 1995. *The Political Economy of Telecommunications Reform in Developing Countries: Privatization and Liberalization in Comparative Perspective*, Praeger: Westport, CT.

Pierson, C. 1996. *The Modern State*, Routledge: London.

Pieterse, J. 2006. 'Globalization as Hybridization', in M. Durham and D. Kellner (eds). *Media and Cultural Studies, Key Works*, Revised edition, Blackwell Publishing: Oxford.

Pogorel, G. (ed.) 1993. *Global Telecommunications Strategies and Technological Changes*, North-Holland: Amsterdam.

Price, M. 1995. *Television, the Public Sphere and National Identity*, Oxford University Press: Clarendon, Oxford.

PricewaterhouseCoopers. 2010. 'The Indian Entertainment and Media Outlook, 2010', Report. Available at www.pwc.de/de_de/de/technologie.

———. 2011. The Indian Entertainment and Media Outlook, 2011 Report. Price Waterhouse Coopers Report. Available at www.Pwc.de.

Puri, N. 2001. 'One Step Closer to Cleaning Up its Act', in *The Economic Times*, Investor's Guide, 14 May.

Radcliffe, S. and Westwood, S. 1996. *Remaking the Nation: Place, Identity and Politics in Latin America*, Routledge: London.

Raghavachari, S. 2001. Professor of Broadcast Journalism, Indian Institute of Mass Communications. Personal Interview, New Delhi, February.

Raizada, V. 2000. 'Straight Answers', *The Times of India, Delhi Times*, 15 September, p. 1.

Raj, R. 2010. 'Zee Learn to Spend Rs. 700 crore, Set up 300 Schools Across India'. Available at http://www.dnaindia.com/india/report_zee-learn.

Rajagopal, A. 2003. *Politics after Television; Religious Nationalism and the Reshaping of the National Public*, Cambridge University Press: Cambridge.

Rao, S. and Koirala, B. 2000. 'Nepal'. in S. Gunaratne. (ed.) *Handbook of the Media in Asia*, Sage: New Delhi.

Rao, N. 2000. *Center for Media Studies*, Personal Interview, New Delhi.

Ramaswami, K. V. 1999. 'Exporting in a Globalized Economy', in K.S. Parikh (ed.) *India Development Report 1999-2000*, Oxford University Press: Delhi.

Rath, A. 2000. 'Global Companies Go Vocal on Local in India', *The Economic Times*, 31 October, p. 1.

Ray, S. 2000. 'Tussles on the Tube', *Outlook*, 13 September, p. 41.

Ray, J. 1989. 'The Abolition of Slavery and the End of International War', in *International Organization*, vol. 43, pp. 405–39.

Robbins, R. 1993. 'Introduction: The Public as Phantom', in B. Robbins, (ed.) *The Phantom Public Sphere*, University of Minnesota Press: Minneapolis, MN.

Robertson, R. 1990. 'Mapping the Global Condition: Globalization as the Central Concept', in M. Featherstone (ed.) *Global Culture: Nationalism, Globalization and Modernity*, Sage: London.

———. 1995. 'Glocalization: Time-Space and Homogeniety-Heterogeniety', in M. Featherstone, S. Lash, and R. Robertson (eds) *Global Modernities*, Sage: London.

Rodrigues, M. 2000. 'Taking a U-Turner', *The Economic Times*, Brand Equity, 13 June, p. 3.

Rosenau, J. 1992a. 'The Relocation of Authority in Shrinking World', *Comparative Politics*, April, pp. 253–72.

Rosenau, J. 1992b. 'Governance, Order and Change in World Politics', in J. Rosenau and E. Czempiel (eds) *Governance without Government: Order and Change in World Politics*, Cambridge University Press: New York.

Rosenau, J. and Czempiel, E. (eds) 1992. *Governance without Government: Order and Change in World Politics*, Cambridge University Press: New York.

———. 1997. *Along the Domestic-Foreign Frontier: Exploring Governance in a Turbulent World*, Cambridge University Press: Cambridge, U.K.

Rothermund, D. (ed.) 1996. *Liberalising India: Progress and Problems*, Manohar: New Delhi.

Roy, B. 2000. 'Turf Wars from Rajiv Era to Ataldom', in *The Times of India*, Government Business, 1 December, p. 1.

———. 2001. 'My Job is Not to Police the Media: Sushma Swaraj', *The Times of India*, 4 April, 2001, p. 11.

Rudolph, L. and Rudolph, S. 1987. '*In Pursuit of Lakshmi, the Political Economy of the Indian State*', The University of Chicago Press: Chicago.

Rushton, D. (ed.) 1993. *Citizen Television: A Local Dimension to Public Service Broadcasting*, John Libbey: London.

Sachs J., Varshney, A. and Bajpai, N. 1999. 'Introduction', in J. Sachs, A. Varshney, and Bajpai N. (eds) *India in the Era of Economic Reforms*, Oxford University Press: New Delhi.

Sahgal, P. 2000. 'Young Turks at War', *Outlook*, 22 May, pp. 22–3.

Said, E. 1978. *Orientalism*, Penguin: Harmondsworth.

Samarajiva, R. and Shields, P. 1990. 'Integration, Telecommunications, and Development: Power in the Paradigms', *Journal of Communication*, vol. 40, no. 3, Summer, pp. 84–105.

Sassen, S. 1991. *The Global City: New York, London, Tokyo*, Princeton University Press: Princeton.

———. 1996. *Losing Control? Sovereignty in an Age of Globalization*, Columbia University Press: New York.

Saunders, R., Warford, J. and Wellenius, B. 1994. *Telecommunications and Economic Development*, Second edition, The Johns Hopkins University Press: Baltimore.

Saxena, P. 2010. 'STAR Plus is Back at No. 1…For Now', *The Hindustan Times*, 19 June, p. 15.

Schramm, W. 1992. *Big Media. Little Media*, Information Center on Instructional Technology: Washington, D.C.

Scott, A. (ed.) 1997. *The Limits of Globalization: Cases and Arguments*, Routledge: London.

Sehgal, R. 1999. 'All at Sea', *The Times of India, Sunday Times*, 5 December, p. 18.

———. 2000a. 'The Most Hotly-contested Territory in India', *The Times of India*, The Sunday Review, 23 January, p. 1.

———. 2000b. 'Cable Wars', in *The Times of India*, The Sunday Review, 26 March, p. 1.

———. 2000c. 'Transmission Boost for Kashmir Channel', *The Times of India*, 2 May, p. 8.

———. 2000d. 'Changing Channels', *The Times of India*, The Sunday Review, 28 May, p. 3

———. 2000e. 'Wild Dreams', *The Times of India*, The Sunday Review, 2 July, p. 9.

———. 2000f. 'Digital Swaraj; Questions and Answers with Sushma Swaraj', *The Times of India*. 10 November, p. 10.

———. 2001. 'The Fall and Fall of Zee', *The Times of India*, 22 April, p. 16.

Sepstrup, P. and Goonasekera, A. 1994. 'TV Transnationalization: Europe and Asia', no. 109, Unesco Publications: Paris.

Servaes, J. 1996. 'Introduction: Participatory Communication and Research in Development Settings', in J. Servaes, T. Jacobson, and S. White (eds) *Participatory Communication for Social Change*, Sage: New Delhi.

Sharan, A. 2009. 'The Drink Drive', *The Hindustan Times*, 31 August, p. 25.

Sharan, A. and Vats, R. 2010a. 'Sporting Magnets', *The Hindustan Times*, 19 July, p. 23.

———. 2010b. 'Sony Films to have TV Premieres on PIX Now,' *The Hindustan Times*, 20 September, p. 25.

———. 2010c. 'Small Town Tales', *The Hindustan Times*, 6 September, p. 23.

Sharma, A. 2000. 'It's Official, Delhi is No. 1', *Delhi Times, Times of India*, 5 October, p. 1.

Sharma, G. 1995. 'Cable, Strong and Stable', *International Cable*, July.

Sharma, P. 1995. 'Too Many Bids Spoil the Broth', *India Today*, September.

Sharma, V. 2011. 'India's Agricultural Development under the New Economic Regime: Policy Perspective and Strategy for the 12th Five Year Plan', Indian Institute of Management, Ahmedabad, W.P. No. 2011-11-01. Available at http://www.iimahd.ernet.in/assets/snippets/workingpaperpdf/1617912601%2011-11-01.pdf. (accessed in November 2011).

Shukla, A. 2009. 'Doordarshan, Half a Century Later', *The Sunday Express*, 20 September, p. 11.

Siebert, F., Peterson, T. and Schramm, W. 1963. *Four Theories of the Press*, University of Illinois Press: Urbana.

Silj, A. 1992. *The New Television in Europe*, John Libbey: London.

Simpson, C. 1994. *Science of Coercion: Communication Research and Psychological Warfare, 1945-1960*, Oxford University Press: New York.

Singh, G. 2000a. 'KBC Catapults Ad Rate to Rs 10 l/30 Sec', *The Economic Times*, 30 August, p. 1.

———. 2000b. 'STAR-BBC Ally to Bring Ji Mantriji to India', *The Economic Times*, 13 October, p. 13.

———. 2000c. 'New Convergence News Product from CNN Stable by Dec', *The Economic Times*, 8 November, p. 20.

———. 2000d. 'Where's the Beeb?', in *The Economic Times*, Brand Equity, 8–14 November, p. 3.

———. 2000e. 'Sony Ropes in Govinda to Take on Big B with Game Show', *The Economic Times*, 10 November, p. 13.

———. 2001a. 'Scandals Bring News Channels Back to Life', *The Economic Times*, 5 April, p. 20.

———. 2001b. 'MTV's Sister Channel VH 1 Likely to See Early Launch', *The Economic Times*, 4 May, p. 2001.

Singhal, A. and Rogers, E. 1989. *India's Information Revolution*, Sage: New Delhi.

———. 2001. *India's Communication Revolution: from Bullock Carts to Cyber Marts*, Sage: New Delhi.

Sinha, A. 1996. 'Development Dilemmas for Indian Television', in D. French and M. Richards (eds) *Contemporary Television: Eastern Perspectives*, Sage: New Delhi.

Sinha, P. 2000. 'Will Junior Murdoch Push for More Foreign Equity in DTH', *The Times of India*, 21 November, p. 13.

Sinha, N. 1996. 'The Political Economy of India's Telecommunication Reforms', *Telecommunications Policy*, vol. 20, no. 1, pp. 23–38.

Sinha, N. 1998. 'Doordarshan, Public Service Broadcasting and the Impact of Globalization: a short history', in M. Price and S. Verhulst (eds) *Broadcasting Reform in India*, Oxford University Press: Delhi, pp. 22–40.

Smith, A. and Patterson, R. (eds) 1998. *Television, an International History,* Oxford University Press: Oxford.

Smith, A. 1998. 'Introduction', in A. Smith and R. Patterson (eds) *Television, An International History,* Oxford University Press: Oxford.

Spruyt, H. 1994. *The Sovereign State and its Competitors: An Analysis of Systems Change,* Princeton University Press: Princeton, NJ.

Sreberny-Mohammadi, A. 1996. 'Globalization, Communication and Transnational Civil Society: Introduction', in S. Braman and A. Sreberny-Mohammadi (eds), *Globalization, Communication and Transnational Civil Society,* Hampton: Cresskill, New Jersey.

Sreberny-Mohammadi, A. and Mohammadi, A. 1997. 'Small Media and Revolutionary Change: A New Model', in A. Sreberny-Mohammadi, D. Winseck, J. Mckenna, and Oliver Boyd-Barrett (eds) *Media in Global Context,* St. Martin's Press: New York.

Sreberny-Mohammadi, A., Winseck, D., McKenna, J. and Boyd-Barrett, O. (eds) 1997. *Media in Global Context: A Reader,* Arnold: London.

Stake, R. 1994. 'Case Studies', in N. Denzin and Y. Lincoln (eds) *Handbook of Qualitative Research,* Sage: Thousand Oaks.

Stephen, L. 1992. 'The World's Media Systems: An Overview', in J. C. Merril (ed.) *Global Journalism,* New York: Longman.

Strange, S. 1986. *Casino Capitalism,* Basil Blackwell: Oxford.

———. 1998. *Mad Money: When Markets Outgrow Governments,* University of Michigan Press: Ann Arbor.

Straubhaar, J. 2006. '(Re) Asserting National Television and National Identity Against the Global, Regional, and Local Levels of World Television', in M. Durham and D. Kellner (eds), 2006. *Media and Cultural Studies, Key Works,* Revised edition, Blackwell Publishing: Oxford.

Stopford, J., Strange, S. and Henley, J. 1991. *Rival States, Rival Firms: Competition for World Market Shares,* Cambridge University Press: Cambridge.

Subramaniam, K. 2000. 'Stop Press', *The Indian Express,* The Express Magazine, 23 April, p. 5.

Sussman, G. and Lent, J. (eds) 1991. *Transnational Communications: Wiring the Third World,* Sage: Newbury Park.

Talbot, I. 2000. *Inventing the Nation; India and Pakistan,* Arnold: London.

Teheranian, M. 1997. 'Discourses of Development and Development of Discourses', *Journal of Development Communication,* no. 2, vol. 8, December.

Thakur, R. 2000. 'HLL to Chant Om Namah Shivay', *The Economic Times,* 8 November, p. 5.

Thakur, R. and Govardhan, D. 2000. 'Lingo, bingo', *The Economic Times,* Corporate Dossier, 13–19 October, p. 3.

Thomas. 1998. 'South Asia', in A. Smith and, R. Patterson (eds) 1998. *Television, an International History*, Oxford University Press: Oxford.

Thomas, P. 2010. *Political Economy of Communications in India*, Sage: New Delhi.

Thurow, L. 1992. *Head to Head: The Coming Economic Battle among Japan, Europe and America*, Morrow: New York.

The Economic Times. 2000a. The ET 500, Entertainment Unlimited, June, pp. 42–4.

———. 2000b. 'Zee Plans Rural Education Initiative', 8 June, p. 13.

———. 2000c. 'Zee-MGM Movie Channel in Feb', 30 August, p. 11.

———. 2000d. 'STAR TV buys 26% of Hathway Cable', 15 September, p. 15.

———. 2000e. 'Summer of 2000'. 27 September, p. 6.

———. 2000f. 'Making Waves'. 31 October, p. 12.

———. 2000g. 'We're Just Helping Prasar Bharati Out of Red: Jaitley', 22 December, p. 2.

———. 2000h. 'Naidu Wants DD, AIR to be Master's Voice', 22 May, p. 3.

The Times of India, 1995. 'Cabinet Approves Ordinance for Telecom Watchdog', November 1.

———. 2000a. 'Murdoch Favours Open Skies Policy', 16 March, p. 12.

———. 2000b. 'Broadcast Worldwide plans Rs 100 cr IPO', 31 May, p. 17.

———. 2000c. 'Foreign Channels Go Hindi', 1 June, p. 8.

———. 2000d. 'TV Channels Must Conform to Have Uplink Rights', 28 July, p. 10.

———. 2000e. 'Zee to Invest Rs 100 cr in Learning Solutions', in *The Times of India*, 9 August, p. 19.

———. 2000f. 'Govt. Cleans Cable of Immorality, Piracy', 9 September, p. 1.

———. 2000g. 'Cable Operators Protest', 10 September, p. 8.

———. 2000h. 'Jaipal Raps Govt. on Prasar Bharati Vacancies'. 16 September, p. 9.

———. 2000i. 'Convergence Bill May see Creation of Super Ministry, 21 October, p. 1.

———. 2000j. 'ZTL will not Launch Sports Channel', 30 December, p. 17.

———. 2000k. 'Q&A with Arun Jaitley', 5 May, p. 14.

———. 2001a. 'Zee to Merge Entertainment with News, 17 November, p. 13.

———. 2001b. 'DTH Cleared, Viewers Rid of Cable Operators', 17 March, p. 1.

———. 2001c. 'Sushma Invites Sonia for Panel Discussion', 22 March, p. 11.

———. 2001d. 'Bollywood Poised to Take the Big Leap, 24 March, p. 13.

The Times of India, Delhi Times, 2000. 'Bollywood Boulevard: From Box Office to Idiot-box?', 14 August, p. 1.

Thomas, P. 1993. 'Broadcasting and the State in India: Towards Relevant Alternatives', *Gazette*, v. 51, pp. 19–33.

Thomas, P. 1998. 'South Asia', in A. Smith and R. Patterson (eds) *Television, An International History*, Oxford University Press: Oxford.

Thussu, D. 1998. 'Localising the Global: Zee TV in India', in D. Thussu (ed.) *Electronic Empires: Global Media and Local Resistance*, Arnold: London.

Tiwari, S. 2001. *Director Broadcasting Policy, Ministry of Information and Broadcasting*. Interviewed by author, Delhi.

Vats, R. 2010. 'Bollywood High on TV', *The Hindustan Times*, 12 July, p. 25.

Verna, T. 1993. *Global Television: How to Create Effective Television for the Future*, Focal Press: Boston.

Vidyasagar, N. 2000a. 'So, Whose Toon is it Anyway?', *The Times of India*, 21 July, p. 12.

———. 2000b. 'Vijay TV Signs Deal with NDTV', *The Times of India*, 28 July, p. 17.

———. 2000c. 'It's Cable + ISP = Cutting Edge in Convergence Era', *The Times of India*, 18 August, p. 17.

———. 2000d. 'Overseas Market Tunes into Indian TV Content', *The Times of India*, 28 August, p. 15.

———. 2000e. 'CNN Looking for Partner to Perk up India Business', *The Times of India*, 4 September, p. 13.

———. 2000f. 'HBO is "popular" among cable operators: Survey', *The Times of India*, 19 November, p. 14.

Viswanath, K. and Karan, K. 2000. 'India', in S. Gunaratne (ed.) *Handbook of the Media in Asia*, Sage: New Delhi.

Vyas, C. 2001. Assistant Controller of Programs, Prasar Bharati. Interviewed by author, Delhi.

Walia, K. 2003. 'Big Houses Push out Small TV Serial-producers'. Available at http://timesofindia.indiatimes.com/city/mumbai/Big-houses

Walia, N. 2000. 'Shoppers Don't Stop', *The Times of India*, Sunday Review, 10 December, p. 1.

Wallerstein. 1990. 'Culture as the Ideological Battleground of the Modern World-System', in M. Featherstone (ed.) *Global Culture: Nationalism, Globalization and Modernity*, Sage: London.

Weber, M. 1978. 'Economy and Society', vol. 1, Bedminster: New York.

Wellenius, B. and Stern, P. 1994. 'Implementing Reforms in the Telecommunications Sector: Background, Overview, and Lessons', in B. Wellenius and P. Stern (eds) *Implementing Reforms in the Telecommunications Sector: Lessons from Experience*, The World Bank: Washington D.C.

Williams, R. 1974. *Television, Technology and Cultural Form*, Fontana: London.

Wilson, R. and Dissanayake, W. (eds) 1996. *Global/ Local: Cultural Production and the Transnational Imaginary*, Duke University Press: Durham.

Wiseman, J. 1998. *Global Nation? Australia and the Politics of Globalization*, Cambridge University Press: Cambridge.

World Trade Organization. 1995. 'International Trade: Trends and Statistics', WTO: Geneva.

Worthy, J. and Kariyawasam, R. 1998. 'Comment: A pan-European Telecommunications Regulator?' *Telecommunications Policy*, vol. 22, no. 1. pp. 1–7.

Yin, R. 1984. *Case Study Research*, Sage: Beverly Hills.

Zee Telefilms Ltd. 2001. Personal Interview with a Marketing Official, April, New Delhi.

Zee Telefilms Ltd. 1997–98. *Zee Telefilms Limited: 16th Annual Report*, Mumbai.

———. 1998–99. *Zee Telefilms Limited: 17th Annual Report*, Mumbai.

———. 1999–2000. *Zee Telefilms Limited: 18th Annual Report*, Mumbai.

INDEX

ABOUT THE AUTHOR

Sunetra Sen Narayan earned her Masters degree in Economics from the Delhi School of Economics, India and her Doctoral degree in Mass Communications from the Pennsylvania State University, USA. She is currently a faculty member of the Indian Institute of Mass Communications, New Delhi. Her research interests include international communications, development, and new media. She has worked in the fields of advertising, print journalism, documentary film production, and media education. She can be contacted at sunetran@gmail.com